Paul McFedries

Microsoft®
Windows Vista™
Unveiled

 SAMS | 800 East 96th Street, Indianapolis, Indiana 46240 USA

Microsoft® Windows Vista™ Unveiled

International Standard Book Number: 0-672-32893-3

Library of Congress Catalog Card Number: 2006922045

Printed in the United States of America

First Printing: June 2006

09   08   07   06   4   3   2   1

Trademarks

All terms mentioned in this book that are known to be trademarks or service marks have been appropriately capitalized. Sams Publishing cannot attest to the accuracy of this information. Use of a term in this book should not be regarded as affecting the validity of any trademark or service mark.

Microsoft is a registered trademark of Microsoft Corporation. Windows Vista is a trademark of Microsoft Corporation.

Warning and Disclaimer

Every effort has been made to make this book as complete and as accurate as possible, but no warranty or fitness is implied. The information provided is on an "as is" basis. The author and the publisher shall have neither liability nor responsibility to any person or entity with respect to any loss or damages arising from the information contained in this book.

Bulk Sales

Sams Publishing offers excellent discounts on this book when ordered in quantity for bulk purchases or special sales. For more information, please contact

U.S. Corporate and Government Sales
1-800-382-3419
corpsales@pearsontechgroup.com

For sales outside the United States, please contact

International Sales
international@pearsoned.com

Associate Publisher
Greg Wiegand

Acquisitions Editor
Loretta Yates

Development Editor
Todd Brakke

Managing Editor
Patrick Kanouse

Project Editor
Tonya Simpson

Copy Editor
Krista Hansing

Indexer
Ken Johnson

Proofreader
Elizabeth Scott

Technical Editor
Terri Stratton

Publishing Coordinator
Sharry Lee Gregory

Cover Designer
Luckenbill Studios

Interior Designer
Susan Geiselman

Contents at a Glance

Table of Contents

About the Author

Paul McFedries runs Logophilia Limited, a technical writing company, and has been writing computer books for more than 15 years. He is the author or coauthor of more than 40 computer books that have sold more than 3 million copies worldwide. His recent titles include the Sams Publishing book *Windows XP Unleashed* (2005) and the Sams Publishing books *Formulas and Functions with Microsoft Excel 2003* (2005), *Tricks of the Microsoft Office Gurus* (2005), and *Microsoft Access 2003 Forms, Reports, and Queries* (2004). He is also the proprietor of Wordspy.com, a website that tracks new words and phrases as they enter the language.

Dedication

To my beautiful wife, Karen, and to Gypsy, the silliest dog ever.

Acknowledgments

Writing books is endlessly fascinating for me because what begins as just a few thoughts ends up as a physical, tangible thing that gets sent out (hopefully) to the far-flung corners of the world. Of course, the trip from thought to thing is a long one, and lots of people get their fingers in a book's pie before it's ready to ship. This book was no exception, so I'd like to thank not only the long list of people that you'll find near the front of this book, but also the following hard-working souls that I worked with directly: acquisitions editor Loretta Yates, development editor Todd Brakke, project editor Tonya Simpson, copy editor Krista Hansing, and technical editor Terri Stratton.

We Want to Hear from You!

As the reader of this book, *you* are our most important critic and commentator. We value your opinion and want to know what we're doing right, what we could do better, what areas you'd like to see us publish in, and any other words of wisdom you're willing to pass our way.

As an associate publisher for Sams Publishing, I welcome your comments. You can email or write me directly to let me know what you did or didn't like about this book—as well as what we can do to make our books better.

Please note that I cannot help you with technical problems related to the topic of this book. We do have a User Services group, however, where I will forward specific technical questions related to the book.

When you write, please be sure to include this book's title and author as well as your name, email address, and phone number. I will carefully review your comments and share them with the author and editors who worked on the book.

Email: feedback@samspublishing.com

Mail: Greg Wiegand
           Associate Publisher
           Sams Publishing
           800 East 96th Street
           Indianapolis, IN 46240 USA

Reader Services

Visit our website and register this book at www.samspublishing.com/register for convenient access to any updates, downloads, or errata that might be available for this book.

"*Testing is the process of comparing the invisible to the ambiguous, so as to avoid the unthinkable happening to the anonymous.*" —James Bach

Being a computer book author offers many advantages to those of us with an inner geek: working at home, enjoying the satisfaction of a freshly printed book, and having a good excuse to purchase (and write off) new tech toys. Another big advantage that comes around every so often is the chance to work with a new version of a software program before it's released to the public. Working with pre-release software is like parachuting into a territory that only a few other people have seen. There are always lots of new things to see and try out, and an in-depth exploration is rewarded with finds and experiences that are unique, interesting, and often quite useful.

This book is a record of my in-depth exploration of several prerelease versions of Windows Vista, Microsoft's next major operating system (OS) and the successor to Windows XP. Don't have Windows Vista yet? That's not a problem because this is *not* a "how-to" book. Instead, it's more of a "what-is" book. That is, *Windows Vista Unveiled* takes you on a detailed tour of all the new and improved technologies, features, tools, and programs that the Microsoft programmers have stitched into the Vista fabric. You'll learn not only *what* features are new in Vista, but also *why* they're important (or not), *who* they were designed for, and *how* they will affect your computing life. My goal is to give you an exhaustive sneak preview of Vista's innovations and changes so that by the end of the book you know whether Vista is for you and what to expect when you sit down in front of this new OS.

What Is a Beta?

When software vendors work on a new or updated program, they perform extensive in-house testing of the new version. This is called *alpha testing*, and each new version of the software-in-progress is called an *alpha*.

A *beta*, a term you've probably heard used 3 or 4 or 20,000 times or so, is a later version of the prerelease program that the company distributes to outside users for testing and feedback. The process of third-party distribution, testing, and feedback is called a *beta test*, and the users who put the program through its paces are called *beta testers*.

> **NOTE**
>
> Because the alpha test is an "in-house" procedure, many a wag has dubbed the beta test an "out-house" procedure. Also, because software with even the most thoroughly tested alpha and beta versions behind it will still ship with more than a few bugs, other wags (or possibly the same ones) have taken to calling the released product the *gamma version*.

The software industry has used the terms *alpha* and *beta* since the early 1980s, but they date back to the 1960s in the hardware world. In fact, the terms are thought to have originated at IBM in the early 1960s and come from that company's use of the terms *A-test* and *B-test* for the initial testing of new hardware components.

Microsoft first started beta-testing its software in the early 1980s, and almost all of its operating systems have run through a beta-testing cycle (the possible exception is the original version of MS-DOS). The old DOS beta cycles had perhaps a few hundred testers, but in recent years the Windows beta test brigade has mushroomed. The Whistler (Windows XP) beta test had a whopping half a million users, who combined to discover tens of thousands of bugs, big and small. The numbers in the Longhorn/Vista beta test have been even bigger. Although the first beta was distributed to just 10,000 users (but was also made available to a few hundred thousand Microsoft Developer Network and TechNet subscribers), it was estimated that up to 2 million people would take a crack at Beta 2, the first build made available to the general public.

What do Windows beta testers do? Those of us who take our beta-testing duties seriously end up doing quite a bit, actually. You have to install each beta, of course, which is no small feat in itself because you have to download a 3GB file, burn that file to a DVD, wipe everything from your test machine, run the setup program, and then tweak your device drivers, depending on the level of driver support in the beta you're installing. Then you need to fill out an installation survey and possibly a hardware survey. Then, most importantly, you need to use the operating system in various scenarios to see if everything works the way it should. If it doesn't, you need to submit a bug report to Microsoft. While you're doing this, you also need to read and participate in the beta newsgroups, follow or contribute to the periodic live chats with the developers, and try out the "feature previews" and report your results. Add to this the necessary (but not for the beta) tasks of studying Microsoft's whitepapers and briefing notes for all the new technologies, following the blogs related to the new OS, keeping tabs on the Microsoft "rumor" sites, and all the while writing up your findings in such a way that people such as yourself will know what to expect. It's hard but very satisfying work, and one of the more tangible results of it all is the book that you now hold in your hands.

NOTE

There's a popular and appealing tale of how the word *bug* came about. Apparently, an early computer pioneer named Grace Hopper was working on a machine called the Mark II in 1947. While investigating a glitch, she found a moth among the vacuum tubes, so from then on glitches were called bugs. Appealing, yes, but true? Not quite. In fact, engineers had already been referring to mechanical defects as "bugs" for at least 60 years before Ms. Hopper's discovery. As proof, the *Oxford English Dictionary* offers the following quotation from an 1889 edition of the *Pall Mall Gazette*:

"Mr. Edison, I was informed, had been up the two previous nights discovering 'a bug' in his phonograph—an expression for solving a difficulty, and implying that some imaginary insect has secreted itself inside and is causing all the trouble."

Who Should Read This Book

All writers write with an audience in mind. Actually, I'm not sure whether that's true for novelists and poets and the like, but it *should* be true for any technical writer who wants to create a useful and comprehensible book. Here are the members of my own imagined audience:

- **IT professionals**—These brave souls must decide whether to move to Vista, work out deployment issues, and support the new Vista desktops. The whole book has information related to your job and Vista.

- **Developers**—Microsoft created many new technologies for Vista developers, including Windows Presentation Foundation, WinFX, RSS, and the Windows PowerShell (now a separate product that will ship around the same time as Vista). Although you won't learn any programming techniques in this book, I've kept you in mind in my discussions of the new Vista architecture and technologies.

- **Power users**—These elite users get their power via knowledge. With that in mind, this book extends the Windows power user's know-how by presenting an exhaustive account of everything that's new and improved in Windows Vista.

- **Business users**—If your company is thinking of or has already committed to moving to Vista, then you need to know what you, your colleagues, and your staff are getting into. You also want to know what Vista will do to improve your productivity and make your life at the office easier. You learn all of this and more in this book.

- **Road warriors**—If you travel for a living, you probably want to know what Vista brings to the remote computing table. Will you be able to synchronize data, connect to the network, and manage power better than before? What other new notebook features can be found in Vista? You'll find out in this book.

- **Small business owners**—If you run a small or home business, you probably want to know whether Vista will give you a good return on investment. Will it make it easier to set up and maintain a network? Will Vista computers be more stable? Will your employees be able to collaborate easier? The answer turns out to be "Yes" for all of these questions, and I'll show you why.

- **Multimedia users**—If you use your computer to listen to music or radio stations, watch TV, work with digital photographs, edit digital movies, or burn CDs and DVDs, then you'll be interested to know that Vista has a handful of new features that affect all of these activities.

- **Gamers**—The PC video game crowd are the ones who, in the end, stand to gain the most from moving to Vista because Microsoft has given its new OS a souped-up graphics engine that should enable game developers to perform some amazing feats that might even outstrip the effects seen on dedicated game consoles. I'll tell you what's new and why it may take gaming to a whole new level.

Conventions Used in This Book

To make your life easier, this book includes various features and conventions that help you get the most out of this book and Windows Vista itself:

Steps	Throughout the book, I've broken many Windows Vista tasks into easy-to-follow step-by-step procedures.
Things you type	Whenever I suggest that you type something, what you type appears in a **bold monospace** font.
Filenames, folder names, and code	These things appear in a `monospace` font.
Commands	Commands and their syntax use the `monospace` font as well. Command placeholders (which stand for what you actually type) appear in an `italic monospace` font.
Pull-down menu commands	I use the following style for all application menu commands—Menu, Command, where Menu is the name of the menu that you pull down and Command is the name of the command you select. Here's an example: File, Open. This means that you pull down the File menu and select the Open command.

This book also uses the following boxes to draw your attention to important (or merely interesting) information:

NOTE

The Note box presents asides that give you more information about the current topic. These tidbits provide extra insights that give you a better understanding of the task at hand. In many cases, they refer you to other sections of the book for more information.

TIP

The Tip box tells you about Windows Vista methods that are easier, faster, or more efficient than the standard methods.

CAUTION

The all-important Caution box tells you about potential accidents waiting to happen. There are always ways to mess things up when you're working with computers. These boxes help you avoid at least some of the pitfalls.

Beta Disclaimer

I used several beta versions of Windows Vista over the 8 months or so between the release of the initial beta and the day this book was sent to the printer. All the information in this book was checked using Beta 2, which Microsoft claimed was "feature complete" and had a user interface that was more or less fixed. Therefore, I'm confident that the Windows Vista that you'll read about in these pages will be an accurate reflection of what you'll see in the final version.

Having said that, however, there are *always* some tweaks that the software designers and programmers make at the last minute. It's even possible that Microsoft could drop or (less likely) add some major feature over the next couple of months. They've done this in the past, and they'll do it again. So although I've got fingers and toes crossed that Microsoft won't throw us any curve balls before Vista is released to manufacturing, it's prudent to assume that every nook and cranny of Windows Vista won't be *exactly* as I describe it here. If so, please accept my apologies in advance.

An Overview of Windows Vista

It's hard to believe, but when Windows Vista ships in 2007, it will be a full quarter of a century after Microsoft released its first version of MS-DOS, and an astonishing 23 years since the company announced the original version of Windows (which eventually shipped—to almost no acclaim—in 1985). Windows 2.0, released in 1987, was marginally more promising, but it resolutely failed to light any fires on the PC landscape. It wasn't until Windows 3.0 was released in 1990 that Windows finally came into its own and its utter dominance of the desktop began. And with the release of Windows 95 on August 24, 1995, Windows became the rock star of the computing world, beloved by many, hated by some, but known to all.

It's also hard to believe that people were actually lining up outside computer stores on the night of August 23, 1995, to be among the first to purchase Windows 95 at midnight. Why on earth would anyone *do* that? Were they insane? Perhaps some were, but most were just caught up in the hype and hope generated, to be sure, by Microsoft's marketing muscle, but also by the simple fact that Windows 95 *was* light-years ahead of any previous version of the operating system.

By comparison, the Windows world since that hot summer night in 1995 has been decidedly—some would say *depressingly*—quiet. There have been plenty of new versions— Windows 98 and Windows Me on the consumer side, Windows NT 4 and Windows 2000 on the corporate side, and then Windows XP in all its flavors—but there has been a distinct lack of *buzz* associated with each release. True, nothing will ever live up to the hype (and hokum) that surrounded Windows 95, but the versions since have had a ho-hum quality to them. Sure, Windows 98 (particularly the Second Edition release) was solid (and is still used by many people to this day), Windows 2000 was a favorite business OS for many years, and XP has been the best Windows yet, but nobody would line up at midnight to buy any of these products.

Will any of this change with the upcoming release of Windows Vista? True, nobody's all that excited about the name, but the name is meaningless in the long run. (In 2001, most folks thought XP—based, head-scratchingly, on the word *eXPerience*—was the dumbest name ever, but everyone got used to it within a month or two and the "controversy," such as it was, faded quickly.) What might get people talking about Vista isn't the name, but the simple fact that we're *finally* seeing some interesting OS technology from Microsoft. Vista is beautiful to look at, promises to make our day-to-day lives a bit easier, and contains some compelling architectural improvements. I doubt people will be camping out to buy Vista in the days before it releases, but many months of delving into Vista's innards has convinced me that it has at least a few things to get excited about.

This chapter gets your Windows Vista introduction off the ground by giving you an overview of the operating system. I start with a brief history of Longhorn/Vista, and then I give you a quick tour of what's new and interesting. Along the way, I point out the relevant sections in the book where you can find more information about each new feature.

The Development of Longhorn

In 2000, Bill Gates, chairman and chief software architect of Microsoft, announced that the successor to the forthcoming Whistler operating system—later renamed as Windows XP—would be a new OS codenamed Blackcomb. A year later, however, just a few months before the release of XP, Microsoft announced a change of plans: Blackcomb would come much later than expected, and between XP and Blackcomb, probably around 2003, we'd see a minor update codenamed Longhorn.

> **NOTE**
>
> Microsoft has long applied codenames to prerelease versions of its products. For Windows, the practice began with Windows 3.1, which used the codename Janus. The first of these temporary monikers that was in any way "famous" (that is, known reasonably widely outside of Microsoft) was Chicago, the codename for Windows 95. Since then, we've seen, among many others, Memphis for Windows 98, Cairo for Windows NT 4.0, Millennium for Windows Me, and Whistler for Windows XP.
>
> So why the codename Longhorn? Legend has it that Bill Gates has fond feelings for British Columbia's Whistler-Blackcomb ski resort (the name of which has given us two codenames for Windows, so it's clear that *someone* at Microsoft loves the place). At the base of Whistler Mountain, in the Carleton Lodge, there is an après-ski bar called the Longhorn Saloon. The burgers, I hear, are quite good.
>
> There is an impressively exhaustive list of Microsoft codenames on the Bink.nu site: http://bink.nu/Codenames.bink.

However, Microsoft's approach to Longhorn soon began to change. By the time the Windows Hardware Engineering Conference (WinHEC) rolled around in mid-2003, Microsoft was describing Longhorn as a "huge, big, bet-the-company move." Windows XP was being kept current with new updates, including Windows XP Service Pack 2, and new versions of Windows XP Tablet PC Edition and Windows XP Media Center Edition. Meanwhile, Longhorn gradually began to accumulate new features that had originally been intended for Blackcomb. By the summer of 2004, Microsoft realized that Longhorn had become the next major Windows OS, so the company revamped the entire Longhorn development process and more or less started the whole thing from scratch. This delayed the release of Longhorn, of course, and the dates kept getting pushed out: to 2005, then to early 2006, and finally to later in 2006. (Microsoft has said that Vista's code will ship to business customers in November, 2006 and will be in the retail channel in January, 2007. As I write this, rumors are swirling that Vista might be delayed yet again, depending on the feedback Microsoft gets from the legions of Beta 2 testers.)

But it wasn't just a revamped development process that was delaying Longhorn. In conferences, demos, and meetings with hardware vendors, developers, and customers, Microsoft had described the new OS and features in the most glowing terms imaginable. This had become a seriously ambitious project that was going to require an equally serious commitment of resources and, crucially, *time* to make the promises a reality. Unfortunately, time was the one thing that Microsoft didn't have a lot of. Yes, XP was a fine OS and was being kept fresh with updates, but even a 2006 ship date for Longhorn meant an unprecedented *five years* between major OS releases. Not even mighty Microsoft could afford to keep XP in the channel any longer than that.

In other words, Longhorn *had* to be complete in 2006 even if it doesn't reach retail shelves until early 2007. Microsoft briefly considered an interim version of Windows that would ship between Windows XP Service Pack 2 and Longhorn. (This stopgap release was codenamed Oasis, but some wags dubbed it Shorthorn.)

"Vista" Unveiled

The codename Longhorn was finally retired when Microsoft announced on July 22, 2005, that the new OS would be called Windows Vista. Why *Vista*? Because, according to one Microsoft spokesperson, the new OS is "about providing clarity to your world and giving focus to the things that are important to you," and it "provides your view of the world." That sounds like a lot of marketing hoo-ha to my ears, but it's true that Vista does offer some new features that enable you to view your documents in radically new ways (radical for Windows, that is).

To give just one example, you can run a local search right from the Start menu. The resulting window displays a list of all the files—documents, email messages, music files, images, and more—that contain the search term. You can then save the results as a search folder. The next time you open the search folder, Vista shows not only the files from the original search, but also any new files you've created that include the search term.

NOTE

Windows version numbers haven't mattered very much since the days of Windows 3.x and NT 4.0. However, all Windows releases do carry a version number. For example, Windows XP is version 5.1. Just for the record, Windows Vista is version 6.0. If you have Vista, you can see this for yourself: Press Windows Logo+R; type `winver`; and click OK.

What's *Not* in Windows Vista

But what of all those fancy new technologies that promised to rock the Windows world? Well, there was simply no way to include all of those features *and* ship Vista in 2006. Reluctantly, Microsoft had to start dropping features from Vista.

The first major piece to land in the Recycle Bin was Windows Future Storage (WinFS), a SQL Server–based file system designed to run on top of NTFS and to make it easier to navigate and find documents. WinFS will ship separately after Windows Vista, although as you'll see in this book, some features of WinFS *did* make it into Vista (see Chapter 4, "File System Improvements").

Microsoft also removed the Windows PowerShell (codenamed Monad and also called the Windows Command Shell or Microsoft Command Shell), a .NET-based command-line scripting language. (However, PowerShell is undergoing a separate beta cycle as I write this, and it's expected to be released around the same time as Vista.)

Microsoft also "decoupled" some important technologies from Vista, which meant that these technologies developed separately and would be released for Vista and "backported" to run on Windows XP and Windows Server 2003. Two major technologies are being backported:

- A new graphics architecture and application programming interface that was code-named Avalon and is now called Windows Presentation Foundation (WPF)

- A new programming platform for building, configuring, and deploying network-distributed services, codenamed Indigo and now called Windows Communications Foundation (WCF)

In both cases, it doesn't mean that Windows XP and Windows Server 2003 will suddenly look and feel like Windows Vista after you install WPF and WCF. Instead, it means that the older operating systems will be capable of running any applications that use WPF and WCF code. This gives developers more incentive to build applications around these technologies because it ensures a much larger user base than they would otherwise have if WPF and WCF ran only on Vista installations.

Finally, there are also several Vista tools that will be XP "down-level" tools. This means they will be made available as XP downloads, although without certain features that you get in the Vista versions.

- **Internet Explorer 7**—The XP version doesn't come with Protected Mode or Parental Controls (see "Security Enhancements" and "Internet Explorer 7," later in this chapter).

- **Windows Defender**—On XP, scan times will be slower because XP doesn't track file changes the way Vista does (see "Transactional NTFS," later in this chapter).

- **Media Player 11**—The XP version won't play content from another PC or device; it won't view content from a Vista Media Library; it won't integrate with the Windows shell; and it won't have Vista's advanced DVD playback features.

The upshot of these deletions, backports, and down-level tools is that Vista is not quite as compelling of a release as it was once touted to be, but there are still plenty of new improvements to make it worth your time.

New Interface Features

You'll be learning about what's new with Vista's interface in detail in Chapter 3, "The Windows Vista Interface." For now, here's a summary of what to expect:

- **The Start "Orb"**—The Start button—a fixture in the computing firmament since Windows 95—has been replaced by an "orb" with the Windows logo, as shown in Figure 1.1.

FIGURE 1.1   Windows Vista replaces the Start button with an orb.

- **The Start Menu**—The Windows Vista Start menu has a new look, as you can see in Figure 1.2. There are still Internet and Email icons pinned to the top of the left side of the menu (although the Email icon now points to Windows Mail, the Vista replacement for Outlook Express), and the collection of links to Windows features on the right has been reconfigured. Also, the icon at the top of the menu changes depending on which link is highlighted. The new Start menu has an integrated Search box as well, which I discuss a bit later in this section.

NOTE

Note also that the names of many Windows features have changed. In particular, Windows Vista no longer tacks on the word *My* to your personal folders (for example, My Documents is now just Documents).

- **The Desktop**—The desktop itself hasn't changed much, although the new high-resolution icons are much prettier than in previous versions. The big change related to the desktop is the new customization interface—called Desktop Background—which is much nicer than the old dialog box of controls and also offers a much wider variety of wallpapers, some of which are quite stunning. Figure 1.3 shows the Control Panel's Desktop Background window.

FIGURE 1.2   The Windows Vista reconfigured Start menu.

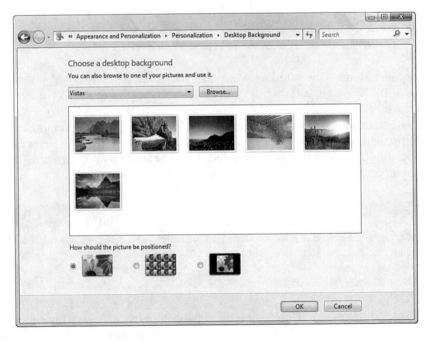

FIGURE 1.3   The Control Panel's Desktop Background window makes it easy to customize the desktop wallpaper, color, and more.

- **Aero Glass**—This is the new look of Vista's window, controls, and other elements. The "Glass" part means that for systems with relatively high-end graphics capabilities, the Vista window title bars and border will have a transparency effect.

- **Window Thumbnails**—These are scaled-down versions of windows and documents. For supported file types, these thumbnails are "live," which means they reflect the current content of the window or document. For example, in folder windows, the icon for an Excel workbook shows the first worksheet, and an icon for a Word document shows the first page. Similarly, a Windows Media Player thumbnail shows live content, such as a running video.

- **Flip and Flip 3D**—When you hold down Alt and press Tab, Vista displays not an icon for each open window, but a thumbnail for each window. Each time you press Tab, Vista "flips" to the next window (hence the name of this new feature: Flip). You can also press Windows Logo+Tab to organize the open windows in a 3D stack. Pressing the arrow keys or scrolling the wheel mouse flips you from one window to another (this feature is called Flip 3D). In Chapter 3, see the section titled "Better Cool Switches: Flip and Flip 3D" for screen shots that show you these features in action.

- **Taskbar Thumbnails**—The live thumbnails idea also extends to the taskbar. If you mouse over a taskbar button, Vista displays a live thumbnail for the window associated with the button, as shown in Figure 1.4.

FIGURE 1.4   When you hover the mouse pointer over a taskbar button, Vista displays a live thumbnail image of the associate window.

- **Folder Windows**—Windows Vista has given folder windows a considerable makeover, as shown in Figure 1.5. The "address" of the folder is hidden in favor of a hierarchical "breadcrumb" folder path, the Task pane is now a strip below the address bar, the Classic (as they're now called) menus are hidden (you can display them by pressing Alt), and the window can be divided into as many as five sections: Besides the folder content, you can display the Navigation pane on the left, the Reading pane on the right, the Search pane above, and the Preview pane below.

- **Instant Search**—Vista's new Windows Search Engine (WSE) promises to be a more powerful alternative to the search capabilities of previous Windows versions. This is partially because WSE supports searching via tags, comments, and other document metadata (see "Support for Document Metadata," later in this chapter). But perhaps the biggest and potentially most useful search innovation in Vista is the Search box that appears at the bottom of the Start menu (see Figure 1.2) and within every folder window (see Figure 1.5). The Search box enables you to perform as-you-type searches, which means that when you type even a single character in the Search box, Vista automatically begins searching all your programs and files (in the case of the Start menu's Search box) or all the files in the current folder (in the case of a folder window's Search box). There are also Instant Search boxes within Windows Media Player, Windows Mail, Windows Photo Gallery, and many other locations.

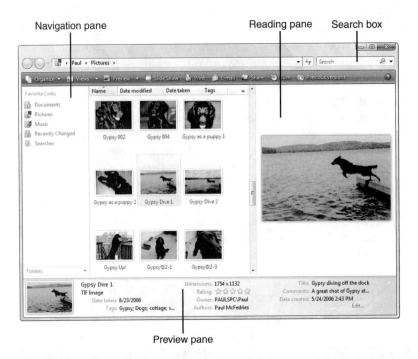

FIGURE 1.5   Folder windows in Windows Vista have been given a serious makeover.

> **NOTE**
>
> Folder windows come with a new Search pane that you can use to perform much more sophisticated searches, including operators such as `starts with` and `doesn't contain`, and also Boolean (AND/OR) searches.

- **Windows Sidebar**—The Windows Sidebar is a pane that appears on the right side of the Vista desktop. You can populate the Sidebar with a new technology called *gadgets*, which are miniapplications that can display the local weather, stock quotes, the current time, RSS newsfeeds, and much more.

What's New Under the Hood

The Windows Vista interface has been garnering most of the attention in the beta program, but Vista also offers plenty of new and improved features under the hood, as the next few sections show.

Support for Document Metadata

Metadata is data that describes data. For example, if you have some digital photos on your computer, you could use metadata to describe each image: the person who took the picture, the camera used, tags that describe the image itself, and so on. Windows Vista comes with built-in support for document metadata, enabling you to add and edit properties such as the Title, Comments, Tags, Author, and Rating (1 to 5 stars).

Windows not only gives you easier ways to edit metadata (for example, you can click the Edit link right in the folder window's Preview pane), but it also makes good use of metadata to make your life easier:

> **NOTE**
>
> For the complete details on metadata, see the section "Metadata and the Windows Explorer Property System" in Chapter 4.

- **Searching**—The Windows Search service indexes metadata (tags) so you can search for documents using any metadata property as a query operand.

- **Grouping**—This refers to organizing a folder's contents according to the values in a particular property. This was also possible in Windows XP, but Windows Vista improves upon XP by adding techniques that enable you to quickly select all the files in a group and to collapse a group to show only its header.

- **Stacking**—This is similar to grouping because it organizes the folder's contents based on the values of a property. The difference is that a stack of files appears in the folder as a kind of subfolder.

- **Filtering**—This refers to changing the folder view so that only files that have one or more specified property values are displayed. For example, you could filter the folder's files to show only those in which the Kind property was, say, Email or Music.

Performance Improvements

When I tell people that I'm testing a prerelease version of Windows, the first question they inevitably ask is, "Is it faster than [insert their current Windows version here]?" Everybody wants Windows to run faster, but that's primarily because most of us are running systems that have had the same OS installed for several years. One of the bitter truths of computing is that even the most meticulously well maintained system will slow down over time. On such systems, the only surefire way to get a big performance boost is to wipe the hard drive and start with a fresh OS install.

The Windows Vista Setup program essentially does just that (preserving and restoring your files and settings along the way, of course). So the short answer to the previous question is, "Yes, Vista will be faster than your existing system." However, that performance gain comes not just from a fresh install, but also because Microsoft has tweaked the Windows code for more speed:

- **Faster startup**—Microsoft has optimized the Vista startup code and implemented asynchronous startup script and application launching. This means that Vista doesn't delay startup by waiting for initialization scripts to complete their chores. It simply completes its own startup tasks while the scripts run in their own good time in the background.

- **Sleep mode**—Actually, you can reduce Vista startup to just a few seconds by taking advantage of the new Sleep mode, which combines the best features of the XP Hibernate and Standby modes. Like Hibernate, Sleep mode preserves all your open documents, windows, and programs, and it completely shuts down your computer. However, like Standby, you enter Sleep mode within just a few seconds, and you resume from Sleep mode within just a few seconds.

- **SuperFetch**—This technology tracks the programs and data you use over time to create a kind of profile of your disk usage. Using the profile, SuperFetch can then make an educated guess about the data that you'll require; like XP's Prefetcher, it can then load that data into memory ahead of time for enhanced performance. SuperFetch can also work with Vista's new ReadyBoost technology, which uses a USB 2.0 Flash drive as storage for the SuperFetch cache, which should provide improved performance even further by freeing up the RAM that SuperFetch would otherwise use.

- **Restart Manager**—This feature enables patches and updates to install much more intelligently. Now you often have to reboot when you install a patch because Windows can't shut down all the processes associated with the application you're patching. Restart Manager keeps track of all running processes and, in most cases, can shut down all of an application's processes so that the patch can be installed without requiring a reboot.

> **NOTE**
>
> I talk about Vista's performance and stability improvements in Chapter 5, "Vista Performance and Maintenance."

Stability Improvements

The second thing that people always ask about a forthcoming version of Windows is, "Will it crash less often? Microsoft has had nearly a quarter of a century to get Windows right, so why can't they produce a glitch-free operating system?" I have to break the news to my frustrated interlocutors that what they seek is almost certainly impossible. Windows is just too big and complex, and the number of software permutations and hardware combinations is just too huge to ensure complete system stability in all setups.

That doesn't mean that Microsoft isn't at least *trying* to make Windows more stable. Here's what they've done in Vista:

- **I/O cancellation**—Windows often fails because some program has crashed and brought the OS down with it. The usual cause of this is that a program has made an input/output (I/O) request to a service, resource, or another program, but that process is unavailable; this results in a stuck program that requires a reboot to recover. To prevent this, Vista implements an improved version of a technology called *I/O cancellation*, which can detect when a program is stuck waiting for an I/O request and then cancel that request to help the program recover from the problem.

- **Reliability monitor**—This new feature keeps track of the overall stability of your system, as well as *reliability events*, which are either changes to your system that could affect stability or occurrences that might indicate instability. Reliability events include Windows updates, software installs and uninstalls, device driver installs, updates, rollbacks and uninstalls, device driver problems, and Windows failures. Reliability monitors graphs these changes and a measure of system stability over time so that you can graphically see whether any changes affected system stability.

- **Service recovery**—Many Windows services are mission-critical, and if they fail, it almost always means that the only way to recover your system is to shut down and restart your computer. With Windows Vista, however, every service has a *recovery policy* that enables Vista not only to restart the service, but also to reset any other service or process that is dependent on the failed service.

- **Startup Repair Tool**—Troubleshooting startup problems is not for the faint-of-heart, but you may never have to perform this onerous core again, thanks to Vista's new Startup Repair Tool (SRT), which is designed to fix many common startup problems automatically. When a startup failure occurs, Vista starts the SRT immediately. The program then analyzes the startup logs and performs a series of diagnostic tests to determine the cause of the startup failure.

- **New diagnostic tools**—Windows Vista is loaded with new and improved diagnostic tools. These include Disk Diagnostics (which monitors the Self-Monitoring, Analysis, and Reporting Technology, or SMART, data generated by most modern hard disks), Windows Memory Diagnostics (which works with Microsoft Online Crash Analysis to determine whether program crashes are caused by defective physical memory), Memory Leak Diagnosis (which looks for and fixes programs that are using up increasing amounts of memory), Windows Resource Exhaustion Detection and Resolution (RADAR, which monitors virtual memory and issues a warning when resources run low, and also identifies which programs or processes are using the most virtual memory and includes a list of these resource hogs as part of the warning), Network Diagnostics (which analyzes all aspects of the network connection and then either fixes the problem or gives the user simple instructions for resolving the situation), and the Windows Diagnostic Console (which enables you to monitor performance metrics).

Security Enhancements

With reports of new Windows XP vulnerabilities coming in with stomach-lurching regu-
larity, we all hope that Vista has a much better security track record. It's still too early to
tell—and nefarious hackers are exceptionally clever—but it certainly looks as though
Microsoft is heading in the right direction with Vista:

> **NOTE**
>
> You can get a detailed look at Vista and security in Chapter 6, "Security Enhancements in
> Windows Vista."

- **User Account Control**—This new—and *very* controversial—feature ensures that
  every Vista user runs with only limited privileges, even those accounts that are part
  of the Administrators group (except the Administrator account itself). In other
  words, each user runs as a "least privileged user," which means users have only the
  minimum privileges they require for day-to-day work. This also means that any
  malicious user or program that gains access to the system also runs with only
  limited privileges, thus limiting the amount of damage they can do. The downside
  (and the source of the controversy) is that you constantly get pestered with security
  dialog boxes that ask for your approval or credentials to perform even trivial tasks,
  such as deleting certain files.

- **Windows Firewall**—This feature is now *bidirectional*, which means that it blocks
  not only unauthorized *incoming* traffic, but also unauthorized *outgoing* traffic. For
  example, if your computer has a Trojan horse installed, it may attempt to send data
  out to the Web, but the firewall's outgoing protection will prevent this.

- **Windows Defender**—This is the Windows Vista antispyware program. (Spyware is a
  program that surreptitiously monitors a user's computer activities or harvests sensitive data on the user's computer, and then sends that information to an individual
  or a company via the user's Internet connection.) Windows Defender prevents
  spyware from being installed on your system and also monitors your system in real
  time to look for signs of spyware activity.

- **Internet Explorer Protected mode**—This new operating mode for Internet Explorer
  builds upon the User Account Control feature. Protected mode means that Internet
  Explorer runs with a privilege level that's enough to surf the Web, but that's about
  it. Internet Explorer can't install software, modify the user's files or settings, add
  shortcuts to the Startup folder, or even change its own settings for the default
  home page and search engine. This is designed to thwart spyware and other malicious programs that attempt to gain access to your system through the web browser.

- **Phishing Filter**—*Phishing* refers to creating a replica of an existing web page to fool
  a user into submitting personal, financial, or password data. Internet Explorer's new
  Phishing Filter can alert you when you surf to a page that is a known phishing site,
  or it can warn you if the current page appears to be a phishing scam.

- **Junk Mail Filter**—Windows Mail (the Vista replacement for Outlook Express) comes with an antispam filter based on the one that's part of Microsoft Outlook. The Junk Mail Filter uses a sophisticated algorithm to scan incoming messages for signs of spam. If it finds any, it quarantines the spam in a separate Junk Mail folder.

- **Windows Service Hardening**—This new technology is designed to limit the damage that a compromised service can wreak upon a system by (among other things) running all services in a lower privilege level, stripping services of permissions that they don't require, and applying restrictions to services that control exactly what they can do on a system.

- **Secure Startup**—This technology encrypts the entire system drive to prevent a malicious user from accessing your sensitive data. Secure Startup works by storing the keys that encrypt and decrypt the sectors on a system drive in a Trusted Platform Module (TPM) 1.2 chip, which is a hardware component available on many newer machines.

- **Network Access Protection (NAP)**—This service checks the *health status* of a computer, including its installed security patches, downloaded virus signatures, and security settings. If any of the health items are not completely up-to-date or within the network guidelines, the NAP enforcement service (running on a server that supports this feature) either doesn't let the computer log on to the network or shuttles the computer off to a restricted area of the network.

- **Parental Controls**—This feature enables you to place restrictions on the user accounts that you've assigned to your children. Using the new User Controls window in the Control Panel, you can allow or block specific websites, set up general site restrictions (such as Kids Websites Only), block content categories (such as Pornography, Mature Content, and Bomb Making), block file downloads, set time limits for computer use, allow or disallow games, restrict games based on ratings and contents, and allow or block specific programs.

Windows Presentation Foundation

The Windows Presentation Foundation (WPF) is Vista's new graphical subsystem, and it's responsible for all the interface changes in the Vista package. WPF implements a new graphics model that can take full advantage of today's powerful graphics processing units (GPUs). With WPF, all output goes through the powerful Direct3D layer (so the CPU doesn't have to deal with any graphics); this output also is all vector based, so WPF produces extremely high-resolution images that are completely scalable.

Desktop Window Manager

The Desktop Window Manager (DWM) is a new technology that assumes control over the screen display. With Vista, applications draw their graphics to an off-screen buffer, and then the DWM composites the buffer contents on the screen.

Improved Graphics

The combination of the WPF and DWM means that Vista graphics are the best Windows graphics ever. Program and document windows no longer "tear" when you move them quickly across the screen, animations applied to actions such as minimizing a window are richer and more effective, icons scale up and down with no loss of quality, and transparency effects are applied to window title bars and borders.

Transactional NTFS

The Windows Vista file system implements a new technology called *Transactional NTFS,* or *TxF,* for short. TxF applies transactional database ideas to the file system. This means that if some mishap occurs to your data—it could be a system crash, a program crash, an overwrite to an important file, or even just imprudent edits to a file—Vista allows you to roll back the file to a previous version. It's a lot like the System Restore feature, except that it works not for the entire system, but for individual files, folders, and volumes.

XML Paper Specification

Windows Vista supports a new Microsoft document format called the XML Paper Specification, or XPS. This is an XML schema designed to create documents that are high-fidelity reproductions of existing documents. In other words, documents published as XPS and opened in an XPS viewer program should look exactly the same as they do in the original application. Microsoft has incorporated an XPS viewer into Windows Vista, so any Vista user will automatically be able to view XPS documents. (The viewer runs within Internet Explorer.)

Microsoft is also licensing XPS royalty-free so developers can incorporate XPS viewing and publishing features into their products without cost. This means it should be easy to publish XPS documents from a variety of applications.

New and Improved Programs and Tools

All new versions of Windows come with a few brand-new programs and tools, as well as a bunch of existing features that have been overhauled, tweaked, or merely prettified. Windows Vista is no exception, and I've talked about a few of these already (including Windows Sidebar, Windows Defender, and the Reliability Monitor). The next few sections take you through the main highlights of the rest of Vista's new and improved programs and tools.

Welcome Center

When you start Windows Vista, you automatically see the new Welcome Center window, shown in Figure 1.6. This window tells you your Vista version and activation status, and provides you with some basic details about your PC (processor, RAM, computer name, and so on). There are also several links for tasks such as setting up devices, working with user accounts, transferring files from your old computer, and viewing more details about your computer.

FIGURE 1.6   The new Welcome Center window appears automatically each time you start Vista.

Control Panel

The Control Panel received a major overhaul in Windows XP, which consisted of a new Category view that divided the icons into 10 categories, such as Appearance and Themes, Printers and Other Hardware, and Network and Internet Connections. This was a boon to novice users because it meant they no longer had to be intimidated by the 30-plus Control Panel icons that came with a default XP install. Power users, of course, *hated* the Category View because it required far too many extra clicks to get at the icon we wanted. Fortunately, Microsoft made it easy to switch between Category view and Classic view, the new name for the old all-icon arrangement of the Control Panel window.

Microsoft has tried again to reconfigure Control Panel in Windows Vista. Perhaps that's because the sheer number of Control Panel icons has exploded in Vista, with a default install foisting more than 50 icons onto your system. That's a lot of icons, even for power users to deal with, so clearly some kind of reorganization is required. Fortunately, Microsoft did *not* simply come up a new set of Control Panel categories that everyone but beginners would ignore. Yes, there are categories, but with a number of twists:

- There are more categories than in XP. There are 11 sections in all (including the Mobile PC category that appears in notebook installations), so the categorization is a bit more fine grained. This is particularly true because several XP "categories"— User Accounts, Add or Remove Programs, and Security Center—were actually icons that launched features.

- The categories are supplemented with links to specific features, as shown in Figure 1.7. For example, besides clicking the Hardware and Sound category to see all of the Control Panel's hardware- and audio-related icons, you can also click Printers or Mouse to go directly to those features.

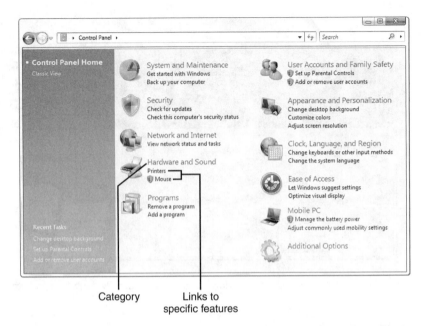

Category   Links to
                specific features

FIGURE 1.7   The Vista Control Panel supplements icon categories with links to specific features.

- Some icons are cross-referenced in multiple categories to make them easier to find. For example, you can find the Power Options icon in both the Hardware and Sound category and the Mobile PC category, and you can find the Windows Firewall icon in both the Security category and the Network and Internet category.

- When you open a category, Control Panel displays a list of all the categories on the left pane, as shown in Figure 1.8. That way, if you pick the wrong category or want to work with a different category, you don't need to navigate back to the Control Panel Home window.

- Control Panel remembers your most recent tasks in each Windows session, as shown in Figure 1.8. This makes it easy to rerun a task that you use frequently.

The Vista Control Panel is clearly superior to its XP predecessor. It's easy to navigate for novices, but it also minimizes mouse clicks for experienced users. However, my guess is that most power users will still use the Classic view and, even faster, will set up the Control Panel as a submenu off the Start menu.

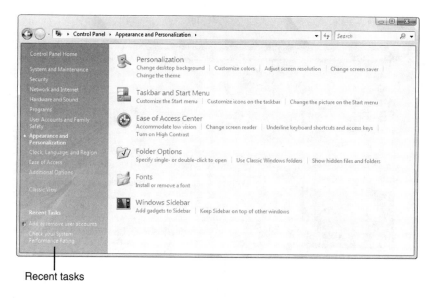

Recent tasks

FIGURE 1.8   When you navigate into a category, Control Panel displays a list of all the categories in the left pane for easy access.

Internet Explorer 7

We haven't seen a new web browser from Microsoft for several years, so you'd expect that Internet Explorer 7 would be chock full of new features. Alas, it's not. The most important new features are the security enhancements that I mentioned earlier (the Phishing Filter and Protected mode). Other than those and a slightly revamped interface, the list of significant new features is disappointingly meager:

- **Tabbed browsing**—Like Firefox, Opera, Safari and quite a few other browsers, Internet Explorer finally has tabbed browsing, in which each open page appears in its own tab within a single Internet Explorer window. Internet Explorer ups the tab ante a bit with a new feature called Quick Tabs that displays a live thumbnail of each tabbed page, as shown in Figure 1.9.

- **Support for RSS feeds**—RSS (Real Simple Syndication) is becoming the preferred method for sites to enable readers to stay up-to-date with changing content. Internet Explorer 7 recognizes when a site has one or more RSS feeds available and enables you to view the feed (see Figure 1.10). You can also subscribe to a feed (see Figure 1.11) to have Internet Explorer alert you when new content is available. Subscribed feeds appear in the new Feeds folder, which is part of the Favorites Center, a pane that also includes the Favorites and History folders.

Click to toggle Quick Tabs   Tabs

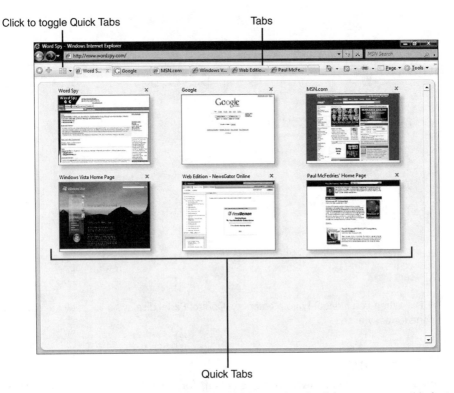

Quick Tabs

FIGURE 1.9   Internet Explorer 7 finally has tabbed browsing, but it improves upon this feature with Quick Tabs, which provides live thumbnails of the tabbed pages.

- **Delete Browsing History**—This new feature gives you an easy way to delete the following data related to your past web browsing: temporary Internet files, cookies, history, saved form data, and remembered passwords. You can delete any one of these options, or you can delete all of them with a single click.

- **Multiple home pages**—Internet Explorer 7 enables you to specify up to eight home pages. When you launch Internet Explorer or click the Home button, Internet Explorer loads each home page in its own tab. This is a great new feature if you always open the same few sites at the start of each browsing session.

CAUTION

There's no such thing as a free browsing lunch, of course. The more home pages you have, the longer it will take Internet Explorer to launch.

- **Manage Add-ons**—If you've installed an add-on program that adds new features such as a toolbar to Internet Explorer, you can use the new Manage Add-ons dialog box to see all the add-ons. You can also use it to enable or disable an add-on and delete an installed ActiveX control.

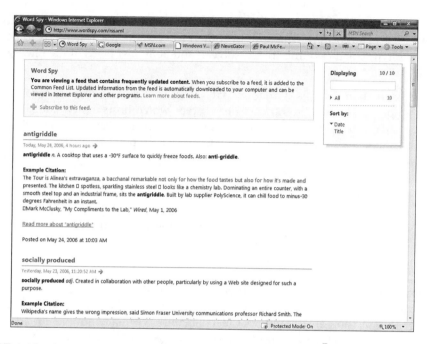

FIGURE 1.10   Internet Explorer can display a site's RSS feed.

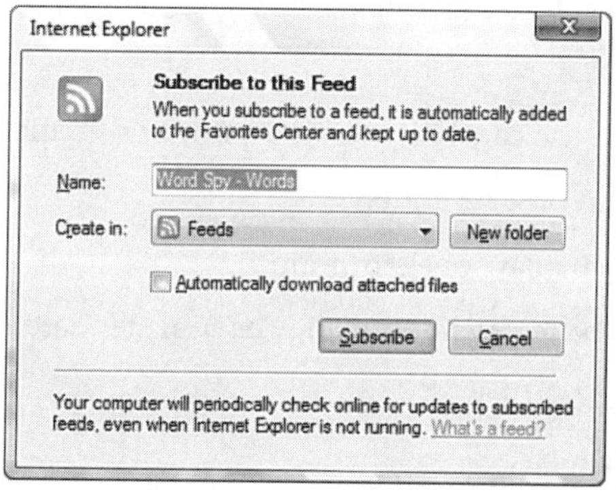

FIGURE 1.11   You can subscribe to an RSS feed to receive alerts about updated site content.

Windows Mail

Windows Mail is the new name for Outlook Express, which Microsoft needed to change because some people were getting it confused with Microsoft Outlook. Unfortunately, the name is just about all that's new with Windows Mail. Only three new features are of any significance:

- **Junk Mail Filter**—Borrowed from Microsoft Outlook's excellent spam filter, this does a fine job of detecting incoming spam and relegating it to the new Junk Email folder.

- **Search box**—Like the Vista Start menu and folder windows, Windows Mail comes with a Search box in the upper-right corner. You can use the Search box to perform as-you-type searches of the To, Cc, subject, and body text fields of the messages in the current folder.

- **Microsoft Help Groups**—Windows Mail comes with a preconfigured account for Microsoft's msnews.microsoft.com news server, which hosts more than 2,000 `microsoft.public.*` newsgroups. If you have a Microsoft Passport ID (such as a Hotmail address), you can log in and rate newsgroup posts as either Useful or Not Useful.

Windows Calendar

Windows is slowly evolving into a complete computing system in the sense that it contains everything that a user with simple needs could want. It has long had a word processor, text editor, graphics editor, web browser, email client, media player, and backup program. What's missing? On the security side, it's essential to have a bidirectional firewall and antispyware tool, and Vista has both of those. Also, all of us need some way to track appointments and to-do lists, so we need a calendar application; Vista now comes with one of those, too, called Windows Calendar, and it's actually not bad for an operating system freebie. It has a nice, clean interface (see Figure 1.12), and it does all the basic jobs that a calendar should:

- Create appointments, both one-time and recurring

- Create all-day events

- Schedule tasks, with the capability to set a priority flag and a completed flag

- Set appointment and task reminders

- View appointments by day, week, or month

- Publish and subscribe to calendars using the iCal standard

- Import Calendar (.ics) files

- Create multiple calendars

Media Player

Vista ships with Windows Media Player 11 (WMP 11), a major update that includes quite a few new features:

- **Cleaner interface**—The overall interface is a bit simpler than in previous versions.

- **Album art**—If you've downloaded or scanned album art, it appears throughout the WMP 11 interface, which is much nicer than previous versions, in which album art appeared only rarely.

- **Grouping and stacking of media**—The grouping and stacking techniques that I mentioned earlier for folder windows also apply to the WMP library. For music, for example, WMP offers several views based on media metadata, including Songs view, which groups songs according the values in the Album Artist property and then by the values in the Album property, and Genre, which stacks the albums using the values in the Genre property. You get a different set of views for each category (Music, Pictures, Video, Recorded TV, or Other Media).

- **Advanced Tag Editor**—You can easily apply media metadata by downloading the relevant information from the Internet, but most WMP metadata is editable. A new innovation in WMP 11 is the Advanced Tag Editor, which gives you a front end for much of the metadata available for a particular media file.

- **As-you-type search**—The WMP 11 window has a Search box in the upper-right corner that enables you to perform as-you-type searches. After you type your text in the Search box, WMP searches filenames and metadata for matching media files; it shows the results in the WMP window.

- **Synching with media devices**—Synching items from the Library to a media device is a bit easier in WMP 11. When you insert a WMP-compatible media device, WMP recognizes it and automatically displays the device, its total capacity, and its available space in the Sync tab. Also, WMP 11 supports two-way synching, which means that you can not only synch files from your PC to a media device, but you can also synch files from a media device to your PC.

- **Easier ripping**—Ripping files from an audio CD is more convenient in WMP 11 because the program gives you easier access to rip settings. For example, if you pull down the Rip tab list, you can select Format to display a list of file formats, including various Windows Media Audio formats (regular, Variable Bit Rate, and Lossless), MP3, and—new in WMP 11—WAV. You can also pull down the Rip menu and select Bit Rate to choose the rate at which you want to rip the media.

- **Burning options**—Burning music or other media to a disc is more flexible in WMP 11. For one thing, WMP supports burning media to a DVD disc. For another, WMP 11 comes with a new Burn tab in its options dialog box, which you can use to select the burn speed, apply volume leveling to audio CDs, select the file list format for a data disc, and set the file quality.

- **URGE support**—WMP 11 automatically downloads and installs the URGE store, which is the online music store that Microsoft has created in collaboration with MTV.

- **Library Sharing**—This feature enables you to share your WMP Library with other network users, just like you'd share a folder or a printer.

- **DVD playback**—When you play a DVD in WMP 11, a DVD button is added to the playback controls. Clicking that button displays the DVD menu, which offers a much wider array of DVD-related commands than in previous versions. Welcome additions to the DVD arsenal are the capabilities to select audio and language tracks (if available), display subtitles (if any), and capture frames.

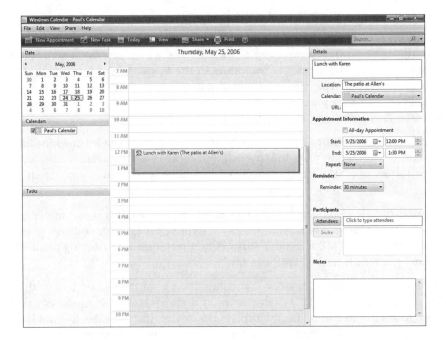

FIGURE 1.12   Windows Calendar is a reasonably competent calendar program.

Media Center

You'll find no separate Media Center Edition of Windows Vista as there was with Windows XP. Instead, Vista comes with Media Center as part of its Home Premium and Ultimate editions. Here's a summary of the changes Microsoft has made to the Vista version of Media Center:

- **Interface improvements**—Microsoft has tweaked the Media Center interface to make it easier to use. The top-level tasks (TV, Music, and so on) appear more like a list than menu choices, as they do in XP Media Center. When you select a top-level task, Vista Media Center bolds the task text and displays the available second-level tasks below. When you select a second-level task, Media Center displays a graphic along with the task text to illustrate the task's function. As the displayed tasks move away from the center of the screen (whether up or down, left or right), they become progressively lighter. This focuses the user's attention on the task at hand in the center of the screen.

- **New menu structure**—The Vista Media Center comes with quite a few top-level tasks, including Pictures + Videos (work with your picture and video libraries), Movies (work with DVD movies), TV (work with your TV tuner), Music (work with music and radio), Spotlight (access media online and run other Media Center programs installed on your computer), Tools (access Media Center tools), and Tasks (run other Media Center features).

- **Show notifications for incoming phone calls**—You can set up Media Center to display these notifications for all incoming calls or just for calls with Caller ID.

- **Wireless networking**—You can now use the Media Center to join your computer to an existing wireless network.

- **Parental controls**—You can set up parental controls to restrict the content that is viewed through Media Center.

- **Program optimization**—Vista Media Center comes with an optimization feature that ensures maximum performance from your system. Optimization occurs automatically every morning at 4 a.m., but you can set your own schedule.

Windows Photo Gallery

Windows Photo Gallery is a new program that can import images and videos from a camera, a scanner, removable media, the network, or the Web. You can then view the images, add metadata such as captions and tags, rate the images, search for images, and even apply common fixes to improve the look of photos. You can also burn selected images to a DVD disc.

DVD Burning and Authoring

Windows Vista offers DVD-burning capabilities in a number of places, including Windows Photo Gallery, Windows Media Player, Media Center, and Windows Movie Maker. Vista also comes with Windows DVD Maker, a program that enables you to author actual DVD discs, complete with menus, chapters, and other elements of a typical DVD disc interface.

Per-Application Volume Control

Windows Vista implements a new technology called *per-application volume control*. This means that Vista gives you a volume-control slider for every running program and process that is currently producing audio output. Figure 1.13 shows the new Volume window that appears when you double-click the Volume icon in the notification area. The slider on the left controls the speaker volume, so you can use it as a system-wide volume control. The rest of the window contains the *application mixer*—sliders and mute buttons for individual programs.

Sound Recorder

Vista's Sound Recorder program is completely new and improves upon its predecessors by offering unlimited record time and the capability to record to the Windows Media Audio file format (previous versions were limited to 1 minute of WAV audio).

Windows Easy Transfer

Windows Transfer is the replacement for the XP Files and Settings Transfer Wizard. It works in much the same way as the XP wizard, but Windows Easy Transfer supports a broader range of transfer media, including Flash drives.

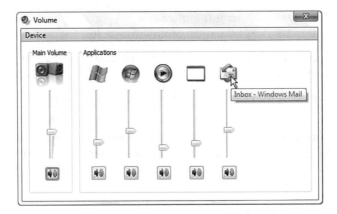

FIGURE 1.13   Windows Vista uses per-application volume control to enable you to set the volume level for each program that outputs audio.

Windows Backup

The Windows Vista new backup program—now called Windows Backup—is quite an improvement on its predecessors:

- You can back up to a writeable disc, USB Flash drive, or other removable media.

- You can back up to a network share.

- When you set up the program, backing up is completely automated, particularly if you back up to a resource that has plenty of room to hold your files (such as a hard disk or roomy network share).

- You can create a *system image backup*—which Microsoft calls a CompletePC backup—that saves the exact state of your computer and thus enables you to completely restore your system if your computer dies or is stolen.

The Game Explorer

The Game Explorer is a special shell folder that offers several new features for gamers and game developers:

- A repository for all installed games.

- Game-related tasks such as launching a game, linking to the developer's website, and setting up parental controls.

- Support for games metadata, such as the game's publisher and version number and the last time you played the game. The Game Explorer also supports ratings from various organizations, including the Entertainment Software Rating Board (ESRB).

- Auto-update of games. With the new Game Update feature, Vista automatically lets you know if a patch or a newer version is available for an installed game.

The Game Explorer is initially populated with the eight games that come in the Vista box. These games include updates to venerable Windows favorites (FreeCell, Hearts, Minesweeper, Solitaire, Spider Solitaire, and InkBall) and a few new additions (Chess Titans, Mahjong Titans, and Purble Place).

Mobility Center

The new Windows Mobility Center offers a convenient overview of the state of various mobility features on your notebook computer. As you can see in Figure 1.14, the Mobility Center enables you to view and control the brightness, volume, battery status, wireless network connection, screen orientation for a Tablet PC, external display, and current synchronization status of your offline files.

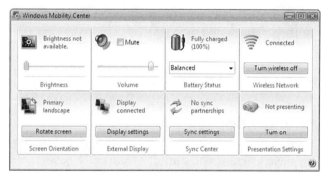

FIGURE 1.14   The new Mobility Center offers a selection of information and controls for note-book-related features.

Network Center

Network Center is the new Vista networking hub that shows you the current status of your connection and gives you quick access to all the most common networking tasks: connecting to a network, browsing a network, setting up a network (including new *ad hoc connections*, which are temporary hookups between two or more nearby PCs), and diagnosing network problems.

Network Map

The Network Center displays a subset of the new Network Map feature, which gives you a visual display of everything your computer is connected to: network connections (wired and wireless), ad hoc connections, Internet connections, and more. Network Map also gives you a visual display of the connection status so you can easily spot problems. Windows Vista comes with a more detailed version of Network Map, an example of which is shown in Figure 1.15.

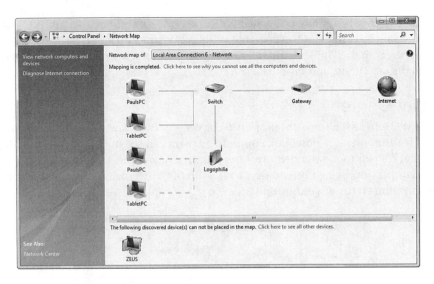

FIGURE 1.15   The full version of the Network Map.

Windows Collaboration

Vista's replacement for NetMeeting is an entirely new program called Windows Collaboration. As with NetMeeting, you can use Windows Collaboration to show a local program or document to any number of remote users, and you can collaborate on a document with remote users. Windows Collaboration uses several new Vista technologies, including Peer-to-Peer Networking, Distributed File System Replicator (DFSR), and People Near Me. The latter is an opt-in list of people on the same network that you are. The idea is that you start a collaboration session and then invite one or more people from the People Near Me list to join the session. You can then start a *presentation*, which involves one of the participants performing some sort of action on his or her computer, and the other participants seeing the results of those actions within their session window. For example, you can demonstrate how a program works, collaborate on a document, or share your desktop, which enables remote users to view everything you do on your computer.

How Windows Vista Affects You

Everybody uses an operating system in a different way and approaches a new operating system with different expectations. Some of those expectations are nearly universal: We all want an OS that's fast, secure, and stable, and if it's pretty to look at as well, that's a bonus. Beyond all that, different types of users focus on different aspects of the system. The rest of this chapter looks at nine different user types—IT professionals, developers, power users, digital media users, business users, road warriors, small business owners, gamers, and parents—and discusses what in Vista should appeal to them (or repel them).

IT Professionals

The big news for IT pros is the new set of deployment tools and technologies that Microsoft has created for Windows Vista. In the past, deploying Windows to multiple desktops was a time-consuming and complex chore that require a hodgepodge of tools from not only Microsoft, but usually a few third-party vendors as well. I discuss Vista deployment in more detail in Chapter 2, "Moving to Windows Vista," but here's a summary of what's new that will make your life easier:

- **Modularized Windows**—Vista begins with a core OS that contains 95% of the functionality, and all the other editions are created by adding the appropriate modules to that core. This includes not only OS features such as Media Player and games, but also language packs.

- **Windows Imaging (WIM)**—This is a new file-based imaging file format that enables you to create images for deployment. WIM files can contain images for multiple SKUs, so you can deploy any edition of Vista, for any computer type, in any language, customized in any way you want, using just a *single* file.

- **System Image Manager**—This new GUI and command-line tool enables you to create a custom Vista deployment.

- **XML answer file**—The customizations and settings created by Setup Manager are stored in a single XML file, usually called `unattend.xml`.

- **XImage**—This command-line tool enables you to capture volume to image files, mount image files to folders for offline editing of the image, and perform other image-based tasks.

Support professionals always want a more stable Windows to make their lives easier. Vista innovations such as I/O Cancellation, Service Recovery, and the Startup Repair Tool should help keep users up and running, and the extra security offered by User Account Control, Windows Defender, and Windows Service Hardening should keep users out of trouble. However, it's also good to know that diagnostic tools such as the Reliability Monitor, Disk Diagnostics, and Network Diagnostics should ease tech support when problems crop up.

However, if there's one technology that has the potential to turn IT engineers into corporate stars, it's probably Transactional NTFS and the previous versions of files that it creates. There probably isn't a support desk pro who hasn't been yelled at because an employee has lost all of his or her work due to a program crash. By restoring a recent version of that work with just a few mouse clicks, there will be kudos and glory for all.

Developers

The big news for independent software vendors (ISVs) and other Windows developers is WinFX, the new application programming interface (API) for Vista. WinFX is based on (actually, it's a superset of) the .NET Framework. That's where the name comes from: WinFX is the Windows .NET Framework Extension. Its .NET underpinnings tell you that

WinFX is a managed API, which means that the runtime environment handles things such as allocating and reclaiming memory. (In the old Win32 API, programmers had to manage memory themselves.) This should mean that WinFX applications are a bit more stable than their Win32 counterparts because there's less chance of memory mismanagement or other programmer error. (Of course, the old Win32 API is still supported in Vista, meaning that most Windows applications built on the Win32 framework will still work in Vista.)

A major component of WinFX is the Windows Presentation Foundation, which developers should love because it replaces the myriad of APIs—including but not limited to the Graphics Device Interface (GDI), Direct3D, OpenGL, DirectShow, USER32, and Windows Forms—with a single API. With WPF, developers can do 2D, 3D, animation, imaging, video, audio, special effects, and text rendering using a single API that works consistently no matter what type of object the developer is working with.

Developers also get to play with a new markup language called XAML—eXtensible Application Markup Language—which acts as a kind of front end for building interfaces. XAML implements a simple markup language that enables developers and designers to work together to build user interfaces.

Microsoft has also put together a number of APIs that enable developers to hook into other new Vista features. Here's a list of just a few of these new features that come with APIs:

- Microsoft has published the API for viewing and manipulating XPS documents, so there's little doubt that third-party developers will come up with XPS viewers for the Mac, Linux, and other systems. Microsoft is also licensing XPS royalty-free, so developers can incorporate XPS viewing and publishing features into their products without cost. This means it should be easy to publish XPS documents from a variety of applications.

- Microsoft is giving PC manufacturers access to the Mobility Center, so we'll likely see the Mobility Center window customized with features that are specific to particular notebooks.

- Microsoft has created an API for SideShow, so third-party developers can create programs and gadgets that you can add to your SideShow menu.

- Microsoft is making I/O cancellation available to developers via an API, so programs, too, can cancel unresponsive requests and recover on their own.

- Microsoft is providing developers with an API for the RADAR tool, thus enabling vendors to build resource exhaustion detection into their applications. When such a program detects that it is using excessive resources, or if it detects that the system as a whole is low on virtual memory, the program can free resources to improve overall system stability.

- There is an API for the Windows System Assessment Tool (WinSAT), so third-party programs—particularly games—can access the assessments and tune program features depending on the WinSAT metrics.

- Windows Vista supports DirectX 10, the latest version of the Windows graphics APIs, which have been completely rewritten to take full advantage of the powerful graphics hardware that's now available for PCs.

Power Users

Power users may at first be disappointed with Windows Vista because, as part of Microsoft's constant quest to make Windows easier for novices and casual users, the OS becomes increasingly encrusted with "user-friendly" features that might get in the way of the power user's goal of efficiency and speed. However, the Windows programmers and designers are mostly power users themselves, so in many cases they've slipped in alternative methods to work around the hand-holding.

For example, most power users will probably be driven to the point of insanity by User Account Control and its endless requests for your permission to do many things. I can attest that you *do* get used to it after a week or two. However, what's truly annoying about UAC is that it simply won't let you do some tasks—it won't even ask for permission. A good example is editing a file in a protected folder. For instance, I often modify the lmhosts file to ensure proper networking, but UAP doesn't let me save my changes. However, I can get around this by right-clicking the Notepad icon and then clicking Run As Administrator.

Power users will get the most out of Vista to the extent that they discover and use such workarounds (which I talk about in more detail in my book *Windows Vista Unleashed*, also from Sams Publishing, 2006).

Digital Media Users

If you're a big digital media user, you should love Windows Vista because so many of its innovations and improvements were made with digital media in mind. Got a massive digital music collection? Then it will find a good home in Windows Media Player 11. The interface lets you view your music in many different ways (such as grouped or stacked), and the new search engine is lightning quick, even with the largest music collections.

> **NOTE**
>
> See Chapter 9, "Digital Media in Windows Vista," to learn more about what's new in Media Player, Media Center, and other media programs.

Microsoft has said that it will ship all the Vista SKUs to each OEM, which gives computer manufacturers complete freedom to put any version of Vista on any machine (as long as the hardware supports it). This should mean that Media Center PCs become more popular because it will no longer be perceived as some "other" version of the OS. That's good news for people looking to set up a PC as a home media hub. With its support for all types of media, as well as TV tuners, radio tuners, and media broadcast hardware, the Vista Media Center should take pride of place as the center of such as hub.

Business Users

Generalizing is always a risky proposition, but I think I'm going out on a pretty sturdy limb when I say that the majority of business users don't care about their computer's operating system. They're more focused on getting their job done as quickly and as efficiently as possible; it's the operating system's job to help when it can, and to get out of the way the rest of the time.

So, will Vista help business users get their jobs done? The new OS does come with quite a few efficiencies that should make many day-to-day chores faster. Features like as-you-type searching, faster and more powerful document searching, the streamlined Start menu, live thumbnails (particularly with Flip and taskbar thumbnails), the capability to group and stack documents, and Windows Sidebar are all productivity boosters. On the other hand, in some cases, Vista requires *more* involvement from the business user. The most obvious example here is document metadata, which is a great way to organize data but requires time to enter the data into each property.

How about getting out of the way of the business user? Most recent versions of Windows do a pretty good job of this, and Vista is no exception. When you're performing normal business chores, you'll probably rarely have to interact with Vista itself. The exception here will be when you try to do anything that runs afoul of the User Account Control policies, and that dialog box comes up yet again. Users will also be getting pestered by Windows Firewall (to block or allow some programs) and Windows Defender (to block or allow certain actions), so I can foresee a backlash against all these so-called "nag" dialog boxes. Also, most existing Windows applications should run well under Vista, but device driver support might be spotty for a while, and that could slow people down. In the end, however, business users want an operating system that works. Nothing sucks up time like an unstable OS that requires constant reboots, tweaking, and repairing. If Vista's promise of increased stability proves true, businesses should flock to the new OS in droves.

Unfortunately, however, the real problem for business users, particularly corporate desktops, will be having enough horsepower—especially graphics power—to run Vista well and to take advantage of its new features. Business machines tend to have only the minimum amount of RAM necessary, and they almost always have a low-end graphics card. Without upgrades, this will mean that Vista runs quite slowly and that the nice Aero Glass interface and other effects will be disabled.

Road Warriors

The legion of mobile users who take their notebooks on the road will find a lot to like in Vista. The new Mobility Center makes it easy to quickly monitor and change important settings such as the screen brightness, speaker volume, and battery. Vista also comes with a new Mobile PC icon in the Control Panel that gives notebook users easy access to other settings related to notebooks, such as the display and audio devices.

NOTE

See Chapter 7, "Mobile Computing with Windows Vista," for more details on all the mobility features I discuss in this section.

Users who lug their notebooks with them to give presentations will make good use of the Vista Presentation Settings. This new feature enables you to specify several different notebook settings relating to giving a presentation, including turning off the screen saver, deactivating system alerts (such as incoming email messages), setting the speaker volume, and choosing a desktop background. When you're about to give a presentation, you can apply all of these settings with just a few clicks of the mouse.

In the long run, perhaps the most useful of Vista's new mobility features will be Windows SideShow, which enables a notebook manufacturer to add a small, secondary display to the outside of a notebook case, and enables Vista to display information on that secondary display—such as calendar data, email messages, and Media Player "now playing" data and playback controls—even if the computer is in sleep mode or turned off.

Small Business Owners

I mentioned earlier that Windows Vista is the closest that a Microsoft OS has come to being a complete system. If you're a small business owner on a budget, the addition of Windows Calendar, Windows Defender, and the bidirectional Windows Firewall should help your bottom line. Of course, you'll still likely need mainstream business tools such as a spreadsheet, database, and accounting package.

Most small businesses lack an IT department, so Vista's simple installation, easy network setups, new monitoring tools such as the Reliability Monitor, and myriad diagnostic tools should help most businesses reduce third-party IT costs.

Gamers

One of Microsoft's goals with Vista is to turn the PC into a viable gaming platform that can compete with or even exceed the capabilities of dedicated platforms such as the Xbox 360 and forthcoming PlayStation 3. To that end, Vista introduces a number of gaming features, including the Game Explorer and support for ESRB ratings that I mentioned earlier. Vista also supports a number of game-related metadata—including the last date you played the game, the game version and release date, and the genre (such as Shooter or Strategy). Vista also comes with built-in support for peer-to-peer gaming, enabling you to play along with others on your network.

NOTE

To learn more about Game Explorer, ESRB ratings, and other Vista gaming innovations, see Chapter 10, "Windows Vista and Gaming."

Microsoft is also making it easier for game developers to write games for the PC by giving programmers access to WinSAT metrics, implementing the powerful DirectX 10 API, defining game-definition files that enable the game to appear in the Game Explorer, and putting developer-friendly touches into the Game Explorer: links to the developer's community and support web pages, automatic update of games, and more.

Parents

When it comes to kids and computers, most parent want to know two things about a new operating system:

- Can it help protect my kids from others?

- Can it help protect my kids from themselves?

Windows Defender, Internet Explorer Protected mode, and the bidirectional Windows Firewall all work to ensure that kids can't download and install viruses, spyware, Trojan horses, and other malware. Also, Vista's support for ESRB and other game-rating systems will help you make decisions about which games your kids can play. Note, too, that it's important to set up younger kids with their own standard user account to ensure the full effects of User Account Control.

With accounts set up for the kids, you can also take full advantage of the new set of Parental Controls in Vista. This will enable you to restrict website content and games, block specific programs, and set time limits on computer usage.

From Here

Here are some other sections in the book where you'll find information related to the topics in this chapter:

- For the details on the Vista look and feel, see Chapter 3.

- For more about file system features such as searching, grouping, stacking, Transactional NTFS, and XPS, see Chapter 4.

- To learn about the performance and stability enhancement in Vista, see Chapter 5.

- What's new in security is the subject of Chapter 6.

- See Chapter 7 for more details on all the mobility features I discussed in this chapter.

- To get the details on what's new with digital media, see Chapter 9.

- Vista's new gaming features are the topic of Chapter 10.

2

Moving to Windows Vista

As I write this, a few months before Windows Vista is slated to hit the shelves, Microsoft's dominance of the desktop remains as solid as ever. Combining the numbers from all Windows versions (particularly XP, Me, 2000, and 98), Microsoft enjoys about a 90% share of the client operating system market, give or take a point or two. That's dominant, with a capital "D."

With numbers like that, it's almost a certainty that any new operating system release from Microsoft is going to be a smashing success. After all, nearly every new non-Macintosh computer is sold with a version of Windows preinstalled, and tens of millions of new computers are sold each year, so any new version of Windows will have instant market clout. I see no reason why that trend won't continue with Windows Vista.

However, when you have a solid lock on 90% of the market, your definition of "success" is likely to be a bit more stringent. Sure, Microsoft is pleased as punch that so many copies of Windows go out the door on new PCs, but what Microsoft desires even more is a brisk retail trade because retail sales mean OS upgrades. And in its secret heart-of-hearts, Microsoft's ultimate goal for every new Windows release is to have each and every Windows user upgrade to the new version. That would be not only immensely profitable, but also cheaper because it would mean only one OS to support. Of course, a complete migration to a new version of Windows or any other OS has never happened and never will. Given that fact, Microsoft's Windows team is happy even if just a significant portion of the current user base makes the move to the new OS.

That did *not* happen with Windows XP, particularly in the corporate market, where many IT managers and chief technology officers decided to stick with the robust and familiar Windows 2000 client. That's not to say that Windows XP was in any sense a failure—not even close. Millions of people *did* upgrade to XP, and tens of millions of people received XP on their new machines. By any measure, XP has been Microsoft's most successful OS yet.

What will happen with Windows Vista? It's too soon to tell, although I'd bet a good percentage of those long-in-the-tooth Windows 2000 desktops will upgrade to the new OS. The real key for Microsoft will be the number of XP users who follow the company to Vista. XP has been a solid performer that gets better with each fix that comes down the Windows Update pipeline. And with Microsoft's decision to backport key new technologies such as Windows Presentation Foundation and Windows Communications Foundation to XP, not to mention the availability of Internet Explorer 7 for XP, it might seem like a tough sell.

If you find yourself on the upgrade bubble, this chapter should help because I take you through everything you need to know about making the move to Windows Vista.

Windows Vista System Requirements

Personal computing is governed by two inexorable, and not unrelated, "laws":

> **Moore's Law**—Processing power doubles every 18 months (from Gordon Moore, cofounder of Intel).

> **Parkinson's Law of Data**—Data expands to fill the space available for storage (from the original Parkinson's Law: Work expands to fill the time available).

These two observations help explain why, when the computers we use are becoming increasingly powerful, our day-to-day tasks never really seem all that much faster. The leaps in processing power and memory are being matched by the increasing complexity and resource requirements of the latest programs. So the computer you're using today might be twice as muscular as the one you were using a year and a half ago, but the applications you're using are twice the size and require twice as many resources.

Windows fits neatly into this scenario. With each new release of Microsoft's flagship operating system, the hardware requirements become more stringent, and our computers' processing power is taxed a little more. Windows Vista is no exception. Even though Microsoft spent an enormous amount of time and effort trying to shoehorn Vista into a minimal system configuration, you need a reasonably powerful computer if you don't want to spend most of your day cursing the dreaded hourglass icon. The good news is that Windows Vista's hardware requirements are nowhere near as onerous as many people believed they would be. In fact, most midrange or better systems purchased in the past year or two should run Vista without a problem. The next few sections present a rundown of the system requirements you need to meet in order to install and work with Windows Vista. Note that I give both the minimum requirements as stipulated by Microsoft, and a set of "reasonable" requirements that I believe you need to make working with Vista more or less pleasurable.

Processor Requirements

Vista desktop minimum: 800MHz modern processor

For adequate Vista performance, you need at least a midrange processor, which means an Intel Pentium 4 or Celeron, or an AMD Athlon or Sempron running at 2.66–3.0GHz. Faster is better, of course, but only if money is no object. Moving up to 3.2GHz or 3.6GHz might set you back a few hundred dollars, but the performance improvement won't be all that noticeable. You'd be better off investing those funds either in extra memory (discussed below) or in a dual-core processor.

> **NOTE**
>
> What does *dual-core* mean? It describes a CPU that combines two separate processors, each with its own cache memory, on a single chip. (The cache memory is an on-board storage area that the processor uses to store commonly used bits of data. The bigger the cache, the greater the performance.) This enables the operating system to perform two tasks at once without a performance hit. For example, you could work in your word processor or spreadsheet program in the foreground using one processor, while the other processor takes care of a background spyware or virus check. Current examples of dual-core processors are the Intel Pentium D series and Pentium Extreme Edition, and the AMD Athlon 64 X2.

The 64-bit processors are becoming more affordable, and they run the 64-bit version of Vista like a dream (one of my Vista test machines was 64-bit, and it was a pleasure to use). Look for a 64-bit Pentium 4 or any of the several x64 chips available from AMD. Note, however, that although these 64-bit machines can run 32-bit applications without a performance hit, those programs will *not* run any faster with the wider bus. To see a speed boost with your applications, you have to wait for 64-bit versions of Windows Vista and the applications you intend to run on it.

Memory Requirements

Vista minimum: 512MB

You can run Vista on a system with 512MB of RAM, but the performance will be quite slow. Admittedly, I've been running beta versions of Vista, which are always slower than release versions because they contain debugging code and are works-in-progress as far as optimization goes. However, I believe that, for most people, 1GB is a more realistic minimum for day-to-day work, and that's how much RAM Microsoft recommends for "Windows Vista Premium Ready" systems. If you regularly have many programs running at the same time, or if you use programs that manipulate digital photos or play music, consider moving up to 1.5GB. If you do extensive work with large files such as databases, or if you use programs that manipulate digital videos, 2GB should be your RAM goal.

Note, however, that if you select a 64-bit processor, you should seriously consider upgrading your system RAM. The conventional wisdom is that because 64-bit machines deal with data in chunks that are twice the size of those in 32-bit machines, you need twice the memory to take full advantage of the 64-bit advantage. So if you'd normally have 1GB of RAM in a 32-bit machine, opt for 2GB in your 64-bit computer.

Finally, consider the speed of the memory. Older DDR (double data rate) memory chips typically operate at between 100MHz (PC-1600) and 200MHz (PC-3200), while newer DDR2 chips run between 200MHz (PC2-3200) and 533MHz (PC2-8500). The up-and-coming DDR3 chips will operate at between 400 and 800MHz, which is a substantial speed boost and should improve Vista performance noticeably.

NOTE

Memory module numbers such as PC-3200 and PC2-8500 tell you the theoretical bandwidth of the memory. For example, PC-3200 implies a theoretical bandwidth of 3200MBps. To calculate theoretical bandwidth, you first multiply the base chip speed by 2 to get the effective clock speed. (Modern memory is *double-pumped*, which means data is transferred at the beginning and the end of each clock cycle.) You then multiply the effective clock speed by 8 (because the memory path is 64 bites wide and there are 8 bits in each byte). So a 100MHz chip has an effective clock speed of 200MHz and, therefore, a theoretical bandwidth of 1600MBps, so it is called PC-1600 memory.

The System Rating

One of the new features in Windows Vista is a *system rating* that Vista calculates for each computer on which it's installed. As shown in Figure 2.1, this rating appears in the System window (on the Start menu, right-click Computer and then click Properties). The rating is a numeric value that's based on the ratings given to your computer's processor, how much RAM is installed on your system, your graphics card and RAM, and the GPU's gaming graphics performance.

Why would Microsoft calculate such a rating? Certainly, it's not to let you know whether your machine is capable of running Vista, because of course you need to install and run Vista to see the rating. Instead, the system rating is part of the performance calculations that the Windows System Assessment Tool (WinSAT) generates. This tool analyzes your system so that applications that support WinSAT (particularly games) can enable or disable certain features based on their performance.

NOTE

For more detailed information on WinSAT, see the section "Windows System Assessment Tool (WinSAT)," in Chapter 5, "Vista Performance and Maintenance."

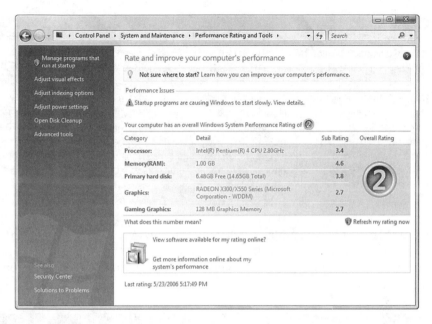

FIGURE 2.1   Windows Vista rates your system's performance.

Storage Requirements

Vista hard disk free space minimum: 15GB

The disk space requirements depend on which version of Vista you're installing, but count on the new OS requiring at least 15GB free space to install. The OS will use perhaps another few gigabytes for the storage of things such as the paging file, System Restore checkpoints, Internet Explorer temporary file, and the Recycle Bin, so Vista will require at least 20GB of storage. These days, of course, it's not the operating system that usurps the most space on our hard drives; it's the massive multimedia files that now seem to be routine for most of us. Multimegabyte digital photos and spreadsheets, and even *multigigabyte* database files and digital video files are not unusual. Fortunately, hard disk storage is dirt cheap these days, with most disks costing less—often *much* less—than a dollar a gigabyte.

Note, too, that the type of hard drive can affect performance. An older IDE drive that spins at 5,400RPM will be a significant performance bottleneck. Moving up to a 7,200RPM drive will help immeasurably, and a 10,000RPM drive is even better if you don't mind the extra expense. You should also consider moving from the older, parallel IDE technology to the new Serial Advanced Technology Attachment (SATA) drives, which are at least theoretically faster (with data-transfer rates starting at 150MBps). Look for a SATA drive with an 8MB cache and Native Command Queuing (NCQ).

NOTE

Native Command Queuing (NCQ) is a relatively new hard-disk technology aimed at solving a long-standing hard-disk performance problem. Requests for hard-drive data are stored in the memory controller and are handled in sequence by the disk's on-board controller. Unfortunately, whenever the controller processes requests for data that is stored in areas that are far away from each other, it causes a significant performance hit. For example, suppose request 1 is for data stored near the start of the disk, request 2 is for data near the end of the disk, and request 3 is again for data near the start of the disk. In a typical hard disk, the read/write heads must travel from the start of the disk to the end, and then back again, processing each request in the order it was received. With NCQ, the controller reorders the requests so that the 1 and 3, which are close to each other, are carried out first, and only then is the distant request 2 carried out.

Finally, you should also bear in mind that one of Windows Vista's new features is the ability to burn data to recordable DVDs. To take advantage of this, your system requires a DVD burner, preferably one that supports both the DVD-RW and DVD+RW disc formats (that is, a DVD±RW drive) .

NOTE

To learn more about Vista's new DVD features, see the section "DVD Authoring," in Chapter 9, "Digital Media in Windows Vista."

Graphics Requirements

Vista graphics memory minimum: 32MB

You'll be learning a lot more about Vista's graphical underpinnings in Chapter 3, "The Windows Vista Interface." For now, however, it's important to note that Microsoft is taking a sensibly cautious route to graphics requirements. Vista's interface is graphics intensive, but it will be smart enough to adopt a less intensive interface based on what your PC can handle. Whether Vista holds back on the visual bells and whistles depends on whether you have a separate AGP or PCI Express graphics adapter (as opposed to an integrated motherboard graphics chip), the capability of the card's graphics processing unit (GPU), and how much graphics memory the card has on board:

- If Vista detects a low-end card, it defaults to the Windows Classic theme, which offers a Windows 2000–like interface.

- If Vista detects a card with medium-range capabilities, it uses the new Aero theme, but without the Glass effects (such as transparency).

- If Vista detects a high-end card, it defaults to the full Aero Glass interface.

To get the beautiful Aero Glass look as well as the new 3D and animated effects, your system should have a graphics processor that supports DirectX 9, Pixel Shader 2.0 (in hardware, not as a software emulation), and 32 bits per pixel, and comes with a device driver that supports the new Windows Vista Display Driver Model (WDDM). (If you purchase a new video card, look for the Windows Vista Capable or Windows Vista Premium Ready logo on the box. If you just need to upgrade the driver for an existing graphics card, look for "WDDM" in the drive name or description.)

The amount of onboard memory you need depends on the resolution you plan to use (assuming you're using a single monitor; for dual monitors, double the memory):

- If you'll be using a basic 800×600 or 1024×768 resolution, 32MB is enough.

- If you want to run up to 1280×1024, then you need at least 64MB.

- If you want to run up to 1920×1200, then you need at least 128MB.

> **TIP**
>
> Graphics memory is like system memory: You can never have too much, and it's always a good investment to buy a card that has much as you can get. One of Microsoft's Vista FAQs said it best: "The most [graphics] memory your bank account can afford is the ticket."

Before the final release of Vista, it wasn't clear whether *any* integrated graphics chips would support the full Aero Glass interface, although I've seen reports that some integrated graphics hardware—such as the Intel 945 and the ATI Radeon XPress X200—can handle Aero Glass.

Hardware Requirements for Various Vista Features

Windows Vista is a big, sprawling program that can do many things, so it's not surprising that there is a long list of miscellaneous equipment you might need, depending on what you plan to do with your system. Table 2.1 provides a rundown.

TABLE 2.1   Equipment Required for Various Windows Vista Tasks

Task	Required Equipment
Using the Internet	For a dial-up connection: A modem, preferably one that supports 56Kbps connections.
	For a broadband connection: A cable or DSL modem and a router for security.
Networking	For a wired connection: A network adapter, preferably one that supports Fast Ethernet (100Mbps) connections, a network switch or hub, and network cables.
	For a wireless connection: A wireless adapter that supports IEEE 802.11a or g and a wireless access point.
Handwriting	A Tablet PC with a digital pen or a graphics tablet.
Photo editing	A USB slot for connecting the digital camera. If you want to transfer the images from a memory card, you need the appropriate memory card reader.
Document scanning	A document scanner or an all-in-one printer that includes scanning capabilities.

TABLE 2.1   Continued

Task	Required Equipment
Faxing	A modem that includes fax capabilities.
Ripping and burning CDs	For ripping: A CD or DVD drive.
	For burning: A recordable CD drive.
Burning DVDs	A recordable DVD drive.
Video editing	An internal or external video-capture device, or an IEEE 1394 (FireWire) port.
Videoconferencing	A webcam or a digital camera that has a webcam mode.
Listening to digital audio files	A sound card or integrated audio, as well as speakers or headphones. For the best sound, use a subwoofer with the speakers.
Listening to radio	A radio tuner card.
Watching TV	A TV tuner card (preferably one that supports video capture). A remote control is useful if you are watching the screen from a distance.

Vista Versions

For many years, the Windows world was divided into two camps: the so-called "consumer" editions—Windows 95, 98, and Me—aimed at individuals and home office users, and the "business" editions—Windows NT and 2000—aimed at the corporate market. With the release of Windows XP, Microsoft merged these two streams into a single code base. However, that didn't mean the end to having multiple editions of the operating system. In fact, XP ended up with six major editions: Starter (for users with low-cost PCs in emerging markets outside North America), Home (individuals), Professional (corporate users and the SOHO crowd), Professional x64 (the 64-bit version for power users), Media Center (multimedia users), and Tablet PC (with digital pen support for Tablet PC users). Many people found the existence of so many versions of XP confusing, and it certainly was a head-scratching situation for anyone not versed in the relatively subtle differences among the editions.

Given this widespread confusion, you would think that Microsoft would simplify things with Windows Vista. After all, a case could be made that the reason so many people did not upgrade to XP was that they simply were not sure which edition they should purchase. So no one would blame you for thinking that the road to Vista is going to be straighter than the twisting XP path.

In the end, Vista will ship with the same number of versions as XP—six in all—although Vista's versions will be configured completely differently than XP's. First, the home market will see two editions:

- **Windows Vista Home Basic**—This edition will be made available in North America and other developed nations, and it represents the simplest Vista option. The Home Basic Edition is aimed at individuals using their computer at home who want security without complexity. Home Basic includes Windows Defender, Windows Mail with its antispam features, Internet Explorer 7 with its antiphishing features and protected mode, the improved Windows Firewall, the revamped Security Center, and Vista's enhanced parental controls. It will also feature Windows Media Player 11, Windows Movie Maker, Windows Photo Gallery, Windows Calendar, Windows Sidebar, Windows Search, the Games Explorer, partial support for the Mobility Center for notebook users, and basic networking (wired and wireless). However, Home Basic will not support the new Aero shell.

- **Windows Vista Home Premium**—This edition includes everything in Home Basic, plus the Aero shell, Media Center, support for Tablet PCs, Windows Collaboration, Windows DVD Maker, scheduled backups, DVD ripping and authoring capabilities, the Mobility Center for notebook users, and advanced networking capabilities (such as ad hoc peer-to-peer networks and multiple-machine parental controls). This edition is aimed at networked household, multimedia enthusiasts, and notebook users.

The business market will also see two editions:

- **Windows Vista Business**—This edition is analogous to Windows XP Professional and includes the same corporate features as XP Pro: support for domains, multiple network protocols, offline files, Remote Desktop, file and folder encryption, roaming user profiles, and group. Vista Business also comes with the Aero shell, Internet Information Server, Windows Fax and Scan, support for Tablet PCs, and the full Mobility Center. This edition does *not* come with Media Center, Movie Maker, and DVD Maker. In short, it's a no-nonsense OS for the business professional.

- **Windows Vista Enterprise**—This edition is optimized for corporate desktops. It includes everything that's in Vista Business, plus features such as Windows BitLocker (drive encryption for sensitive data), Virtual PC Express, Multilanguage User Interface (MUI), and Subsystem for UNIX-Based Applications (SUA). It also allows IT personnel to deploy the OS in different languages using a single disk image. Note, however, that Enterprise Edition will be made available only to Enterprise Agreement (EA) and Software Assurance (SA) volume-licensing customers. (Or, of course, you can just buy the Ultimate Edition, which I discuss next.)

Bestriding the canyon that exists between the home and business editions is an everything-but-the kitchen sink version:

- **Windows Vista Ultimate**—This edition comes with all the features of the Home Premium and Enterprise editions. It also offers enhanced game performance, access to online subscription services, custom themes, and enhanced support.

Here's the sixth Vista version:

- **Windows Vista Starter**—This is a stripped-down edition of Vista that will be made available only in emerging markets. It's designed for low-cost PCs and is optimized to run on machines with relatively slow CPUs and small memory footprints. This means that the Starter Edition won't support features such as the Aero shell, networking, image editing, and DVD burning. As with XP Starter Edition, Vista

Starter Edition will be limited to an 800×600 display and won't allow users to open more than three programs or three windows at once.

In addition to these editions, there will be OEM equivalents for all versions, as well as 64-bit versions for everything except the Starter Edition. Finally, Microsoft will also make available special versions of Vista—a Home Edition and a Professional Edition—that are customized for Europe to satisfy antitrust legal obligations in that region, which means these editions come without Microsoft's media features, including Media Player and Media Center.

Windows Anytime Upgrade

One of the big advantages of shipping multiple Vista SKUs in a single disc image is that all the modules I listed in the previous section are present on the disc. Therefore, it should be easy to "upgrade" to a higher version of Vista by simply adding the appropriate modules. That's exactly what Microsoft is doing with its new Windows Anytime Upgrade feature in the Home Basic, Home Premium, and Business editions. For example, if you are currently running the Home Basic edition of Windows Vista, you can use Windows Anytime Upgrade to jump up to Home Premium or even Ultimate. Similarly, Vista Business users can move to Vista Ultimate.

Figure 2.2 shows the Windows Anytime Upgrade window for Home Basic users (select Start, Control Panel, System and Maintenance, Windows Anytime Upgrade).

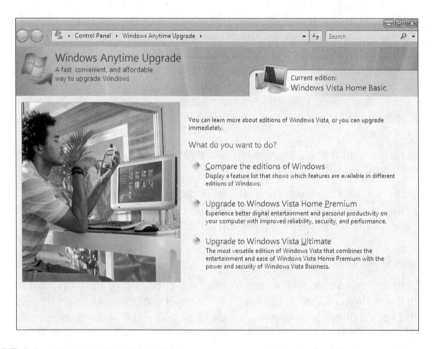

FIGURE 2.2   Windows Vista Home Basic users can upgrade to Home Premium or Ultimate.

Clicking one of the upgrade links takes you to another window that explains the upgrade process (see Figure 2.3):

1. Purchase a license from a Microsoft partner.

2. Download and install the license.

3. Insert your original Vista disc and follow the instructions to add the modules for the new version to your system.

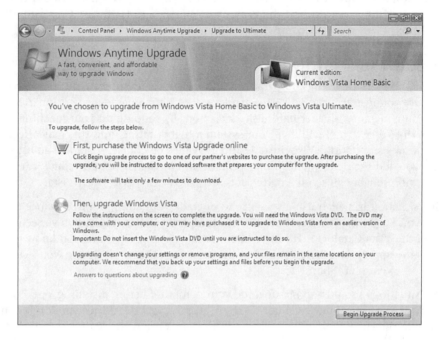

FIGURE 2.3   Clicking an upgrade link takes you to this page, where you can begin the upgrade process.

Preparing for Windows Vista

Installing a new operating system is definitely a "look before you leap" operation. Your computer's operating system is just too important for a willy-nilly install, so you shouldn't dive blindly into the installation process. To make sure that things go well, and to prevent any permanent damage in case disaster strikes, you need to practice "safe" installing. This means taking some time beforehand to run through a few precautionary measures and to make sure that your system is ready to welcome Windows Vista. Even if you won't be installing Vista for a while, you should still do a few things now to prepare your system.

To that end, the next few sections run through a checklist of items you should take care of before inserting the Vista disc. You might be wondering why there's no "Format Your Disk and Start Fresh" section. That's because you don't need to do that with Windows

Vista: Every Vista install is essentially a clean install. I talk more about this a bit later in the chapter (see the section "The Windows Vista Installation Process").

Check Your System Requirements

Now is a good time to make sure that your computer is capable of running Windows Vista. Go back over the system requirements I outlined earlier to make sure that your machine is Windows Vista–ready. If you're not sure about something, it's a good bet that Microsoft will maintain a catalog of Vista-compliant hardware, as it does with Windows XP and Windows 2000. You can find the Windows Catalogs and Hardware Compatibility Lists at http://www.microsoft.com/whdc/hcl/default.mspx.

Upgrade Your Hardware

In general, if you're planning to upgrade or change your computer hardware, it's best to do it before you install Vista. This is particularly true if the upgrade is performance related: more memory, a faster hard disk, and so on. By souping up your machine in advance, the WinSAT tool will give your system a higher rating, and this may affect which features and options Vista installs and activates. Of course, Vista will adjust the rating if you add the performance improvements after installation, but doing it in advance will probably give you a better out-of-the-box experience with Vista.

Another situation in which it makes sense to upgrade your computer in advance of Vista is when you know the new hardware is Vista-compliant (for example, you've seen the device in the Vista Catalog or Hardware Compatibility List). This way, you know that Vista has the appropriate drivers and that the presence of the new device won't cause the installation to crash and burn.

In what situations should you *not* upgrade your computer before installing Vista? When you know that a critical device is not on the Vista HCL *and* the device vendor does not offer a Vista driver. Yes, many devices should work in Vista with XP drivers, but that is not universally true. Most major hardware vendors have been working on Vista drivers for many months (if not years) before the Vista launch date, so updated drivers should be fairly easy to come by. If not, either pester the hardware vendor to update drivers, or try a different vendor that has its Vista act together.

Back Up Your Files

Although I'm sure the vast majority of Windows Vista installations will make it through without a hitch, there's a third law that software (particularly complex operating system software) always seems to follow: Murphy's Law (that is, if anything can go wrong, it will). Windows Vista Setup has a recovery option that should get you out of most jams, but you should still make backup copies of important files, just to be safe. Whether it's critical corporate data or precious family photos, you absolutely *do not* want to be in the position of lamenting, "If only I had backed up those files...."

Even if you're not planning on moving to Vista for a while, it's still a good idea to start backing up now so that you get into the habit of it. Here are some backup notes to bear in mind:

- First and foremost, back up your documents and data. These are nothing short of irreplaceable and should be treated accordingly.

- Back up important items from your Application Data folders, which contain things such as your Internet Explorer Favorites folder, your Outlook Express folder files, and application-specific data. These folders are usually found here:

```
C:\Documents and Settings\UserName\Application Data
C:\Documents and Settings\UserName\Local Settings\Application Data
```

- Consider using Microsoft Backup to set up an Automated System Recovery disk and backup set. This enables you to recover your entire system in case the Vista installation fails miserably.

- For maximum protection, consider "ghosting" or imaging your system, which means making a backup copy of your entire system (essentially a second version—a *ghost* or *image*—of your system). Products such as Norton Ghost (http://www.symantec.com) and Acronis True Image (http://www.acronis.com/) make this easy. Ideally, you should have a second hard drive (preferably external) or network share with enough free space to hold the image.

Clean Up Your Hard Disk

If you're upgrading to Vista, to maximize the amount of free space on your hard disk (and just for the sake of doing some spring cleaning), you should go through your hard disk with a fine-toothed comb, looking for unnecessary files you can delete. Here are some candidates:

- **Programs you no longer use**—Most of us have hard disks that are littered with the rusting hulks of programs we tried a few times and then gave up on. Now is as good a time as any to remove this detritus from your system once and for all. Use the Control Panel Add/Remove Programs icon or the program's own uninstall feature to kick an old program off your machine.

- **Old downloads**—If you have a folder in which you store downloaded programs (it's a good idea to keep such archives in one place), delete those that you're sure you will no longer need, or those in which a newer version of the program is available.

- **Disk cleanup**—Run this tool to rid your system of unused temporary files, Internet Explorer cache files, temporary Remote Desktop files, Recycle Bin contents, and more. (In My Computer, right-click a drive, click Properties, and then click Disk Cleanup. Note that this program is not available if you're upgrading from Windows 98.)

Check and Defragment Your Hard Disk

Because hard disks store our programs and, most important, our precious data, they have a special place in the computing firmament. They ought to be pampered and coddled to ensure a long and trouble-free existence, but that's rarely the case, unfortunately. Just consider everything that a modern hard disk has to put up with:

- **General wear and tear**—If your computer is running right now, its hard disk is spinning away at between 5,400 and 10,000RPM. That's right, even though you're not doing anything, the hard disk is hard at work. Because of this constant activity, most hard disks simply wear out after a few years.

- **The old bump-and-grind**—Your hard disk includes *read/write heads* that are used to read data from and write data to the disk. These heads float on a cushion of air just above the spinning hard-disk platters. A bump or jolt of sufficient intensity can send them crashing onto the surface of the disk, which could easily result in trashed data. If the heads happen to hit a particularly sensitive area, the entire hard disk could crash. Notebook computers are particularly prone to this problem.

- **Power surges**—The current that is supplied to your PC is, under normal conditions, relatively constant. It's possible, however, for your computer to be assailed by massive power surges (for example, during a lightning storm). These surges can wreak havoc on a carefully arranged hard disk.

So unless your computer is brand new, it's a good idea to use the Check Disk tool to scan your hard disk for errors before you install Vista. Note, however, that I'm not talking about the basic disk scan that looks for things such as lost and invalid clusters file system. It's important to fix those, of course, but I'm also talking about a deeper scan that uncovers bad sectors on your hard drive.

> **NOTE**
>
> Large hard disks are inherently inefficient. When you format a disk, the disk's magnetic medium is divided into small storage areas called sectors, which usually hold up to 512 bytes of data. A large hard disk can contain tens of millions of sectors, so it would be too inefficient for the operating system to deal with individual sectors. Instead, the operating system groups sectors into clusters, the size of which depends on the file system and the size of the partition. For example, on NTFS volumes that are 2GB or larger, the cluster size is 4KB.

When you run Check Disk (in My Computer, right-click the drive, click Properties, click the Tools tab, and then click Check Now), be sure to activate the Scan for and Attempt Recovery of Bad Sectors check box.

When that's done, you should defragment the files on your hard drive. This ensures that the install program will store the Windows Vista files with optimal efficiency, which improves performance and lessens the risk of corrupted data. (In My Computer, right-click the drive, click Properties, click the Tools tab, and then click Defragment Now.)

The Windows Vista Installation Process

The installation process for Windows Vista is probably the easiest—and, certainly, the least interactive—Windows install to date. Upgrading takes just a few mouse clicks, and even a clean install is a simple affair, although it does come with some welcome new tools for managing partitions.

Before going through the process, it's important to mention here that with Windows Vista, there's no longer a major distinction between upgrade installs and clean installs. In the past, you had a big decision to make before installing a new operating system:

- Do I upgrade over my existing OS, thus ensuring that my settings, customizations, programs, and documents remain in place?

- Do I back up my files, wipe the hard drive, and install the new OS on the clean partition, thus ensuring that the new system is free of any baggage from the old OS?

You no longer have to make this choice with Vista because *every* Vista install is a clean install. Even if you choose the upgrade path, Vista's Setup program puts all your settings, programs, and documents aside; wipes the partition; installs Vista; and then restores your settings, programs, and documents. The old method of doing a clean OS install was known as a *wipe-and-load* install. With a Vista upgrade, however, you now do a *wipe-and-reload* install.

After the Setup program boots from the disc, it copies a file named boot.wim (located in the \sources subfolder on the Vista disc) into RAM. This file is a scaled-down OS called the Windows Preinstallation Environment (Windows PE) that boots after a few seconds, so the rest of the install takes place in GUI mode. Windows PE begins by displaying the window shown in Figure 2.4, which acts as kind of a Welcome screen for Windows PE.

Click to get the install underway. At this point, you are running in the Windows PE OS. The next major screen asks for your Windows Vista product key; then the installer displays the license agreement and asks whether you accept its terms. The install program next asks you what type of installation you want to perform. You have two choices, as shown in Figure 2.5:

- **Upgrade**—Click this choice to upgrade Vista over your existing operating system, which preserves your existing settings and configuration.

- **Custom**—Click this choice to install a clean version of Vista.

TIP

When Windows PE is running, you can display the command line at any time by pressing Shift+F10.

FIGURE 2.4   This window is the first stop in the Windows Vista installation process, which uses a GUI for all user interaction.

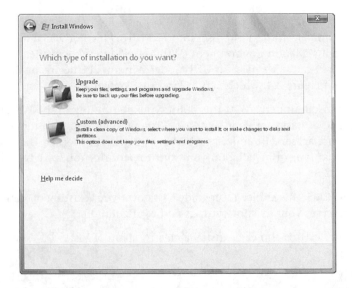

FIGURE 2.5   You can install Vista either as an upgrade or as a clean version.

If you choose the Custom option, you come to the most interesting part of the setup process. The installer begins by showing you a list of your system's available partitions, and you click the one on which you want to install Vista. The real install fun begins if you click the Drive Options (Advanced) link (which appears for only unformatted partitions). As you can see in Figure 2.4, depending on the partition, one or more of the following commands become available:

- **Delete**—Click this command to delete the selected partition.

- **Format**—Click this command to format the selected partition. Note that the installer formats the partition using NTFS.

- **New**—Click this command to create a new partition out of the selected unallocated disk space. As shown in Figure 2.6, this displays a spin that you can use to set the partition size. Click Apply to create the new partition.

- **Extend**—Click this command to increase the size of the selected partition by extended it into adjoining unallocated disk space.

- **Load Driver**—Click this command to load a third-party device driver for the selected partition. Note that Vista can install the drivers from a CD, DVD, or USB Flash drive.

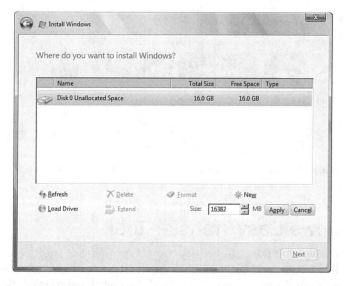

FIGURE 2.6   The installer gives you a number of options for manipulating the partition on which you want to install Windows Vista.

Clicking Next here ends the interactive portion of the installation. From here on, the installer handles everything from copying files to rebooting the machine without prompting you.

When the installation is complete, the Set Up Windows dialog box appears and you're taken through a few dialog boxes to configure Vista. Configuration chores include the following:

- Specifying your country or region and the keyboard layout you prefer
- Typing a username, password (twice), and password hint, as well as selecting an initial picture for this user account
- Typing a computer name and selecting a desktop background (see Figure 2.7)
- Specifying how Vista should handle updates
- Setting the date, time, and time zone

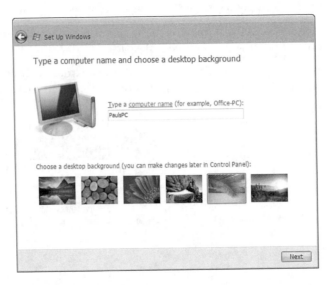

FIGURE 2.7   Part of the Vista configuration process includes typing a name for your computer and choosing a desktop background.

The Windows Easy Transfer Tool

In the old days, when you purchased a new computer to replace another machine, copying your documents and configuring the new system to use the same settings as the old one often took a full day or more. Windows XP enabled you to save all that time for more productive pursuits by offering the Files and Settings Transfer Wizard. This tool transfers those files and settings from your old computer and applies them automatically to your new computer. Windows Vista takes this useful tool to a slightly higher level with the Windows Easy Transfer program, shown in Figure 2.8.

This utility copies to Vista the configuration of your old Windows 2000 or Windows XP machine. Windows Transfer enables you to transfer any or all of the following:

- **Files and folders**—Windows Easy Transfer gathers the contents of several folders, including My Documents, My Pictures, Desktop, Favorites, Shared Documents, and

Shared Pictures. It also gathers a long list of specific document file types, including WordPad documents, text files, all media files, and any file types associated with your installed third-party programs, including all Microsoft Office file types.

- **User accounts and settings**—Windows Easy Transfer gathers display settings, such as the screen colors and fonts, desktop background, screen saver, and so on; your taskbar settings; your mouse and keyboard settings; your regional settings, such as number and currency formats, country location, and installed languages; and your sound and multimedia settings; network connections, drives, and printers; Start menu items; and accessibility options.

- **Programs and settings**—As with the Files and Settings Transfer Wizard, Windows Easy Transfer brings over the options and data for Internet Explorer, Outlook Express, MSN Explorer, Windows Media Player, and Microsoft Messenger. The wizard also gathers settings from certain third-party programs, including the Microsoft Office programs, Microsoft Works, Netscape, Photoshop, Quicken, RealPlayer, and others, depending on what is installed on your computer.

- **Internet settings**—This includes your Internet connections, Internet Explorer properties, favorites, and cookies. It also transfers your email accounts, messages, and address book entries.

FIGURE 2.8 Use Vista's Windows Easy Transfer program to copy your old files and settings on your new computer.

When you launch Windows Easy Transfer (Start, All Programs, Accessories, System Tools, Windows Easy Transfer), the program prompts you for a location to store a copy of itself to run on your old computer. A shared network folder is best for this. After the copy of Windows Easy Transfer is created, you run the program on your old machine and specify the items you want to transfer. You can elect to transfer everything, just your user account, documents and settings, or a custom selection, as shown in Figure 2.9.

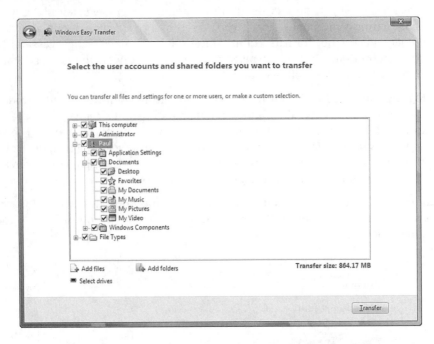

FIGURE 2.9   Use the Transfer Wizard's Custom option to specify exactly which users, documents, programs, and settings you want to transfer.

Logging On Under the Administrator Account

For security reasons, Windows Vista doesn't give you access to the all-powerful Administrator account. I explain why in Chapter 6, "Security Enhancements in Windows Vista." Actually, I should say that it doesn't give you *easy* access to this account. The logon screen doesn't include an option to choose the Administrator, and there is no option anywhere in the main Vista interface to enable this account to log on.

That's probably just as well because it will keep most users much safer, but it's annoying for those of us who occasionally require the Administrator account. For example, the Windows Automated Installation Kit that I discuss in the next section requires the Administrator account.

Fortunately, there are a couple of workarounds, both of which involve editing the Registry. Begin by opening the Registry Editor: Select Start, All Programs, Accessories, Run. Type **regedit** and click OK, and then click Allow in the Windows Security dialog box.

With the Registry Editor open, navigate to the following key:

```
HKLM\SOFTWARE\Microsoft\Windows NT\CurrentVersion\Winlogon
```

You now have two choices:

- **To log on automatically as Administrator**—Double-click the AutoAdminLogon setting and change its value to 1. You should also create a String setting named DefaultPassword and change its value to your Administrator password.

- **To include Administrator in the logon screen**—Create a new subkey under Winlogon named SpecialAccounts, and then create a new subkey under SpecialAccounts named UserList. In the UserList key, create a DWORD value named Administrator and set its value to 1.

Windows Vista Deployment

Deploying Windows has never been easy because Microsoft has never set up its operating systems with efficient deployment in mind. Yes, there have long been decent tools for customizing install parameters and creating unattended setups. However, the real deployment problem has always been the monolithic nature of the Windows editions, in which each edition exists as a separate chunk of code. That's not so bad if you don't have to worry about language support, but when you get into international editions, the code chunks proliferate because each edition has language support built in from the code base up. Russian and Japanese versions of XP Professional aren't just XP Professional with Russian and Japanese language support layered on top. No, these are entirely separate editions of XP Pro and must be deployed as such. And the situation gets even worse when it comes to deploying patches such as service packs and hot fixes because you must apply separate patches for each edition and language. Most IT shops turned to third-party utilities that created separate *images*—essentially, the entire operating system is turned into a single file—for deployment, but they still had to deal with many different images.

Finally, it appears that this IT nightmare is ending because Microsoft has made two major changes that directly affect deployment: modularization and built-in imaging courtesy of the Windows Imaging file format.

Modularization

Microsoft is building Windows Vista as a *modularized* OS. This means that *every* edition of Vista rests on a subset—sometimes called *MinWin*—that contains the core functionality of the OS. Microsoft says that base contains about 95% of the Vista functionality. To create any of the Vista editions that you learned about earlier in this chapter, Microsoft simply adds the appropriate module (or *SKU*) on top of the base. This also works for language packs. The base OS has no language-specific code (it's *language-agnostic*, in the vernacular). Not even English is in the base OS. Therefore, you can apply only the languages you need on top of the base.

NOTE

SKU—short for *stock keeping unit* and pronounced *skew*—is a retailing term that refers to a unique code assigned to a product, which makes it easy for retailers to receive, identify, and inventory their stock. It also has the broader meaning of "a separate product," which is the meaning that Microsoft is using with the Vista components.

Windows Imaging Format

Imaging is now part of Windows Vista, and for this purpose, Microsoft has developed a new file-based imaging format called Windows Imaging format (WIM), which uses the .wim extension. The boot.wim file I mentioned earlier is a WIM file that contains the Windows PE image. The WIM file for Vista itself is called install.wim, and it also resides in the \sources folder of the Vista disc.

WIM files can contain images for multiple SKUs, so you can deploy any edition of Vista, for any computer type, in any language, customized in any way you want, using just a *single* file. And those files aren't huge, either, because WIM files are highly compressed and WIM supports *single instancing*—that is, a particular file is stored only once in the WIM file, even if it's required multiple times for the different SKUs.

Even better, WIM files are editable, which means you can make changes to the OS configuration without having to rebuild the entire image from scratch (a process that could take several hours).

Maintaining WIM Files with XImage

The Windows Automated Installation Kit (WAIK) comes with a new command-line utility, called XImage, that is responsible for the creation and maintenance of WIM files. Table 2.2 lists the switches that XImage supports.

TIP

At the command line, change to the Windows AIK\Tools\x86 folder and run the following command to see the complete XImage syntax:

```
ximage /?
```

TABLE 2.2   Switches Supported by the XImage Command-Line Utility

Switch	Description
/append	Appends an image into an existing WIM file
/apply	Applies an image to the specified drive
/capture	Captures an image into a new WIM file
/commit	Commits the changes made to a mounted WIM
/compress	Sets the WIM file's compression type: use

TABLE 2.2   Continued

Switch	Description
/delete	Deletes an image from a WIM file
/dir	Displays a list of files and folders within a image
/export	Transfers an image from one WIM file to another
/info	Returns the XML descriptions for the specified WIM
/split	Splits an existing WIM file into multiple read-only WIM parts
/verify	Verify duplicate and extracted files
/mount	Mounts a read-only image to the specified folder
/mountrw	Mounts a read/write image to the specified folder
/unmount	Unmounts the image mounted to the specified folder

Of particular note here is the /mountrw switch, which places the image in the specified folder where you can view and work with the image contents just like any other folder. This enables you to make whatever changes you need to the image. When you then unmount the image, your changes are applied immediately without having to rebuild the image from scratch.

> **NOTE**
>
> Before you can use XImage to work with a mounted image, you need to install the Windows Imaging File System Filter tool. Begin by opening the WAIK folder that contains XImage.exe, which is usually the following:
>
> C:\Program Files\Windows AIK\Tools\x86
>
> Right-click the wimfltr.inf file and then click Install.

For example, if install.wim is in the c:\vistawim folder and you want to mount it to the c:\vistamount folder, run the following command:

ximage /mountrw c:\vistamount c:\vistawim\install.wim 1

Automating Installations with System Image Manager

The secret to a successful deployment is, of course, the unattended installation. Windows Vista doesn't require much feedback during the install, but no one in IT these days has the time to wait around to type in even the few bits of information that Vista asks for, especially if you have a large number of systems to upgrade. To create unattended Vista setups, you use a new tool called the Windows Automated Installation Kit (WAIK), which enables you to specify information such as the user's name, organization, computer name, and product key. You can also configure a disk partition and specify one or more "run once" commands to execute after the installation. Note that you must install the WAIK on a computer running Windows XP with Service Pack 2, Windows Server 2003 with Service Pack 1, or Windows Vista.

You use the System Image Manager (Start, All Programs, Microsoft Windows AIK, Image Manager) to specify the details of the unattended setup. Figure 2.10 shows the System Image Manager with a WIM file loaded (select File, Select Windows Image) and a new answer file started (select File, New Answer File). You add items from the image file to the answer file (right-click a component and then click the part of the answer file you want the component to appear in), and then use the Properties pane to customize the component.

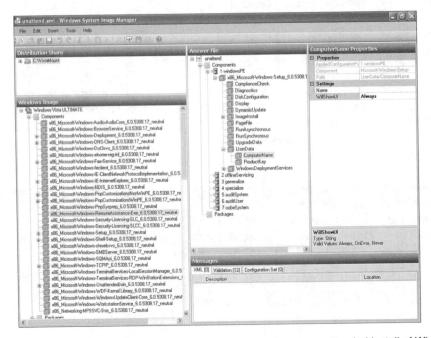

FIGURE 2.10   Use the WAIK System Image Manager to set up an unattended install of Windows Vista.

Deploying Windows Vista

With these and other new tools, deploying Windows Vista becomes a relatively simple process:

1. Create a folder to hold the Vista `install.wim` file.

2. Copy `install.wim` from the Vista disc's `\sources` folder to the folder you created in step 1.

3. Create a folder to hold the mounted `install.wim` image.

4. Use XImage to mount the Vista image. For example, if `install.wim` is in the `c:\vistawim` folder and you want to mount it to the `c:\vistamount` folder, run the following command:

```
ximage /mountrw c:\vistamount c:\vistawim\install.wim 1
```

5. Navigate the folder to which you mounted the Vista image. This folder contains all of the folders and files that normally appear after you install Vista, as shown in Figure 2.11.

6. Customize the mounted image by editing file contents, adding folders and files, and so on.

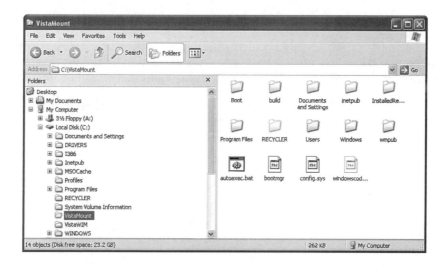

FIGURE 2.11   After you mount a Vista image, it appears in the folder.

7. Unmount the mounted image and save your changes by running XImage with the /unmount and /commit switches. For example, if you mounted install.wim to the c:\vistamount folder, run the following command:

```
ximage /unmount /commit c:\vistamount
```

8. Use System Image Manager to customize the Vista configuration and create the unat-tend.xml answer file.

9. Install Vista on a reference computer using the image you created earlier and the unat-tend.xml file.

10. Install the applications you want to include as part of the client desktop, along with any patches and drivers required by those applications.

11. Capture the desktop volume into a WIM file by booting to Windows PE, invoking the command line (Shift+F10), and running XImage from there. For example, the follow-ing command captures drive C: to a file named myinstall.wim:

```
ximage /capture d: c:\images\myinstall.wim
```

12. Copy the image to a network share (or a distributable medium, such as a DVD disc).

13. Use the final image to install Vista on the client computers.

From Here

Here are some other sections in the book where you'll find information related to the topics in this chapter:

- For a broad look at what's new in Windows Vista, see Chapter 1, "An Overview of Windows Vista."

- For the details on Vista's graphical underpinnings, see Chapter 3, "The Windows Vista Interface."

- For more detailed information on WinSAT, see the section "Windows System Assessment Tool (WinSAT)," in Chapter 5, "Vista Performance and Maintenance."

- To learn more about Vista's new DVD features, see the section "DVD Authoring," in Chapter 9, "Digital Media in Windows Vista."

The Windows Vista Interface

Whenever Microsoft releases a new operating system, the one thing anyone seems to want to talk about is the new interface. What does it look like? Is it cool? Can I run it? On the surface this seems superficial because, after all, Windows is and should be more than just a pretty interface. Don't things such as stability and security mean more? Shouldn't the goal of any OS be to just get out of the way and let us get on with our work, perhaps a tad more productively than before?

That's all true, but the operating system interface shouldn't be relegated to mere eye candy status. After all, we use the operating system's interface for many nontrivial tasks during a typical day: starting programs; saving our work; finding documents; moving, copying, and deleting files; maintaining the computer; troubleshooting problems; networking with others; and so much more. If the interface to all these tasks is ugly, inefficient, or confusing, then we'll simply get less work done or have less fun than we would otherwise.

So how does Vista's interface rate? As you'll see in this chapter, the answer has to be "pretty darned good," although with a few reservations. Vista's interface is almost certainly the best that Microsoft has come up with so far (some would claim that's not saying much), and it's got plenty of eye-popping and jaw-dropping features without descending into gaudiness and mere trickery.

The Windows Presentation Foundation

All the interface changes that come in the Vista package are a direct or indirect result of Vista's new graphical subsystem. Code-named Avalon but now officially called Windows Presentation Foundation (WPF), Vista's graphical underpinnings should prove to be a boon to both developers *and* end users. But it won't be just the Vista community that benefits from WPF because Microsoft has decided to backport WPF for Windows XP and Windows Server 2003.

Developers will (and, by all accounts, already do) love WPF because it provides a one-stop shop for all their graphical needs. Before WPF, developers had to work with a rather alarming number of technologies and application programming interfaces (APIs). For example, to draw a simple 2D shape, they called on the Graphics Device Interface (GDI); for 3D objects, they used Direct3D or OpenGL; for media objects, they used DirectShow; and for user interface objects, they used USER32 or Windows Forms, to name just a few. Some of these technologies (such as the GDI) have been around since Windows 1.0. Clearly, it was time for a change.

With WPF, developers can do 2D, 3D, animation, imaging, video, audio, special effects, and text rendering using a single API that works consistently no matter what type of object the developer is working with. This greatly simplifies user interface programming, resulting in more robust applications that are delivered to market faster than ever.

WPF also introduced a new markup language called XAML—eXtensible Application Markup Language—which acts as a kind of front end for building application interfaces. The idea here is that by using relatively simple markup code, developers and designers can work together to build user interfaces.

From the user's perspective, the main problem has been that although our graphics processing units (GPUs) have been getting ever more powerful, and our video adapters have been populated with more graphics memory, our operating systems and applications—with the notable exception of the gaming sphere—have not been programmed to take advantage of all this powerful hardware.

WPF changes all that by implementing a new graphics model that can take full advantage of today's powerful GPUs and scads of video RAM. With WPF, all output goes through the powerful Direct3D layer, which means that all graphical work is offloaded to the GPU, thus saving the CPU for more important tasks. (Technically, WPF will only pass the graphics load to the GPU in video adapters that support DirectX 7 or later.) Also, the output uses *vector graphics*, a rendering technology in which each image on the screen is composed of points, lines, polygons, and curves (these are called *primitives*). Unlike *raster graphics*, in which each screen image is composed of pixels, vector graphics support extremely high-resolution images and are completely scalable (that is, you can zoom in and zoom out) without any loss of quality in the image.

Also, WPF implements a new technology called the Desktop Window Manager (DWM), which assumes complete control over what's displayed on the screen. In previous versions of Windows, applications used APIs to display their graphics directly on the screen. Now the DWM takes over that chore. Each application draws its graphics to an off-screen buffer, and then the DWM composites the buffer contents on the screen.

All this means that WPF brings some significant changes to Windows graphics:

- **No more window "tearing"**—When you move a window quickly in any GDI-based version of Windows, the edges of the window appear to temporarily "tear" because the system has trouble keeping up with the graphical changes that are happening onscreen. On WDF systems, however, the graphics route through the hardware-accelerated GPU, so window movement remains smooth and seamless no matter how quickly you drag across the screen.

- **Better and more useful animations**—Microsoft realized a few years ago that some sort of animation effects were necessary, particularly for novice users. For example, new Windows users are often surprised at the abrupt disappearance of a window when they click the Minimize button. The user either thinks he has closed the program or that he has done something wrong. With an animated minimize, however, the user can "see" the window going down to the toolbar, which offers a vital visual clue about what just happened. With the power of WPF available, Microsoft has implemented animations of much higher quality than those seen in, say, Windows XP. For example, windows that are being moved quickly or minimized have a motion blur effect, which effectively highlights the movement of the window.

- **Improved scaling**—With vector-based graphics, you can scale any image bigger or smaller without any loss in the image quality. This is simply not possibly with raster-based graphics. For example, if you have ever tried using larger icons in Windows or a program toolbar, you know that the resulting icons look blurry and jagged. With WPF, everything is drawn with vectors, so you can scale windows and icons as big (or as small) as you want, and the objects will display with no loss in quality.

- **Transparency**—Drawing an object so that it offers some level of transparency has always been a tall order for the GDI because transparency effects require hardware acceleration, and the GDI didn't have access to that part of the GPU (for the most part). Any developer trying to get transparency via the GDI would end up with a program that slowed the system to a crawl. With WPF, however, transparency effects are easy because a dedicated GPU is much more capable of rendering them without any effect on overall performance.

- **Video as just another graphical object**—Most of us think of video as a real performance killer. Just running video in a single window can slow your system noticeably, and video doesn't move or scale well: If you try, you get dropped frames by the cartload. That all changes in WPF because it treats video as though it were any other graphic object. Thanks to WPF's direct access to the GPU's hardware acceleration, you can move and animate running videos without dropping frames or affecting the performance of the CPU. On a practical level, this enables Vista to show running video when you press Alt+Tab to switch windows (see the section "Better Cool Switches: Flip and Flip 3D," later in this chapter) and when you move your mouse over the video window's icon in the taskbar (see "Taskbar Thumbnails," later in this chapter).

General Interface Changes

The first thing you might notice upon loading Windows Vista for the first time is the new Welcome screen, shown in Figure 3.1, which replaces the XP Welcome screen. (If you're running Vista with just a single user account and no password, you won't see the Welcome screen; it appears only if you have multiple user accounts or after you have assigned a password to at least one account.) Click the user you want to log on as; then type your password and press Enter.

FIGURE 3.1   The Windows Vista Welcome screen.

The Vista Desktop

After Vista loads, the main thing you'll notice is that the overall look of the desktop has changed. As you can see in Figure 3.2, the most obvious change is the new wallpaper (although the one you see might be different; when you install Windows Vista, it gives you a choice of several wallpapers) and the new Windows Sidebar on the right.

If you're into the wallpaper thing (I rarely see my desktop these days), you'll be happy to know that Vista ships with some stunning new images, as shown in Figures 3.3 and 3.4.

FIGURE 3.2   The Windows Vista desktop.

FIGURE 3.3   The Windows Vista desktop showing an image from the Textures series of backgrounds.

FIGURE 3.4   The Windows Vista desktop showing an image from the Black and White series of backgrounds.

As you can see in Figure 3.2, the desktop also comes with updated icons for the Recycle Bin, Computer (formerly My Computer), and Network (formerly My Network Places), as well as a new desktop icon for the Control Panel. The default desktop just shows the Recycle Bin icon, but you can customize which icons appear on the desktop by using the Desktop Items dialog box, shown in Figure 3.5. (Right-click the desktop, click Properties, click Change Desktop Icons, and then click Customize Desktop.)

The Vista Taskbar

At the bottom of the Vista screen, you see the slightly revamped taskbar, shown in Figure 3.6.

The most obvious change here is that the Start button has morphed from XP's rounded rectangle to a translucent orb showing just the Windows Vista logo. It sure looks nice, but I have to wonder if it will confuse novice users because in the past they saw the word Start and at least had a logical place in the interface to get something going.

To the right of the Start button, the taskbar itself has a new look. If your video card supports the Aero Glass interface, the taskbar appears with the transparency effect so you can see the desktop behind it. Also, the taskbar now appears as an integrated whole, meaning that you no longer see any visual breaks between the Quick Launch toolbar on the left, the taskbar's icon area in the middle, and the notification area on the right. (The breaks are still there, but they don't appear with the taskbar locked. Right-click the taskbar and then deactivate the Lock the Taskbar command to do things such as resize the Quick Launch toolbar and display more taskbar rows.)

FIGURE 3.5   Use the Desktop Items dialog box to customize the Windows Vista desktop.

FIGURE 3.6   The Windows Vista taskbar.

Speaking of the notification area, it's now a bit more customizable in Vista. As you can see in Figure 3.7, the Taskbar and Start Menu Properties dialog box (right-click an empty section of the taskbar and then click Properties) now comes with a Notification Area tab. You can hide inactive icons, as you could in XP, but there's a new System Icons group that enables you to toggle the icons for four different items: Clock, Volume, Network, and Power.

The Start Menu

Clicking the Start button reveals the Windows Vista version of the Start menu, shown in Figure 3.8. The overall layout of the Start menu hasn't changed too much from Windows XP, but there are subtle differences in the way the Vista Start menu works. For example, the left side of the XP Start menu showed a list of the programs that you've used most often. In Vista, the left side of the Start menu shows a list of the programs you've used most recently; those that you've used most often appear closer to the top of the list. As with XP, the Internet and Email items are "pinned"—that is, they appear in bold at the top of the program list and are a fixed part of the Start menu. However, just as in XP, you can pin any icon to the Start menu by right-clicking the icon and then clicking Pin to Start Menu.

FIGURE 3.7   In Windows Vista, you can control the notification area view by toggling several different system icons.

TIP

You can tell Windows Vista not to display recently used programs on the Start menu. Right-click the Start button, click Properties, and then deactivate the Store and Display a List of Recently Opened Programs check box.

TIP

One of the biggest disappointments on the new Start menu is the missing Run command that gives you access to a command-line interface. If, like me, you use Run frequently, you can add it back where it belongs. Right-click the Start button, click Properties, and then click Customize. In the list of Start menu items, activate the Run Command check box and then click OK to exit all dialog boxes. Remember that you can also fire up the Run dialog box by pressing Windows Log+R.

The right side of the Start menu—it's called the Start panel—contains links to various Windows Vista folders and features. There are three changes to note:

- Windows Vista does away with the old "My X" paradigm that began with Windows 95 and the My Computer icon, and reached absurd heights in Windows XP (My Music, My Pictures, My Videos, My Received Files, and on and on). In Vista, the corresponding folders are named simply Documents, Pictures, Music, Recent Items, and Computer.

- The new Games icon opens the Games folder, which has icons for the games that come with Vista, as well as most third-party games you install yourself. See Chapter 10, "Windows Vista and Gaming," for more details.

- If you're connected to a network, the Network icon appears on the Start menu. Launching this icon shows you the computers and devices in your workgroup or network, so it's the equivalent of XP's View Workgroup Computers command. (Vista has no equivalent to XP's My Network Places feature.)

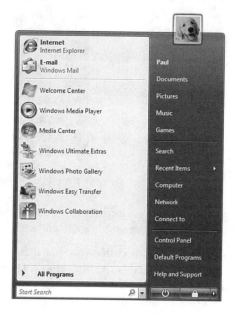

FIGURE 3.8   The Windows Vista Start menu.

One of the major changes to the Start menu is the All Programs link, which works a bit differently than it did in previous versions of Windows. When you click all Programs, instead of a menu flying out to the right, Vista simply converts the Start menu's program list to a list of items in the All Programs folder, as shown in Figure 3.9.

If you then click a folder icon, the folder's menu items appear in place, as shown with the Accessories folder in Figure 3.10. To return to the list of recently used programs, click Back. In other words, Vista's Start menu is self-contained; when you get used to the new method, it's a relief not have to chase menus and submenus across the screen.

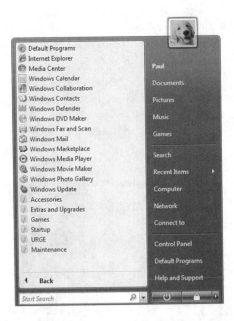

FIGURE 3.9   In Vista, clicking All Programs displays the submenu within the main Start menu.

The bottom of the Start menu has been revamped considerably from XP. For starters, there are replacements for XP's Shut Down and Log Off links:

- **Sleep**—Click this button to save your current programs and documents and put your computer into a low-power mode that's the next closest thing to being completely shut off. The next time you power up your computer, Vista resumes in just a few seconds; after you log on, it restores your running programs and documents.

- **Lock**—Click this button to lock your computer. This displays the logon screen; you can return to the desktop only by entering your password. You can also click the arrow to the right of the Lock button to display a menu consisting of several items, including Switch User, Lock, Log Off, Shut Down, Restart, and Undock (for docking stations only).

Perhaps the most interesting and potentially most useful and time-saving of Vista's Start menu innovations is the Instant Search box that appears on the bottom left. Thanks to Vista's high-powered search engine, the Start menu's Instant Search box offers on-the-fly searches. Type in the text you want to search for, and Vista immediately displays a list of programs, folders, files, email messages, contacts, and other user data that have names containing the text, as shown in Figure 3.11. Vista also displays Search the Computer and Search the Internet links so that you can easily expand your search. See "Desktop Searching with the Windows Search Engine" in Chapter 4, "File System Improvements," to get more details on this and other Vista search features.

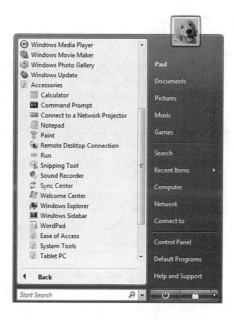

FIGURE 3.10　Clicking a folder icon opens the folder's menu items in place.

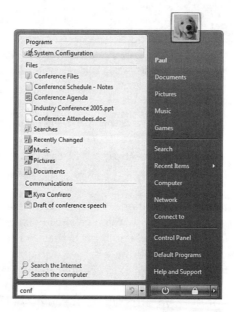

FIGURE 3.11　Type text in the Start menu's Instant Search box, and Vista returns a list of programs, folders, and files with the text contained in the name.

The Aero Glass Theme

Perhaps the most talked about of Windows Vista's new features is the Aero theme with its Glass color scheme. Part of the discussion has centered on Microsoft's controversial decision to run Aero Glass only on systems with relatively powerful graphics capabilities (as I talked about in Chapter 2, "Moving to Windows Vista"). It's not so much an issue with home machines because the hardware required to run Aero Glass is becoming more mainstream, thanks to the influence of gaming and media applications. However, the corporate sector has been doing most of the griping, and that's because in most corporate IT departments, graphics are barely considered during purchasing decisions. The thinking seems to be that if the graphics hardware is good enough to run PowerPoint, it's good enough for a corporate desktop. The entire discussion might be moot, however, because when corporate IT departments finally get around to adopting Vista en masse in 2 or 3 years, Aero Glass-capable graphics should be standard on the kind of midrange PCs that corporate purchasers favor.

TIP

Windows Vista performs a hardware check on your system to see if it can handle the Aero Glass interface. If not, Vista shuts off Aero Glass. However, you can use a trick to force Aero Glass on, as long as you're using a WDDM-compliant video driver. In the Registry Editor (Start, Run, type `regedit`, and click OK), navigate to the following key:

`HKLM\Software\Microsoft`

Add a new subkey named DWM and then create a DWORD setting named `EnableMachineCheck`. Leave the value of this setting at 0, which disables Vista's DWM-related hardware checking. Some caveats concerning this hack:

- It does not work on all systems.
- Even if it does work, it can make your system run extremely slowly. (There's probably a reason Windows shut off Aero Glass.)
- Microsoft might not support the EnableMachineCheck setting in the final version of Vista.

The rest of the Aero Glass talk has centered on what this new theme brings to the Vista interface. The most obvious change is one that you've already had a brief taste of in your brief tour of the Vista interface: the transparency effects that you see in the taskbar and the Start menu. Transparency extends to all the windows and dialog boxes Vista displays. It even extends to the windows and dialog boxes of applications that weren't built with Aero Glass in mind because the DWM displays all screen output, so it can apply the transparency effect—indeed, any of the Aero Glass effects—to any window or dialog box.

Figure 3.12 shows Vista with a window and a dialog box displayed. You can see (hopefully—the effects could be difficult to discern in black and white) that the transparency effect is most apparent in the title bar, but it also applies to the window and dialog box borders. What's the point, you may ask? I think Microsoft's goal here is both simple and subversive: to change the user's focus from the window to what's *inside* the window. In other words, by reducing the visual presence of the window title bar and borders, Vista shifts the focus from the container to the content. Many of the features that you learn about in Chapter 4—including desktop search, virtual folders, document metadata, and a de-emphasis on the traditional disk-and-folder storage model—are also designed to bring content to the fore.

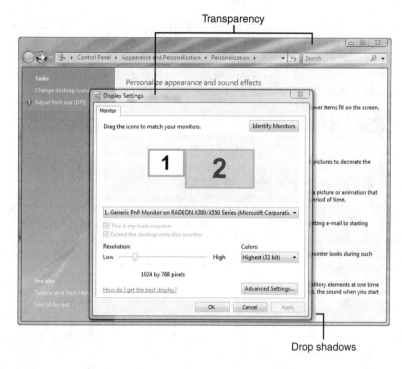

Transparency

Drop shadows

FIGURE 3.12   The Aero Glass theme brings a number of graphical innovations to the Windows Vista interface.

Aero Glass also applies the following effects to the Vista interface:

- Each open window and dialog box has a drop-shadow effect.

- When you hover the mouse pointer over a window button, the button "lights up": You see a blue glow for the Minimize and Maximize buttons, and a red glow for the Close button.

- Almost anything that's live (in the sense that clicking it will trigger some action) gets highlighted when you hover your mouse pointer over it.

- In a dialog box, the default button (usually the OK button) uses a repeating fade effect in which the color that normally appears when you hover the mouse over a command button appears to fade in and out.

These interface changes are, thankfully, subtle. With access to Direct3D and graphics hardware accelerations, Microsoft could have cranked up the eye candy and turned Vista into a version of Halo or some other frenetic game. Instead, they opted for muted effects that enhance the look of the interface while also making users' lives easier. (For example, it's going to be much harder in Vista to accidentally click Close when you meant to click Maximize because that glowing red Close button will put an instant "Stop!" message into your brain.)

Another useful Aero innovation is the use of animations to enhance interface actions. For example, when you minimize a window, it noticeably shrinks down to its taskbar icon. When you restore it, the window expands to its previous size and position. Similarly, when you close a window, it fades from view. Aero Glass also implements blur effects when an action is performed quickly.

Better Cool Switches: Flip and Flip 3D

One of the first keyboard shortcuts almost all Windows users master is Alt+Tab for switching programs. As you hold down Alt and press the Tab key, a small window of icons appears, one icon for each open program window.

This handy shortcut—generally known as the *cool switch*—has served us well since Windows 95, but it suffers from a glaring drawback: The Alt+Tab window shows only the program icons and titles. You can usually figure out which window you want to switch to, but sometimes the limited size of the cool switch window text box means that you can't tell whether the current window is the one you want.

> **NOTE**
>
> If you installed any of Microsoft's PowerToys utilities for XP, you might have used the Alt+Tab Replacement PowerToy. This small utility intercepted Alt+Tab keystrokes and displayed a large window that, as you pressed Tab, showed you not only each icon, but also a copy of the entire program window, making it easier to select the one you want.

If you have a video card that supports the Windows Vista Device Driver Model, Vista's version of the cool switch is similar to the Alt+Tab Replacement PowerToy. When you hold down Alt and press Tab, Vista displays not an icon for each open window, but a scaled-down version of each window. (There's also an icon for the desktop, which gives you a quick way to minimize all open windows and get to the desktop.) The power of WPF brings two considerable benefits to this so-called Flip method of switching windows:

- The WPF vector-based graphics ensure that the scaled-down windows are easily viewed and that the contents of these miniature windows are still fully readable.

- The WPF access to the GPU and its hardware acceleration mean that the scaled-down windows are "live" in the sense that they reflect the current state of each window, even if a window is playing full-motion video.

Figure 3.13 shows the Flip feature in action.

Live thumbnail of playing video clip

FIGURE 3.13   Press Alt+Tab to flip through live thumbnails of your running windows.

Flip is a nice update to the Alt+Tab cool switch, but Vista has another trick up its window-switching sleeve: Flip 3D. Press Windows Logo+Tab to convert the open windows to a 3D stack, as shown in Figure 3.14. To flip through the thumbnails, hold down the Windows Logo key and press Tab. Alternatively, press Windows Logo+Ctrl+Tab to get a 3D stack that doesn't require you to hold down any keys. When you have the stack displayed, you have two choices:

- **Use the arrow keys**—Press the down arrow or right arrow to move thumbnails toward the front of the stack; press the up arrow or left arrow to move thumbnails toward the back of the stack.

- **Use the scroll wheel on your mouse**—Scroll forward to move thumbnails toward the front of the stack; scroll backward to move thumbnails toward the back of the stack.

As with the Flip method, Flip 3D thumbnails show live content. When you bring the thumbnail you want to the front, press Enter to switch to that window.

> **TIP**
>
> As I write this, there is talk that some keyboard manufacturers will be adding a Flip 3D key in upcoming configurations. It's a certainty that Microsoft's own keyboards will include this feature, and I'm sure other manufacturers will follow suit.

FIGURE 3.14   Press Windows Logo+Tab and then scroll the mouse wheel to flip through a 3D stack of live thumbnails.

Taskbar Thumbnails

The taskbar's main duty is to play host to a set of buttons that represent the open windows on the desktop. You can switch to any window by clicking its taskbar button. In theory, it should be straightforward to choose the taskbar button for the window you want to activate because each button shows the window title and the icon associated with the program. In practice, however, picking out the correct taskbar button is often problematic because many window titles don't fit entirely inside the button. This is particularly true of documents, which tend to have longish names. The situation worsens as you open more windows because the more buttons there are on the taskbar, the smaller each button becomes.

The "solution" to this dilemma has long been the pop-up banners that appear when you hover the mouse pointer over a taskbar button. These banners show you the full title of the window. The pop-ups help, but you can still have problems figuring out the correct button if you have opened several documents that use similar names.

What you really need to know in these cases is what's *inside* each window, and Vista has just the thing: taskbar preview windows. When you hover your mouse pointer over a taskbar button in Vista, the WPF displays not only the window title, but also a thumbnail image of the window. As you've probably guessed by now, these thumbnails are live, so they show real-time changes to the window state, such as a running video. Figure 3.15 shows an example of a taskbar preview window.

FIGURE 3.15   When you hover the mouse pointer over a taskbar button in Windows Vista, a live thumbnail of the window appears.

One of Windows XP's solutions to taskbar clutter was to group similar taskbar buttons together. For example, if you had several Internet Explorer windows open, XP would show just a single Internet Explorer taskbar button with an arrow. Clicking the arrow displayed a list of the open Internet Explorer windows, and you could then click the window you wanted to activate.

Windows Vista keeps this feature, but with a slight twist. When you hover your mouse pointer over a button representing a group of windows, a stacked thumbnail appears, as shown in Figure 3.16. The thumbnail that appears at the front of the stack is the window that you opened first. Note, however, that you cannot navigate the stack, so this version of the taskbar thumbnails is not all that useful.

FIGURE 3.16   When you hover the mouse pointer over a grouped taskbar button, a stacked thumbnail appears.

New Folder Windows

Microsoft has spent a lot of time rethinking document storage and has incorporated into Vista some substantial changes in the way we view, navigate, and use folders. I discuss many of these innovations in Chapter 4. For now, let's take a tour of the new interface features that you'll find in Vista's folder windows. Figure 3.17 shows a typical example of the species, the Documents window (formerly My Documents).

Navigating Folders

One of the most fundamental and possibly far-reaching of Vista's innovations is doing away with—or, technically, hiding—the old drive-and-folder-path method of navigating the contents of your computer. You could go your entire Vista career and never have to view or type a backslash. Instead, Vista implements drives and folders as hierarchies that you navigate up, down, and even across. As you can see in Figure 3.17, the Address bar doesn't show any drive letters or blackslashes. Instead, you get a hierarchical path to the current folder. The path in Figure 3.17 has three items, separated by right-pointing arrows:

- **Desktop icon**—This icon represents the top of the hierarchy. You'll see a bit later that you can use this icon to navigate to your computer drives, your network, the Control Panel, your user folder, and more.

- **Paul**—This represents the second level of the example hierarchy. In the example, this level represents all the folders and files associated with the account of a user named Paul.

- **Documents**—This represents the third level of the example hierarchy. In the example, this level represents all the folders and files that reside in the user Paul's Documents folder.

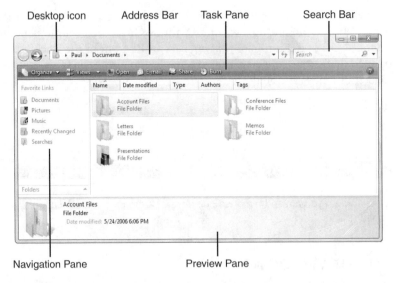

FIGURE 3.17   Vista's folder windows boast a radical new design.

> **TIP**
>
> If you miss the old pathname way of looking at folders, you can still drive letters and backslashes in Vista. Either right-click the path and click Edit Address, or press Alt+D. To return to the hierarchical path, press Esc.

This is a sensible and straightforward way to view the hierarchy, which is already a big improvement over previous versions of Windows. However, the real value here lies in the navigation features of the Address bar, and you can get a hint of these features from the nickname that many people have applied to the new Address bar: the *breadcrumb bar*.

Breadcrumbing refers to a navigation feature that displays a list of the places a person has visited or the route a person has taken. The term comes from the fairy tale of Hansel and Gretel, who threw down bits of bread to help find their way out of the forest. This feature is common on websites where the content is organized as a hierarchy or as a sequence of pages.

Vista introduces breadcrumb navigation to Windows not only by using the Address bar to show you the hierarchical path you've taken to get to the current folder, but also by adding interactivity to the breadcrumb path:

- You can navigate back to any part of the hierarchy by clicking the folder name in the Address bar. For example, in the path shown in Figure 3.17, you could jump immediately to the top-level hierarchy by clicking the Desktop icon on the far left of the path.

- You can navigate "sideways" to any part of any level by clicking the right-pointing arrow to the right of the level you want to work with. In Figure 3.18, for example, you see that clicking the Paul arrow displays a list of the other navigable items that are in the `Paul` folder, such as Downloads, Music, and Pictures. Clicking an item in this list opens that folder.

Click the arrow to see the items in that level

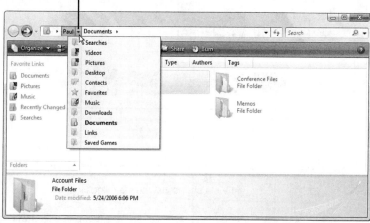

FIGURE 3.18   Breadcrumb navigation: In the Address bar, click a folder's arrow to see a list of the navigable items in that folder.

Instant Search

The next major change to the folder window interface in Windows Vista is the Instant Search box, which appears to the right of the Address bar in all folder windows. Search is everywhere in Vista, and I go into it in much more detail in Chapter 4. For folder windows, however, the Instant Search box gives you a quick way to search for files within the current folder. Most of us nowadays have folders that contain hundreds or even thousands of documents. To knock such folders down to size in Vista, you need only type a word or phrase into the Instant Search box, and Vista instantly filters the folder contents to show just the files with names or content that match the search text, as shown in Figure 3.19. Vista also matches those files that have metadata—such as the author or tag—that match your text.

> **NOTE**
>
> For more on metadata in Vista, see the section in Chapter 4 titled "Metadata and the Windows Explorer Property System."

Type text in the Instant Search box...

...and Vista shows just the matching files

FIGURE 3.19   With as-you-type folder searching, Vista displays just those files with names or metadata that match your search text.

The Task Pane

The Task pane resides just below the Address bar and the Search bar. This pane contains task-related buttons, and its configuration depends on the type of folder you're viewing. For example, in the Pictures folder (see Figure 3.20), there are buttons related to images, such as Preview and Slide Show.

However, all folder windows have the following two buttons:

- **Organize**—This button drops down a menu that enables you to perform basic file tasks (such as renaming, moving, copying, and deleting). It also has a Layout command that displays a submenu of options for configuring the folder window's layout by toggling the Preview pane, Reading pane, and Navigation pane (discussed in the next three sections), the Search pane (see Chapter 4), and the Classic menu bar (see the following Tip).

- **Views**—This button drops down a slider that enables you to change the folder view (such as Details, Tiles, or Large Icons).

3

TIP

Yes, the "classic" menus (as they're now called) are still available. If you want to use them only occasionally, press Alt to display the menu bar. (Press Alt again to hide the menu bar.) If you want the menus to remain onscreen in the active Windows Explorer window, click Organize, Layout, Classic Menus. (To hide the menu bar, click Organize, Layout, Classic Menus to deactivate it.) If you want the menus to appear by default in all Windows Explorer windows, click Organize, Folder Options; display the View tab; and activate the Always Show Classic Menus check box.

The Preview Pane

The Preview pane resides at the bottom of the folder window, and it gives you information about either the current folder (if no files are selected), the currently selected file or folder, or the current multiobject selection. If a document is selected (see Figure 3.20), the Preview pane shows the following data:

- **A thumbnail of the document**—Vista's document thumbnails are much more informative than XP's. Here are some examples:

  - **Image**—The thumbnail shows a scaled-down version of the image.

  - **Video**—The thumbnail shows the first frame.

  - **Word document**—The thumbnail shows the first page.

  - **PowerPoint presentation**—The thumbnail shows the first slide.

  - **Excel workbook**—The thumbnail shows the first worksheet.

- **The document's metadata**—This includes the title, rating, and tags, as well as metadata specific to the document type, such as Genre for a music file and Camera Model for a digital photo. Some of this data is editable, and you can modify that data by clicking the Edit link.

Preview Pane

FIGURE 3.20   The Preview pane shows information about the selected file or folder.

The size of the Preview pane is also configurable. You can use two methods:

- Click and drag the top edge of the Preview pane up or down.

- Right-click an empty part of the Preview pane, click Size, and then click Small, Medium, or Large.

The Reading Pane

The Reading pane offers yet another thumbnail view of the selected object. (It should be apparent to you by now that Vista is big on thumbnails.) As with the thumbnail in the Preview pane, the Reading pane shows you the actual content from file types that support this feature, including images, videos, text files, and Office documents. Figure 3.21 shows the opening text from a text document previewed in the Reading pane.

The Navigation Pane

The Navigation pane appears on the left side of each folder window and offers access to a few common folders. The top three icons—Documents, Pictures, and Music—are shortcuts to those folders. The other two items in the Navigation pane are special folders called *search folders*, which I discuss in detail in Chapter 4. For now, here's a summary of what these three search folders represent:

- **Recently Changed**—Items from your Documents folder that you have created or modified in the past 30 days.

- **Searches**—A collection of search folders, including Recently Changed, Unread Email, and Favorite Music. Any searches that you save also appear in this folder.

Reading pane

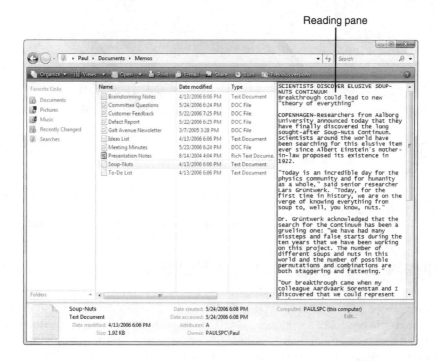

FIGURE 3.21   The Reading pane shows a thumbnail version of the selected file.

TIP

What happened to the Folders list? It's still around, but it's hard to pick out among all the new gewgaws. However, it's easy enough to get at it: just click Folders at the bottom of the Navigation pane.

Live Folder Icons

Do you ever wonder what's inside a folder? In previous versions of Windows, the only way to find out was to open the folder and take a look at the files. With Vista, however, that extra step might not be necessary. That's because Vista introduces a remarkable new feature called Live Icons; each folder icon is an open folder filled not with generic "documents," but with actual folder content. For example, if you have a folder that you use to store PowerPoint presentations, that folder's icon will show the first slides from several of those presentation files. Figure 3.22 shows an example.

Actual first slides from PowerPoint presentation files

FIGURE 3.22   With live icons, the folder icon is filled with actual content from the folder.

Gadgets and the Windows Sidebar

Remember the Active Desktop that Windows 98 foisted on an unsuspecting world? If not, don't worry about it—it was about as forgettable a technology as Microsoft has ever shipped (with the possible exception of Microsoft Bob). The idea wasn't a terrible one: enable the desktop to support mini-applications downloadable from the Internet. Why not convert the desktop wasteland into something that does more than just provide a home for a few icons? The problem was that the Active Desktop items were ugly, slow, barely functional, and hungry: Their appetite for system resources seemed boundless, and just a few of them running at the same time could bring the most powerful system to its knees. Microsoft quietly dropped the Active Desktop and it sank from view, never to be heard from again.

Now, however, Microsoft seems to be trying again. No, the Active Desktop hasn't risen from the dead. Instead, Microsoft is touting a new technology called *gadgets,* which are, once again, mini-applications. The big different between gadgets and Active Desktop items is that gadgets are much more versatile:

- You can run *web gadgets* from a website, such as Microsoft's Live.com site, shown in Figure 3.23.

- You can run *desktop gadgets* in Windows Vista's new Sidebar or on the desktop itself, as shown in Figure 3.24. (To display the Sidebar, select Start, All Programs, Accessories, Windows Sidebar.) In this example, the Sidebar is running three gadgets (from top to bottom): Slide Show (images from your `Pictures` folder), Clock, and Feed Viewer (RSS feeds from Internet Explorer). As you can see from the accompanying window, there are a number of other gadgets you can add.

- You can run *device gadgets* on external devices.

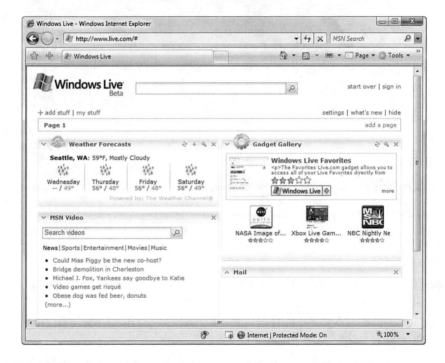

FIGURE 3.23   Websites can implement gadgets, as shown here on Microsoft's Live.com site.

Also, gadgets should prove to be far more robust and efficient than their Active Desktop predecessors because developers can build gadgets using either standard DHTML or the Windows Presentation Foundation.

FIGURE 3.24   Gadgets running in the new Windows Sidebar.

From Here

Here are some other sections in the book where you'll find information related to the topics in this chapter:

- To learn the system requirements to run Vista's Aero Glass interface, see the section in Chapter 2 titled "Graphics Requirements."

- For information on metadata in Vista, see the section in Chapter 4 titled "Metadata and the Windows Explorer Property System."

- See "Desktop Searching with the Windows Search Engine" in Chapter 4 to get the details on Vista's new search features.

- To learn about search folders, see the "Search Folders" section of Chapter 4.

- For information on Vista's new Games folder, see the section "The Game Explorer" in Chapter 10.

File System Improvements

Windows Vista was supposed to be the operating system that finally realized Microsoft's long-sought dream of a major file system breakthrough. Windows Vista was supposed to include WinFS (Windows Future Storage), a file-storage subsystem that runs on NTFS. WinFS not only uses SQL Server–related technology to create sophisticated indexes of a wide variety of data—documents, images, email messages, and so on—but it also leverages the power of XML to create metadata schemas for your data. *Metadata* is information that describes data. For example, you could implement a Tags property to hold keywords. If you then applied the tag Budget2006 to all your data related to this year's budget—Excel workbooks, Word documents, PowerPoint presentations, Access databases, Outlook email messages, and so on—WinFS would not only index all this content, but it also would relate them together based on the common Tags metadata.

It's really the Holy Grail of file systems, but, alas, Microsoft had to drop support for WinFS in Vista so it could ship in a reasonable timeframe. Not that WinFS is dead: On the contrary, a group at Microsoft is still working on this technology, and Microsoft has promised that WinFS will be available for Windows Vista sometime after Vista hits the shelves.

In the meantime, you'll have to content yourself with the changes that Microsoft made to Vista's implementation of the NTFS file system. As you'll see in this chapter, Vista has cobbled quite a few WinFS-like features onto NTFS, including some support for metadata and advanced searching.

Overall, what we're seeing in Vista is a move away from the venerable drive-and-directory storage model that has been the only way of doing things in the PC world since MS-DOS 1.0. For the past quarter-century, we've been taught to think of a file as something that resides, say, on hard disk 0, in partition C:, in the directory/folder named Data. This location-based storage model worked more or less efficiently in the days of 100MB hard drives, but now 100GB drives are common, and mainstream terabyte (1000GB) drives are just around the corner. We fill these massive disks, of course (remember Parkinson's Law of Data), so these days we're dealing with anywhere from 1,000 to 10,000 times the amount of data that we were 10 years ago.

But it's not just the amount of data to deal with—it's also the number of places where that data is stored. If you have a floppy drive, a couple of hard disks, several partitions on each hard disk, a couple of optical drives, and a memory card reader, your system could easily use 15 drive letters. A well-used system might have more than 10,000 folders scattered across those drives. And, of course, plenty of data is stored in hundreds of email folders, RSS feeds, address books, and calendars. With numbers like these, it's clearly time to look for an alternative to location-based file storage. Vista is the first step toward that new storage mechanism, and this chapter gives you a preview of what's new.

Metadata and the Windows Explorer Property System

If file location will become less important, what can you use to take its place? Content seems like a pretty good place to start. After all, it's what's inside the documents that really matters. For example, suppose you're working on the Penske account. It's a pretty good bet that all the Penske-related documents on your system actually have the word *Penske* inside them somewhere. If you want to find a Penske document, a file system that indexes document content sure helps because then you need only do a content search on the word *Penske*.

However, what if a memo or other document comes your way with an idea that would be perfect for the Penske account, but that document doesn't use the word *Penske* anywhere? This is where purely content-based file management fails because you have no way of relating this new document with your Penske documents. Of course, you could edit the new document to add the word *Penske* somewhere, but that's a bit kludgy and, in any case, you might not have write permission on the file. It would be far better if you could somehow identify all of your documents that have "Penske-ness"—that is, that are directly or indirectly related to the Penske account.

This sounds like a job for metadata, and that's appropriate because metadata is all the rage these days, particularly on the Web. At sites such as Flickr.com and del.icio.us, surfers are categorizing the data they find online by applying descriptive keywords—called *tags*—to the objects they come across. *Social software*—software that enables users to share information and collaborate online—makes these tags available to other users, who can then take advantage of all this tagging to search for the information they need. At the del.icio.us site, for example, users bookmark interesting pages and assign tags to each site, and those tags can then be searched. This is called *social bookmarking*. Certainly, metadata is nothing new in the Windows world, either:

- Digital photo files often come with their own metadata for things such as the camera model and image dimensions, and some imaging software enables you to apply tags to pictures.

- In Windows Media Player, you can download album and track information that gets stored as various metadata properties: Artist, Album Title, Track Title, and Genre, to name just a few.

- The last few versions of Microsoft Office have supported metadata via the File, Properties command.

- For all file types, Windows XP displays in each file's property sheet a Summary tab that enables you to set metadata properties such as Author, Comments, and Tags.

What's different in Vista is that metadata is a more integral part of the operating system. With the new Windows Search Engine, you can perform searches on some or all of these properties (see "Desktop Searching with the Windows Search Engine" later in this chapter). You can also use them to create virtual folders, file stacks, and file filters (see "Grouping, Stacking, and Filtering with Metadata," later in this chapter).

Windows Explorer displays some of a document's metadata in the Preview pane, as shown in Figure 4.1. Click and drag the top edge of the Preview pane up to see more metadata, as shown in Figure 4.2.

FIGURE 4.1   The Windows Explorer Preview pane shows some of the metadata for the selected document.

FIGURE 4.2   Expand the Preview pane to see more metadata.

To edit a document's metadata, you use the document's property sheet, and Vista gives you two ways to display it:

- Click the Edit link in the Preview pane.
- Right-click the document and click Properties to display the property sheet, and then click the Details tab.

As you can see in Figure 4.3, this tab displays a list of properties and their values. To edit a property, click inside the Value column to the right of the property.

Putting metadata at the heart of the operating system is a welcome innovation. Throw in the capability to sort, group, stack, filter, and create search folders based on such metadata, and few would dispute the value of this enhanced file system.

It's also a good thing that metadata is easy to implement for individual files, but will people get into the habit of adding metadata for each new document that they create? Time will tell, but it's certainly true that metadata has been underutilized so far. I think people will have to be convinced that taking a little time now to add metadata will save them more time in the future because the metadata makes documents easier to find and manage. It also helps if software vendors can make it easier for users to add metadata to documents. Having to switch over to Windows Explorer to add or edit metadata is not a big productivity booster. Instead, I hope Vista-aware programs will offer metadata-friendly interfaces and prompt for properties when users save new documents.

Click the Value cell of the property you want to edit

FIGURE 4.3   You can edit all of a document's configurable metadata in the document's property sheet.

A much bigger problem is applying metadata to existing documents. I have thousands of them, and you probably do, too. Who has the time or motivation to set even just a few property values for thousands of old files? Nobody does, of course, and I suspect most of us will simply ignore the vast majority of our existing files (after all, we might never use 95% of them again) and move forward into the metadata future.

Desktop Searching with Windows Search

Searching your computer in Windows XP wasn't a terrible experience, but no one raved about it, either. First there was Microsoft's inexplicable decision to ship XP with the

Indexing service turned off by default. Without the Indexing service, search was next-to-useless in XP, but turning it on required several relatively obscure clicks in the Search Companion. Even with the Indexing service running, searches that included entire partitions could take a frustratingly long time to complete.

Microsoft's goal in Vista is to make search a truly useful tool that provides complete results quickly. Did they succeed? For the most part, yes. The Windows Search service is started by default, which all by itself is a big improvement over XP. On the downside, it can still take Vista an absurdly long time to search, say, all of drive C:. However, that's because Windows Search does *not* index the entire drive. Instead, it just indexes the following:

- Your user folder, which includes not only Documents, Music, and Pictures but also Contacts, Favorites, and the hidden AppData folder, which stores application data such as your Windows Mail messages

- Your offline files

- Your Start menu contents

If you're searching for documents in any of these locations, Vista searches are lightning quick.

Note that you can control what Window Search indexes and force a rebuild of the index by selecting Start, Control Panel, System and Maintenance, Indexing Options. This displays the dialog box shown in Figure 4.4. To customize the search engine, you have two choices:

- **Modify**—Click this button to display the Indexed Locations dialog box, which enables you to change the locations included in the index. Activate the check box for each drive or folder you want to include.

- **Advanced**—Click this button to display the Advanced Options dialog box, which enables you to specify the file types (extensions) that you want to include in or exclude from the index. Note that for each file type you can tell Windows Vista to include in the index either just the metadata for documents of that type, or both the metadata and the contents (the latter is the default).You can also click Rebuild to re-create the index.

NOTE

If you click the Run As Administrator button, Vista includes the folders for the Administrator account in the index.

CAUTION

Windows Search takes a *long* time to index even a relatively small amount of data. If you're asking Windows Search to index dozens of gigabytes of data, wait until you're done working for the day and let the indexer run all night.

As-You-Type Searches with Instant Search

Vista's searching interface is also radically different from XP's simple but forgettable Search Companion. The most obvious—and, for simple searches, certainly the most useful—innovation is the Instant Search box on the Vista Start menu. As shown in Figure 4.5, as you type characters in the Instant Search box, the Start menu replaces the list of pinned and recently used programs with a new list that displays the following search links:

- A list of programs with names that include the typed characters.

- A list of files (documents) with content or metadata that include the typed characters.

- Other data—such as Contacts and email messages—with content or metadata that includes the typed characters.

- A Search the Computer link.

- A Search the Internet link.

If you see the program or file you want, click it to open it. Otherwise, you can click Search the Computer to see the complete list of matches from the files in your user profile. If you prefer to search the Web for your text, click the Search the Internet link instead.

FIGURE 4.4   Use the Control Panel's Indexing Options to control the Windows Search Service.

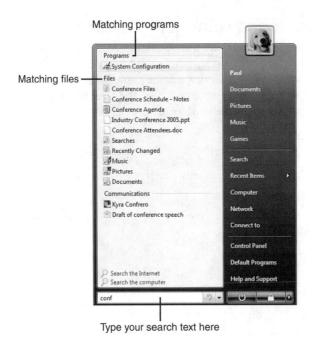

FIGURE 4.5   As-you-type searching using the Start menu's Instant Search box.

You can also perform these as-you-type searches in any folder by using the Instant Search box that appears in every Explorer window. As you type, Explorer displays those files in the current folder with names or metadata that matches your search text, as shown in Figure 4.6. You also get two options for continuing the search, and you can see those options by pulling down the Instant Search box menu:

FIGURE 4.6   As-you-type searching using the Explorer window's Instant Search box.

4

TIP

In a folder window, you can access the Instant Search box via the keyboard by pressing Ctrl+E.

- **Search the Computer**—Click this link (or press Alt+Enter) to extend the search to all the folders in your user profile.

- **Search the Internet**—Click this link (or press Shift+Enter) to extend the search to the Internet.

Advanced Searches

As-you-type searches are handy and fast, but they tend to return too many results because they look for your search text in documents' metadata and contents. However, to find what you're looking for in a hard disk with dozens or even hundreds of gigabytes of data and many thousands of files, you need a more sophisticated approach. Windows Vista can help here, too.

In any folder window, pull down the Instant Search box menu and click Search Pane (or select Organize, Layout, Search Pane) to add the Search pane, as shown in Figure 4.7.

FIGURE 4.7   Use the Search pane to perform more advanced searches.

Vista assumes that you want to search by file type, so click one of the displayed types: All Kinds (matches any file type), E-mails, Documents, Pictures, or Music. You can also click the More Kinds button (>>) to display a much longer list of document types (such as Contacts, Instant Messages, RSS, and Web History; see Figure 4.7).

To modify the search location, either type a new path in the Search In text box, or pull down the In list and click a default location. You can also click Choose Search Locations to display the Choose Search Locations dialog box, shown in Figure 4.8. The bottom part of the dialog box tells you the locations that are included in the search. You have three ways to modify these locations:

- To add a folder, activate the check box beside the folder in the Change Selected Locations list.

- To add any path, type it in the Or Type a Location Here text box, and then click Add.

- To remove a folder, deactivate the check box beside the folder in the Change Selected Locations list.

Finally, you can add metadata filters that specify the properties in which you want Vista to look and how you want it to look there. Click Show Advanced Filters to add a filter to the search criteria, as shown in Figure 4.9. The filter includes three fields:

- **Property**—Pull down this list to select the property you want to use.

- **Operator**—Pull down this list to specify the comparison operator you want to use (for example, Is, Is Not, Starts With, Ends With, Contains, Doesn't Contain, <, and >).

- **Value**—Use this text box to specify the text you want to use for the filter.

FIGURE 4.8   Use the Choose Location dialog box to configure the folders included in your search.

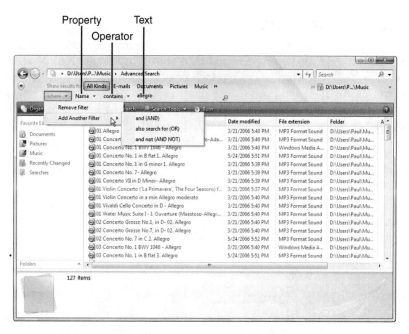

FIGURE 4.9   You can specify a property, operator, and text to add a search filter.

For even more sophisticated searches, you can combine multiple filters using Boolean operators. After creating your first filter, pull down the where list, select Add another Filter, and then select one of the following (see Figure 4.9):

- **And (AND)**—Choose this option to tell Vista to match files that meet *all* of your filter criteria. Note that this is the default choice, and Windows Vista automatically adds this type of filter when you run your initial metadata search.

- **Also Search For (OR)**—Choose this option to tell Vista to match files that meet *at least one* of your filter criteria.

- **And Not (AND NOT)**—Choose this option to tell Vista to match files that do not meet the filter criteria.

Saving Searches

After taking all that time to get a search just right, it would be a real pain if you had to repeat the entire procedure to run the same search later. Fortunately, Windows Vista takes pity on searchers by enabling you to save your searches and rerun them anytime you like. After you run a search, you save it by clicking the Save Search button in the task pane. In the Save As dialog box that appears, type a name for the search and click Save.

Vista saves your searches in the Searches folder, appropriately enough. To rerun a search, click the Searches folder in the Navigation pane and then double-click the search.

Windows Mail Searches

One of the nicest features in the new Windows Mail program (second only to the sorely needed junk mail filter) is as-you-type searching within Windows Mail folders. As in the Explorer window, the Mail window has a search box in the upper-right corner. Type your search text in this box (you can press Ctrl+E to select it), and Mail filters the message list to show only those messages that contain the search text in the From, To, or Cc fields; the subject line; or the body text, as shown in Figure 4.10.

Type your search text here

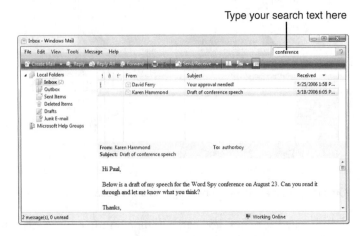

FIGURE 4.10   As-you-type searching in Windows Mail enables you to search for text in the message From, To, and Cc fields, as well as the subject and body.

Grouping, Stacking, and Filtering with Metadata

I mentioned earlier that people might not be motivated to apply metadata to their documents unless they could be convinced that metadata is worth the short-term hassle. The Windows programmers seem to understand this because they built three new file-management techniques into Windows Explorer, all of which become more powerful and more useful the more metadata you've applied to your files. These techniques are grouping, stacking, and filtering.

Grouping Files

Grouping files means organizing a folder's contents according to the values in a particular property. You could do this in Windows XP, but you'll see that Windows Vista implements a couple of new techniques that make its grouping feature far more useful.

The first thing that Vista does better than XP is display property headers full time, while in XP they appeared only in Details view. This means that you can group your files (as well as stack and filter them, as you'll see in the next two sections) no matter which view you're using.

In the Vista version of Windows Explorer, each property header has a drop-down list that includes a Group command. Clicking this command groups the files according to the values in that property. Figure 4.11 shows the Pictures folder grouped by the values in the Type property.

Click here to select the group

FIGURE 4.11   Windows Vista enables you to group and work with files based on the values in a property.

As Figure 4.11 shows, Vista enhances the grouping feature with two new techniques:

- You can select all the files in a group by clicking the group title.

- You can collapse the group (that is, show just the group title) by clicking the upward-pointing arrow to the right of the group title. (You can collapse all the groups by right-clicking any group title and then clicking Collapse All Groups.)

Stacking Files

Stacking files is similar to grouping them because it organizes the folder's contents based on the values of a property. The difference is that a stack of files appears in the folder as a kind of subfolder. You stack files according to a property's values by pulling down the list associated with that property's header and clicking the Stack command (see Figure 4.13, in the next section). For example, Figure 4.12 shows the Pictures folder stacked according to the values in the Size property.

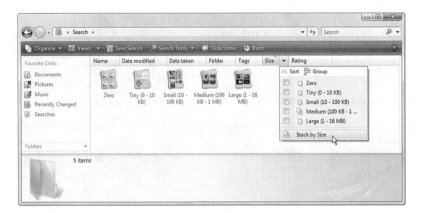

FIGURE 4.12   The Pictures folder stacked according to the values in the Size property.

Filtering Files

Filtering files means changing the folder view so that only files that have one or more specified property values are displayed. Returning to the Type example, you could filter the folder's files to show only those where the Type property was, say, JPEG Image or File Folder.

When you pull down the list associated with a property's header, you see an item for each discrete property value, along with a check box for each value. To filter the files, activate the check boxes for the property values you want to view. For example, in Figure 4.13 I've activated the check boxes beside the Bitmap Image and TIF Image values in the Type property, and only those two types appear in the folder.

Activate the check boxes to filter the files

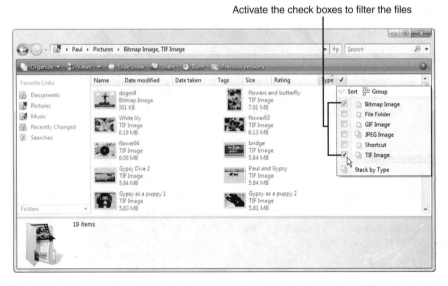

FIGURE 4.13   You can filter a folder to show only those files that have the property values you specify.

Search Folders

File-management gurus exhort users to organize their documents by creating folders and subfolders to store related files. Microsoft decided to force the issue a bit by automatically creating folders such as My Documents, My Pictures, and My Music (now called just Documents, Pictures, and Music in Vista). However, even if you used these dedicated folders religiously and scrupulously, you still ended up with lots of subfolders for different topics, artists, albums, and so on. That's as it should be according to the file-management pros, but it can lead to problems:

- How can you view all of your image files?

- How can you view all the documents written by a particular person?

- How can you view all the music files with the word *love* in the title?

These are thorny conundrums, and they're all created by the fact that users have similar files that are scattered among dozens or even hundreds of subfolders.

One of the design goals of Windows Vista is to maintain the usefulness and organizational clarity of storing similar documents in their own subfolders, while at the same time eliminating the difficulties inherent in viewing similar documents across all those subfolders.

Microsoft's solution to these difficulties is a new concept called the *search folder*. The idea behind this new technology is simple but radical: The operating system knows (or can be told) enough about your files that it can organize all related files into a single, virtual location. Here, "virtual" means that although your files still physically reside in specific folders and subfolders on your hard disk, they simultaneously reside in a separate object— a kind of virtual folder—that stores similar files.

The best way to understand these "virtual" folders is to think of the results of a file search. When you enter your criteria and run the search, Windows returns a list of files that match your criteria. That result set is "virtual" in the sense that the files still reside on disk, but they simultaneously and temporarily reside in the search results. For example, if you rename or even delete a file in the search results, you rename or delete the actual file. In other words, the items in the search results are actual files, not shortcuts or pointers to the files.

In Vista, a virtual folder is essentially a saved search result, which is why Microsoft now uses the term *search folder* instead of *virtual folder*. When you open a search folder, Vista runs the search and displays the results.

Selecting Files with Check Boxes

So far you've seen quite a few substantive changes to the Windows file system: metadata, the Windows Search engine, grouping, stacking, filtering, and search folders. Later in this chapter, you'll learn about shadow copies and transactional NTFS, innovations that are just as sophisticated and useful. However, sometimes it's the small, incremental changes that make your life with a new operating system easier and more efficient. In this section and the next, I give you a bit of a break from the heavier file system updates by telling you about two small but quite useful tweaks to the way you select files and drag and drop them.

Selecting files and folders is one of those workaday tasks that has become second nature to most users over the years. You probably have a favorite technique that you use and are comfortable with, particularly when selecting multiple, noncontiguous objects. For me, I hold down the Ctrl key and click each item I want to select.

However, when I use this technique to select more than a few files, I *always* end up accidentally selecting one or more files that I don't want. It's not a big deal to deselect these extra files, but it's one of those small drains on productivity that just bugs me (and a lot of other users).

Windows Vista introduces a new file-selection technique that promises to eliminate accidental selections. It's called Use Check Boxes to Select Items, and you activate it by selecting Organize, Folder Options to open the Folder Options dialog box. (You can also open this dialog box via the Control Panel's Folder Options icon.) In the View tab, activate the Use Check Boxes to Select Items check box, and then click OK.

As you can see in Figure 4.14, when you turn on this feature, Explorer creates a column to the left of the folder contents. When you point at a file or folder, a check box appears in this column, and you select an item by activating its check box. You don't need to hold down Ctrl or use the keyboard at all. Just activate the check boxes for the files and folders you want to select. Bonus technique: You can also select all the items in the folder quickly by clicking the check box that appears in the Name column.

Activated check boxes remain visible

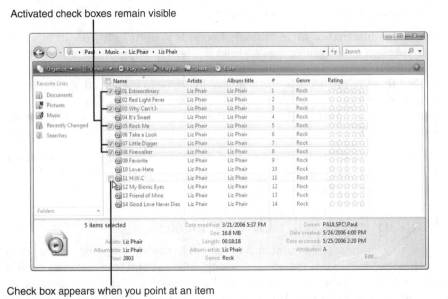

Check box appears when you point at an item

FIGURE 4.14   In Windows Vista, you can select files and folders using check boxes.

Dragging and Dropping Files

One of the biggest complaints that new users have with Windows is that although it's fun (relatively speaking) to click-and-drag files and folders and drop them on new locations, they can never figure out whether the items are going to be copied or moved. There are, of course, rules for this kind of things:

- If you drop the item on a folder in the same disk or partition, Windows moves the item.

- If you drop the item on a folder in a different disk or partition, Windows copies the item.

The only bit of help Windows offered novices was to make a slight change to the mouse pointer (the addition of a tiny plus sign) when dropping the file or folder would result in copying the item.

Windows Vista improves on this by making the result of a drag-and-drop operation explicit when you're in mid-drag. As you can see in Figure 4.15, when you're dragging an item, the mouse pointer changes to display text that tells you exactly what will happen when you drop the item ("Move to Desktop" in this case).

Drag-and-drop result

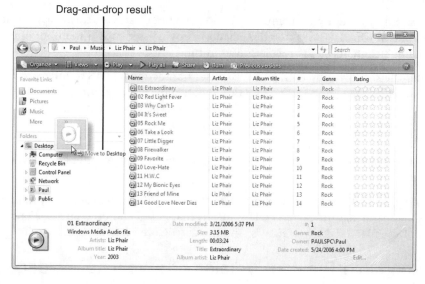

FIGURE 4.15   Windows Vista provides more explicit clues about the result of a file drag-and-drop.

Shadow Copies and Transactional NTFS

High-end databases have long supported the idea of the *transaction*, a collection of data modifications—inserts, deletions, updates, and so on—treated as a unit, meaning that either all of the modifications occur or none of them does. For example, consider a finance database system that needs to perform a single chore: transfer a specified amount of money from one account to another. This involves two discrete steps (I'm simplifying here): debit one account by the specified amount and credit the other account for the same amount. If the database system did not treat these two steps as a single transaction, you could run into problems. For example, if the system successfully debited the first account but for some reason was unable to credit the second account, the system would be left in an unbalanced state. By treating the two steps as a single transaction, the system does not commit any changes unless both steps occur successfully. If the credit to the second account fails, the transaction is *rolled back* to the beginning, meaning that the debit to the first account is reversed and the system reverts to a stable state.

What does all this have to do with the Vista file system? It's actually directly related because Vista implements an interesting new technology called *Transactional NTFS*, or *TxF*, for short. TxF applies the same transactional database ideas to the file system. Put simply, with TxF, if some mishap occurs to your data—it could be a system crash, a program crash, an overwrite of an important file, or even just imprudent edits to a file— Vista enables you to roll back the file to a previous version. It's kind of like System Restore, except that it works not for the entire system, but for individual files, folders, and volumes.

Windows Vista's capability to restore previous versions of files and folders comes from two new processes:

- Each time you start your computer, Windows Vista creates a *shadow copy* of the volume in which Vista is stored. A shadow copy is essentially a snapshot of the volume's contents at a particular point in time.

- After the shadow copy is created, Vista uses transactional NTFS to intercept all calls to the file system, and Vista maintains a meticulous log of those calls so that it knows exactly which files and folders in the volume have changed.

Together these processes enable Vista to store *previous versions* of files and folders, where a previous version is defined as a version of the object that changed after a shadow copy was created.

For example, suppose you reboot your system three mornings in a row, and you make changes to a particular file each day. This means that you'll end up with three previous versions of the file: today's, yesterday's, and the day before yesterday's.

Reverting to a Previous Version of a Volume, Folder, or File

Windows Vista offers three different scenarios for using previous versions:

- If a system crash occurs, you might end up with extensive damage to large sections of the volume. Assuming that you can start Windows Vista, you might then be able to recover your data by reverting to a previous version of the volume (although this means that you'll probably lose any new documents you created since then). Note, however, that this means that *every* file that changed since the associated shadow copy was created will be reverted to the previous version, so use this technique with some care.

- If a system crash or program crash damages a folder, you might be able to recover that folder by reverting to a previous version.

- If a system crash or program damages a file, or if you accidentally overwrite or misedit a file, you might be able to recover the file by reverting to a previous version.

To revert to a previous version, open the property sheet for the object you want to work with and then display the Previous Versions tab. Figure 4.16 shows the Previous Versions tab for a volume, while Figure 4.17 shows the Previous Versions tab for a file.

Clicking a version activates the following three command buttons:

- **Open**—Click this button to view the contents of the previous version of the volume or folder, or to open the previous version of the file. This is useful if you're not sure which previous version you need.

- **Copy**—Click this button to make a copy of the previous version of the volume, folder, or file. This is useful if you're not sure you want to restore *all* of the object, so by making a copy you can restore just part of it (say, a few files from a volume or folder, or a section of a file).

- **Restore**—Click this button to roll back changes made to the volume, folder, or file to the previous version.

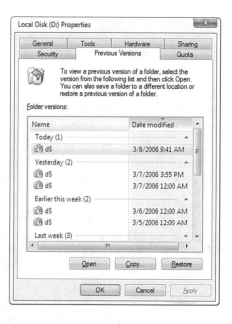

FIGURE 4.16   The Previous Versions tab for a volume.

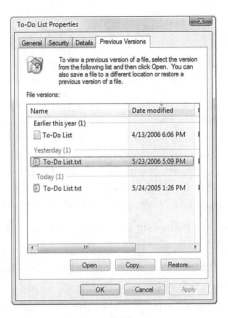

FIGURE 4.17   The Previous Versions tab for a file.

XML Paper Specification (XPS)

The global nature of our connected world means that we often need to share information with people who don't use the same technology that we do. They might not use the same programs that we do, they might run a different version of Windows, or they might be using an entirely different operating system. How do you share the information contained in a document on your system in such circumstances? Currently, you have several different options:

- Convert the document to plain text, a format supported by all systems. This enables you to share the raw data, but you lose all your document's fonts, formatting, and graphics, which could dilute or distort your information.

- Put the document on the Web, enabling the other person to view it using any web browser. This usually offers a reasonable facsimile of the original file, but generally without any rights management. The other user can easily copy the information and republish it.

- Publish the document as a PDF file. Almost all systems have (or can get) PDF viewers, the document looks identical to the original, and you can apply digital rights to the PDF to control its use. However, PDF is a proprietary standard (it's owned by Adobe Systems), and you might prefer to use a format based on open standards.

In other words, you face four problems when it comes to sharing a document:

- The shared document should be viewable by all, regardless of the programs or operating systems they use.

- The shared document should be a faithful rendition of the original, including fonts, formatting, and high-fidelity images.

- The shared document should have some kind of rights management built in so that you can control what other users can do with the document.

- The document's format should be based on open standards.

Attempting to solve these four problems is why Microsoft has come up with a new document format called the XML Paper Specification, or XPS (the original codename was Metro). Here's how XPS solves the document-sharing problems:

- Microsoft has also pledged to create XPS viewers for Vista and for older versions of Windows. The Vista viewer loads in Internet Explorer, as you can see in Figure 4.18 (no viewer for older versions was available as this book went to press). Also, Microsoft has published the programming interface for viewing and manipulating XPS documents, so there's little doubt that third-party developers will come up with XPS viewers for the Mac, Linux, and other systems.

- The XML syntax XPS uses is complex, but that complexity is required to create XPS documents that are high-fidelity reproductions of the original file. Documents published as XPS should look exactly the same as they do in the original application.

- XPS supports digital signatures, which enables the publisher to apply rights to what users can and cannot do with an XPS document.

- XPS uses XML for the document syntax and ZIP for the document container file, so it's based on open and available technologies.

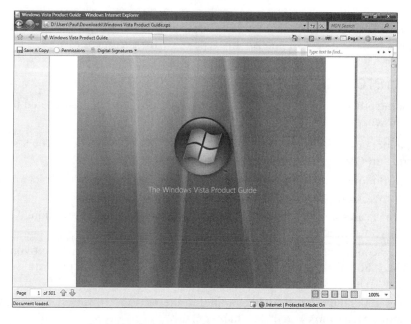

Figure 4.18 The Vista XPS viewer loads XPS documents within Internet Explorer.

Because Microsoft is licensing XPS royalty-free, developers can incorporate XPS viewing and publishing features into their products without cost. This means it should be easy to publish XPS documents from a variety of applications. Note, too, that XPS publishing is built into Windows Vista via the Microsoft XPS printer driver, shown in Figure 4.19. This is a print-to-file driver, so clicking Print publishes your original file to an XPS document in the folder you choose.

FIGURE 4.19   You can publish files as XPS documents in Windows Vista by using the Microsoft XPS printer driver.

I should note here, as well, that a Save as XPS feature will be built into all the Office 2007 applications, making it easy to publish any type of Office document as an XPS container.

From Here

Here are some other sections in the book where you'll find information related to the topics in this chapter:

- For a more detailed look at Vista's new Start menu, see the section "The Start Menu," in Chapter 3.
- To learn more about folder windows in Vista, see the section "New Folder Windows," in Chapter 3.
- System crashes should be rarer in Vista. To find out why, see the section "Vista's Stability Improvements," in Chapter 5.
- Shadow copies and transactional NTFS are welcome improvements, but you should still back up your files. To learn what's new in the Vista Backup program, see the section "Windows Backup," in Chapter 5.
- I cover junk mail rules and related topics in the section "Thwarting Spam with Windows Mail's Junk Filter," in Chapter 6.

Vista Performance and Maintenance

We often wonder why our workaday computer chores seem to take just as long as they ever did, despite the fact that hardware is generally bigger, better, and faster than ever. The answer to this apparent riddle is related to Parkinson's Law of Data, which I mentioned back in Chapter 2, "Moving to Windows Vista." On a more general level, Parkinson's Law could be restated as follows: The increase in software system requirements is directly proportional to the increase in hardware system capabilities. For example, imagine that a slick new chip is released that promises a 30% speed boost; software designers, seeing the new chip gain wide acceptance, add 30% more features to their already bloated code to take advantage of the higher performance level. Then another new chip is released, followed by another software upgrade—and the cycle continues *ad nauseum* as these twin engines of computer progress lurch codependently into the future.

So, how do you break out of the performance deadlock created by the immovable object of software code bloat meeting the irresistible force of hardware advancement? By optimizing your system to minimize the effects of overgrown applications and to maximize the native capabilities of your hardware. Of course, it helps if your operating system gives you a good set of tools to improve and monitor performance, diagnose problems, and keep your data safe. Windows XP came with a decent set of client tools, and Vista improves upon them, although not with anything radically new or earth-shattering. Vista's performance and maintenance improvements are evolutionary, not revolutionary, but they're definitely better than anything we've seen in a Microsoft client operating system.

Vista's Performance Improvements

Certain computer pastimes—hard-core gaming, software development, database administration, and digital video editing, to name just a few—require hardware help to maximize performance. Whether it's scads of system RAM, a mountain of hard drive storage space, or a state-of-the-art graphics card, these intense computer tasks require the best hardware that users can afford.

Those of use who are not into these intense computing pursuits generally don't need the fastest machine on the market to write memos, build spreadsheet models, or design web pages. What we really need is a system that doesn't get in our way by making us wait for seemingly routine tasks. For example, in Windows XP I often right-click a document in Explorer with the intention of clicking a command such as Cut, Copy, or Rename. Along the way, however, my mouse pointer has to pass over the Send To command. XP populates the Send To menu by going to the Registry and searching for items that it can add to this menu. For some reason, that sometimes takes several seconds, so my mouse pointer remains stuck on Send To, even though that's not the command I want.

This kind of interface annoyance must have bugged the Windows programmers one too many times also because they've rewritten the interface code from the ground up to make actions such as choosing menu options (including displaying the Send To menu) much faster. Even the in-place All Programs menu (see Chapter 2) is a huge improvement over XP and enables you to launch items much more quickly from deeply nested folders such as System Tools and Ease of Access.

Besides these fit-and-finish performance improvements, Vista comes with a host of new features and updated technologies designed to make Vista the fastest Windows ever. The next few sections take you through the most important of these performance enhancements.

Faster Startup

The first thing you'll notice about Windows Vista is that it starts up *much* faster than any previous version of Windows. I don't mean that it's a second or two faster, either. My own testing reveals that Vista starts up in approximately *half* the time compared to an equivalent XP setup. For example, on an XP machine that takes 60 seconds from power-up to the point that you can actually start working with the interface, the equivalent Vista system would take 25 to 30 seconds. Remember, too, that I was testing with a beta version of Vista, so the release version you'll use should be even faster.

> **NOTE**
>
> One Microsoft document claimed that Vista startups would take "typically 2 to 3 seconds." This seems *extremely* unlikely, but it sure would be nice if it was true! (but see my discussion of the new sleep mode, later in this chapter).

Where does the startup speed boost come from? Some of it comes from optimizing the startup code. However, most of the improvement comes from Vista's asynchronous startup script and application launching. Older versions of Windows were hobbled at startup because they had to wait for each startup script, batch file, and program to launch before Windows handed the desktop over to the user.

Vista handles startup jobs asynchronously, which means they run in the background while Vista devotes most of its startup energies to getting the desktop onscreen. This means that it's not unusual to notice startup scripts or programs running well after the desktop has made its appearance. Because all startup items run in the background, theoretically it shouldn't matter how many script or programs you run at startup; Vista should start up just as fast as if you had *no* startup items.

CAUTION

The Vista team was right to give the user top startup priority because it's frustrating to wait forever for startup items to execute. However, asynchronous startup could lead to problems if a script or program that you require for your work has not finished its chores before you're ready. In most cases, this should just mean enduring the usual waiting game, but it's something to bear in mind whenever you or one of your programs adds a script, program, or service to the startup.

Sleep Mode: The Best of Both Worlds

In the last few versions of Windows, you had a number of options at your disposal for turning off your computer. You could use the Shut Down option to turn off the system entirely, which saved power but forced you to close all your documents and applications; you could put the system into Standby mode, which preserved your work and enabled you to restart quickly, but didn't entirely shut off the machine's power; or you could go into Hibernate mode, which preserved your work and completely shuts off the machine, but also took a relatively long time to restart (faster than Shut Down, but slower than Standby).

I think it's safe to say that most users were confused by these options, particularly by the (subtle) difference between the Standby and Hibernate modes. By far the most common power-management complaint I've heard over the past few years is, "Why can't Windows be more like a Mac?" That is to say, why can't we turn off our machines instantly, and have them resume instantly with our windows and work still intact, as Apple has done with OS X?

The new answer to these questions is that Vista is heading in that direction with a new Sleep state that combines the best of the old Standby and Hibernate modes:

- As in Standby, you enter Sleep mode within just a few seconds.

- As in both Standby and Hibernate, Sleep mode preserves all your open documents, windows, and programs.

- As in Hibernate, Sleep mode shuts down your computer (although, as you'll see, it doesn't quite shut down everything).

- As in Standby, you resume from Sleep mode within just a few seconds.

How can Vista preserve your work *and* restart in just a few seconds? The secret is that Vista doesn't really shut off your computer when you initiate sleep mode. Instead, it shuts down everything except a few crucial components such as the CPU and RAM. By preserving power to the RAM chips, Vista can keep your work intact and redisplay it instantly upon waking. Don't worry, though: Vista *does* make a copy of your work to the hard disk, so if your computer completely loses power, your work is still preserved.

To use Sleep mode, open the Start menu and click the Sleep button, shown in Figure 5.1. Vista saves the current state and shuts off the computer in a few seconds. To resume, press your computer's power button; the Vista Welcome screen appears almost immediately.

Sleep button

FIGURE 5.1   Click the new Sleep button to quickly shut down your computer and save your work.

SuperFetch with ReadyBoost: The Faster Fetcher

Prefetching was a performance feature introduced in Windows XP that monitored your system and anticipated the data that you might use in the near future. It then loaded (prefetched) that data into memory ahead of time. If that data was indeed what your system required, performance would increase because XP wouldn't have to fetch the data from your hard disk.

Windows Vista introduces a new and improved version of the Prefetcher: SuperFetch. This technology tracks the programs and data you use over time to create a kind of profile of your disk usage. Using the profile, SuperFetch can then make a much more educated guess about the data that you'll require and, like the Prefetcher, can then load that data into memory ahead of time for enhanced performance.

However, SuperFetch goes even further by taking advantage of Vista's new ReadyBoost technology. If you insert a 512MB (or larger) USB 2.0 Flash drive into your system, Vista displays the AutoPlay dialog box shown in Figure 5.2. If you click Speed Up My System Using Windows ReadyBoost, SuperFetch uses that drive's capacity as storage for the SuperFetch cache. This frees up the system RAM that SuperFetch would otherwise use, which should result in an automatic (and probably quite dramatic) performance boost. Not only that, but you still get an extra performance nudge from SuperFetch itself because even though data access via the Flash drive is slower than with system RAM, it's still many times faster than even the fastest hard drive.

FIGURE 5.2   If you insert a USB Flash drive into your system, SuperFetch can use it as its cache to improve system performance.

You can also control the amount of storage space that SuperFetch uses on the Flash drive. Select Start, Computer; right-click the Flash drive; and then click Properties to open the device's property sheet. In the Memory tab, shown in Figure 5.3, click Use This Device to let SuperFetch access the Flash memory and then use the slider to set the maximum amount of memory SuperFetch can use.

NOTE

SuperFetch usually sets the maximum memory it can use to a value less than the total capacity of the Flash drive. That's because most Flash drives contain both fast and slow Flash memory, and SuperFetch can use only the fast variety.

NOTE

As I was writing this, an interesting rumor was circulating—started by, of all people, Jim Allchin, Microsoft's President of Platforms and Services (that is, the Windows Vista head honcho; at least until he retires when Vista ships)—that claimed ReadyBoost was also going to be configured to take advantage of memory on unused computers on your network. It was not clear when this eyebrow-raising idea would be incorporated into Vista.

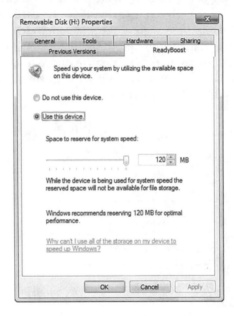

FIGURE 5.3   In the Flash drive's property sheet, use the Memory tab to set the maximum amount of memory that SuperFetch can use.

Restart Manager

In the old days, "updating" an operating system or program meant installing an entirely new version of the software. Then Microsoft and some software vendors started posting "patches" on bulletin boards, then FTP sites, and eventually on the Web. Strangely, they didn't actually *tell* anyone that those patches were there, but they assumed that intrepid power users would unearth them and somehow get them installed.

This primitive state of affairs ended a few Windows versions ago when Microsoft introduced Windows Update, a service that made it much easier to find, download, and install security patches, bug fixes, software and certified driver updates, and service packs. Software vendors followed suit, and it soon become common to have a "Check for Updates" feature in a software package so that you could remain up-to-date.

Having the latest Windows updates and the latest versions of programs is a real boon because it makes computers more secure and more robust. However, it doesn't come without a cost. One of the biggest productivity killers today is the "Reboot Required" message you see all too often after installing even what seems like a minor patch. This dreaded message means that you have to save all your work, shut down your running programs, restart the system, and then open all your programs, windows, and documents all over again. It's frustrating, and it almost always seems so unnecessary. Why is there so often a need for a restart after patching Windows or a program?

The short answer is that it's not possible to overwrite a running executable file or dynamic link library (DLL), which the operating system locks while the program is in use. If the update includes a new version of a running executable or DLL, and that executable or DLL can't be shut down, the only way to perform the update is with a reboot, which ensures that *all* executables and DLLs are unloaded.

Why can't you just close the running program? It's not that easy, unfortunately. For one thing, you can't be sure these days when you shut down a program that you're shutting down *all* instances of the program in memory. Consider Microsoft Word, for example, which can be running not only in the Word window, but also in Outlook as the email editor, in Internet Explorer when it displays a .doc file, and so on. For another thing, many executable files operate in the background, and you don't even know they're running, so there's no interface for shutting them down.

Of course, it's silly to unload the entire system just to patch what could be a single running file. Fortunately, Windows Vista is tackling this absurdity with the new Restart Manager technology. Restart Manager does three things:

1. It looks for all the processes that are using the file that needs to be updated.

2. It shuts down all those processes.

3. After the updates are applied, it restarts those processes.

The real trick here is the *way* that Restart Manager performs these restarts in programs designed to work with Restart Manager. It doesn't just start up the program and leave you to fend for yourself by reopening all your documents. Instead, Restart Manager preserves the *exact* state of each running process and then restores that state upon restarting the process. So if you're working in Word on a document named Budget.doc and the cursor was in line 10, column 20, Restart Manager not only restarts Word, but it also opens Budget.doc *and* restores the cursor to line 10, column 20. (Microsoft calls saving a program state in this way "freeze-drying" the program.) Note that the full functionality of Restart Manager is available only to applications written to take advantage of it. Office 2007 is the only program I know of that has this capability, but expect most major applications to become Restart Manager–aware in their next versions.

For programs that don't support Restart Manager, Windows Vista introduces a new idea called "side-by-side compliant" DLLs. This technology enables an installation program to write a new version of a DLL to the hard disk, even if the old version is still in use. When you shut down the program, Vista replaces the old version of the DLL with the new one, so the update will be complete the next time you start the application.

All of this means that updates should require far fewer reboots in Vista than in XP. Not that reboots will never be required, however. In particular, there will always be patches that must update one or more core operating system files. By definition, core operating system files run at startup and remain running as long as the system is turned on, and it's not possible to shut them down without shutting down the entire OS. (Technically, you *can* rename the file and then install the new version under the old name, but that can lead to all kinds of system problems.) In these situations, there will be no choice but to reboot to apply the patch. Hopefully, however, Vista's faster shutdown and startup times will make this less of a headache as well.

Windows System Assessment Tool (WinSAT)

From a high-level perspective, each version of Windows XP was exactly the same no matter what hardware it ran on. Yes, the set of device drivers running on each system could be vastly different, but from the user's perspective, it didn't matter whether you were running a bare-bones budget PC or a 64-bit behemoth: The look and feel of XP, and the programs and features that were available, didn't change. On the surface, that seems more than a little strange because there's a huge performance gulf between a box that meets only the minimal requirements for running Windows and a top-end machine with a fast 64-bit processor, scads of RAM, and a state-of-the-art GPU. Unfortunately, this situation meant that all too often the system opted for lowest-common-denominator settings that worked for low-end machines but did nothing to take advantage of high-end hardware.

Fortunately, this one-size-fits-all approach to Windows will be history after Windows Vista ships. That's because Vista tailors certain aspects of itself depending on the capabilities of the system on which it's installed. I mentioned in Chapter 2 that the Vista interface will change depending on the graphics hardware on the machine, with low-end machines getting the straightforward Classic interface, midrange adapters getting the regular Aero theme, and high-end GPUs getting the full Aero Glass treatment.

But Vista also scales other aspects up or down to suit its hardware home. With games, for example, Vista enables certain features only if the hardware can support them. (I talk about this in more detail in Chapter 10, "Windows Vista and Gaming.") Other features that are scaled for the computer's hardware are TV recording (for example, how many channels can be recorded at once?) and video playback (for example, what is the optimal playback size and frame rate that doesn't result in dropped frames?).

The tool that handles all of this not only for Vista itself, but also for third-party programs, is the Windows System Assessment Tool, or WinSAT. This tool runs during setup and whenever you make major performance-related hardware changes to your system. It focuses on four aspects of your system performance: graphics, memory, processor, and storage. For each of these subsystems, WinSAT maintains a set of metrics stored as an *assessment* in XML format. Vista then needs to examine only the latest assessment to see what features the computer can support. Note, too, that third-party programs can use an application programming interface that gives them access to the assessments, so developers can tune program features depending on the WinSAT metrics.

Five metrics are used:

- **Processor**—This metric determines how fast the system can process data. The Processor metric is measured in megabytes per second processed.

- **Memory (RAM)**—This metric determines how quickly the system can move large objects through memory. The Memory metric is measured in megabytes per second.

- **Primary hard disk**—This metric determines how fast the computer can write to and read from the hard disk. The Storage metric is measured in megabytes per second.

- Graphics—This metric determines the computer's capability to run a composited desktop like the one created by the Desktop Window Manager. The Graphics metric is expressed in frames per second.

- **Gaming Graphics**—This metric determines the computer's capability to render 3D graphics, particularly those used in gaming. The Gaming Graphics metric is expressed in effective frames per second.

Windows System Performance Rating

Besides WinSAT, Windows Vista comes with Windows System Performance Rating tool that rates your system based on its processor, RAM, hard disk, regular graphics, and gaming graphics. To launch this tool, open the Control Panel, click System and Maintenance, and then click Performance Rating and Tools. As you can see in Figure 5.4, Vista supplies a subrating for each of the five categories and also calculates an overall rating. You can get a new rating (for example, if you change performance-related hardware) by clicking the Refresh My Rating Now link.

Interpreting the ratings is a bit of a black art, but I can tell you the following:

- In general, the higher the rating, the better the performance.

- The lowest possible value is 1.0.

- There doesn't seem to be a highest possible value, which I assume is a reflection of the simple fact that hardware will improve over time. (Microsoft has said, however, that it will attempt to keep the ratings constant over time. So, for example, a machine rated 3.0 today will have the same relative performance as a machine rated 3.0 two years ago or two years from now.) I've seen ratings as high as 5.5 (this was a Memory [RAM] subrating given to a machine with 2GB RAM).

- The Overall Rating takes a weakest-link-in-the-chain approach. That is, you could have nothing but 5.0 scores for everything else, but if you get just 1.0 because your notebook can't do gaming graphics, then your Overall Rating will be 1.0.

Handling Performance Problems

The Performance Rating and Tools window also contains a Performance Issues section that provides alerts that warn you about problems affecting Vista's performance. If you click one of these links, Vista launches a Solutions to Performance Problems dialog box that gives you more details and usually offers a View Help button that displays a Help system article. Figure 5.5 shows an example.

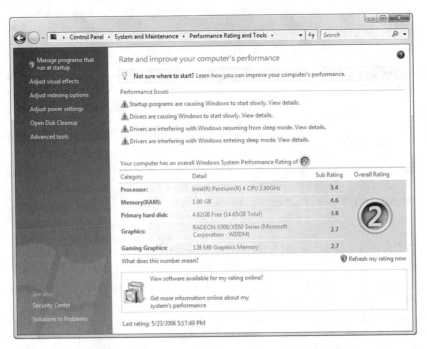

FIGURE 5.4   Vista calculates a Windows System Performance Rating based on five categories.

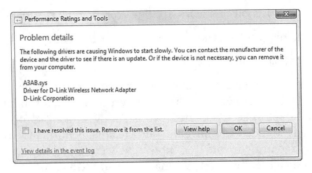

FIGURE 5.5   Click a link in the Performance Issues section to see a dialog box such as the one shown here.

Vista often warns you that startup programs are causing Vista to start slowly. The associated Help article recommends that you shut down some programs that run automatically at startup. In Windows Vista, you do that using Software Explorer, the Windows Defender feature that controls your startup programs (see Chapter 6, "Security Enhancements in Windows Vista," to learn more about Windows Defender). In Windows Defender, select Tools, Software Explorer, and then click Startup Programs in the Category list to see the

Windows Defender window shown in Figure 5.6. From here, you can prevent a program from running at startup by clicking it and then clicking Disable.

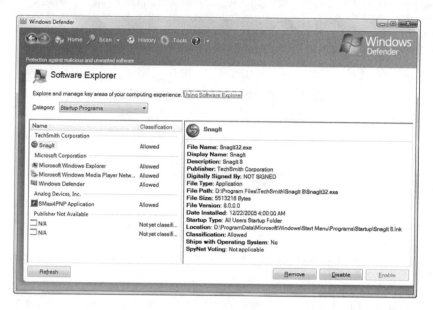

FIGURE 5.6   You can use Windows Defender to disable programs that run at startup.

Vista's Stability Improvements

Few things in this life are as frustrating as an operating system that won't operate, either because Windows itself has given up the ghost or because some program has locked up solid and taken Windows down with it. Unfortunately, computer problems, like the proverbial death and taxes, seem to be one of those constants in life. Fortunately, each new version of Windows seems to be a little more stable and a little better at handling misbehaving programs than its predecessor, so at least we're heading in the right direction.

It's still early, but it looks as though Windows Vista is continuing this positive trend. Vista will ship with a passel of new tools and technologies designed to prevent crashes and to recover from them gracefully if they do occur. The next few sections take you through the most important of these stability improvements.

I/O Cancellation

If you've used Windows for a while, you've probably come across a Windows Error Reporting dialog box similar to the one shown in Figure 5.7. This error message is generated by the Windows Dr. Watson debugging tool, and it includes not only a description of the error, but also the option to send an error report to Microsoft.

NOTE

Many people who have clicked Send Error Report have wondered why they've never heard back from Microsoft—not even a simple "Thank you." That's not surprising because Microsoft has probably received hundreds of thousands, perhaps even millions, of these reports. Even token responses are out of the question.

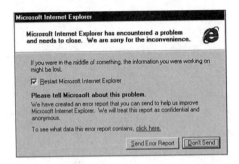

FIGURE 5.7   If Windows handles a program error, it displays a Windows Error Reporting dialog box similar to this one.

This program continues with Vista's new Windows Feedback services. This is an opt-in error-reporting service designed to provide Microsoft and program developers with much more detailed information about program crashes.

That can only be a good thing because it's clear that these kinds of reports are useful. Microsoft has received and studied many such reports over the years, and we're starting to see the fruits of this labor in Windows Vista, which comes with built-in fixes for many of the most common causes of program crashes. The most common of these by far is when a program has made an input/output (I/O) request to a service, resource, or another program, but that process is busy or otherwise incommunicado. In the past, the requesting program would often simply wait forever for the I/O data, thus resulting in a hung program and requiring a reboot to get the system running again.

To prevent this all-too-common scenario, Windows Vista implements an improved version of a technology called *I/O cancellation*, which can detect when a program is stuck waiting for an I/O request and then can cancel that request to help the program recover from the problem. Microsoft is also making I/O cancellation available to developers via an API, so programs, too, can cancel their own unresponsive requests and automagically recover themselves.

Reliability Monitor

In previous versions of Windows, the only way you could tell whether your system was stable was to think about how often in the recent past you were forced to reboot. If you couldn't remember the last time your system required a restart, you could assume that your system was stable. Not exactly a scientific assessment!

Windows Vista changes all that by introducing the Reliability Monitor. This new feature is part of the Windows Performance Diagnostic Console, which I discuss in more detail later (see "Windows Performance Diagnostic Console"). You load this Microsoft Management Console snap-in by pressing Windows Logo+R, typing **perfmon.msc**, and clicking OK. In the console window that appears, click Reliability Monitor.

Reliability monitor keeps track of the overall stability of your system, as well as *reliability events*, which are either changes to your system that could affect stability or occurrences that might indicate instability. Reliability events include the following:

- Windows updates

- Software installs and uninstalls

- Device driver installs, updates, rollbacks, and uninstalls

- Application hangs and crashes

- Device drivers that fail to load or unload

- Disk and memory failures

- Windows failures, including boot failures, system crashes, and sleep failures

Reliability monitors graph these changes and generate a measure of system stability over time so that you can graphically see whether any changes affected system stability (see Figure 5.8). The System Stability Chart shows the overall stability index. A score of 10 indicates a perfectly reliable system, and lower scores indicate decreasing reliability.

Service Recovery

A *service* is a program or process that works in the background to perform a specific, low-level support function for the operating system. You can see all the services on your system by opening Computer Management (right-click Computer or My Computer, and click Manage) and then selecting Services and Applications, Services. On most systems you'll see more than 125 different services listed.

Many services are mission-critical, and if any of these crucial services fail, it almost always means that the only way to recover your system is to shut down and restart your computer. With Windows Vista, however, every service has a *recovery policy* that enables Vista to restart not only the service, but also any other service or process that is dependent on the failed service.

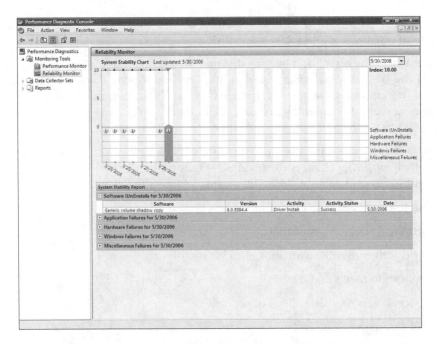

FIGURE 5.8   Reliability Monitor compares system stability with reliability events over time.

Startup Repair Tool

When your computer won't start, it's bad enough that you can't get to your programs and data and that your productivity nosedives. What's even worse is that you can't get to your normal troubleshooting and diagnostics tools to see what the problem might be. Yes, there are startup troubleshooting techniques, but they can often be time-consuming, hit-or-miss affairs. If Windows is in its own partition, or if there's a solid backup ready, many people would prefer to simply reinstall Windows than spend an entire day tracking down a startup problem.

Such drastic solutions could be a thing of the past, thanks to Vista's new Startup Repair Tool (SRT), which is designed to fix many common startup problems automatically. When a startup failure occurs, Vista starts the SRT immediately. The program then analyzes the startup logs and performs a series of diagnostic tests to determine the cause of the startup failure. The SRT looks for a number of possible problems, but three are the most common:

- Incompatible or corrupted device drivers

- Missing or corrupted startup configuration files

- Corrupted disk metadata

If the SRT determines that the startup failure is being caused by one of these problems or some other common snag, the SRT attempts to fix the problem automatically. If it's successful, it lets you know what repairs it made and writes all changes to a log file so you can see exactly what transpired.

If the SRT can't fix the problem, it tries the system's Last Known Good Configuration. If that doesn't work, it writes all of its diagnostic data to a log and offers you support options to try to fix the problem yourself.

New Diagnostics Tools

Fixing computer problems is only as effective and as reliable as your diagnosis of the problem in the first place. Without an accurate diagnosis, you can't hope to effect a proper repair or recovery. It's also true that a diagnosis need not only be an after-the-unpleasant-fact task. Instead of waiting to deal with computer difficulties after they've occurred (what I call *pound-of-cure mode*), it would be great if users' diagnostics could tell them about potential problems in advance (call it *Ounce of Prevention mode*).

Windows Vista comes with new diagnostic tools—together, they're called the Windows Diagnostic Infrastructure (WDI)—that not only do a better job of finding the source of many common disk, memory, and network problems, but that can also detect impending failures and alert you to take corrective or mitigating action (such as backing up your files).

Disk Diagnostics

A hard disk can suddenly bite the dust thanks to a lightning strike, an accidental drop from a decent height, or an electronic component shorting out. However, most of the time hard disks die a slow death. Along the way, hard disks almost always show some signs of decay, such as the following:

- Spin-up time gradually slows.

- Drive temperature increases.

- The seek error rate increases.

- The read error rate increases.

- The write error rate increases.

- The number of reallocated sectors increases.

- The number of bad sectors increases.

- The cyclic redundancy check (CRC) produces an increasing number of errors.

Other factors that might indicate a potential failure are the number of times that the hard drive has been powered up, the number of hours in use, and the number of times the drive has started and stopped spinning.

Since about 1996, almost all hard-disk manufacturers have built into their drives a system called Self-Monitoring, Analysis, and Reporting Technology, or SMART. This system monitors the parameters just listed (and usually quite a few more highly technical hard disk attributes) and uses a sophisticated algorithm to combine these attributes into a value that represents the overall health of the disk. When that value goes beyond some predetermined threshold, SMART issues an alert that hard-disk failure may be imminent.

Although SMART has been around for a while and is now standard, taking advantage of SMART diagnostics has, until now, required third-party programs. However, Windows Vista comes with a new Diagnostic Policy Service (DPS) that includes a Disk Diagnostics tool that can monitor SMART. If the SMART system reports an error, Vista displays a message that your hard disk is at risk. It also guides you through a backup session to ensure that you don't lose any data before you can have the disk replaced.

Memory Diagnostics

Few computer problems are as maddening as those related to physical memory defects because they tend to be intermittent and they tend to cause problems in secondary systems, forcing you to waste time on wild goose chases all over your system.

So it is welcome news indeed that Vista ships with a new Windows Memory Diagnostics tool that works with Microsoft Online Crash Analysis to determine whether defective physical memory is the cause of program crashes. If so, Windows Memory Diagnostics lets you know about the problem and schedules a memory test for the next time you start your computer. If actual problems are detected, the system also marks the affected memory area as unusable to avoid future crashes.

Windows Vista also comes with a Memory Leak Diagnosis tool that's part of the Diagnostic Policy Service. If a program is leaking memory (using up increasing amounts of memory over time), this tool will diagnose the problem and take steps to fix it.

Resource Exhaustion Detection

Your system can become unstable if it runs low on virtual memory, and there's a pretty good chance it will hang if it runs out of virtual memory. Older versions of Windows displayed one warning when they detected low virtual memory and another warning when the system ran out of virtual memory. However, in both cases, users were simply told to shut down some or all of their running programs. That often solved the problem, but shutting *everything* down is usually overkill because it's often the case that just one running program or process is causing the virtual memory shortage.

Vista takes this more subtle point of view into account with its new Windows Resource Exhaustion Detection and Resolution tool (RADAR), which is part of the Diagnostic Policy Service. This tool also monitors virtual memory and issues a warning when resources run low. However, RADAR also identifies which programs or processes are using the most virtual memory, and it includes a list of these resource hogs as part of the warning. This enables you to shut down just one or more of these offending processes to get your system in a more stable state.

Microsoft is also providing developers with programmatic access to the RADAR tool, thus enabling vendors to build resource exhaustion detection into their applications. When such a program detects that it is using excessive resources, or if it detects that the system as a whole is low on virtual memory, the program can free resources to improve overall system stability.

> **NOTE**
>
> The Resource Exhaustion Detection and Recovery tool divides the current amount of committed virtual memory by the *commit limit*, the maximum size of the virtual memory paging file. If this percentage approaches 100, RADAR issues its warning. If you want to track this yourself, run System Monitor (see "Performance Monitor," later in this chapter) and add the % Committed Bytes In Use counter in the Memory object. If you want to see the exact commit numbers, add the Committed Bytes and Commit Limit counters (also in the Memory object).

Network Diagnostics

Resolving networking connectivity issues has never been an easy task for people who aren't networking professionals. Solutions often entail such arcane actions as "renewing the DHCP lease" and "flushing the ARP cache." Even if you are a networking pro, solving a user's network connectivity and access issues can't be done remotely (by definition) and so requires a visit to the user's desk.

Windows Vista aims to make diagnosing and solving network problems easier with a new Windows Network Diagnostics Tool. This feature analyzes all aspects of the network connection and then either fixes the problem or provides the user with simple instructions for resolving the situation. You can access the Windows Network Diagnostic Tool easily by viewing the connection status from the Network Center, and then clicking the Diagnose button, as shown in Figure 5.9. (See Chapter 8, "New Networking Features," to learn more about the Network Center.)

Windows Performance Diagnostic Console

Besides the automatic diagnostic tools mentioned in the previous few sections, Windows Vista comes with a new tool for monitoring your system yourself: the Windows Performance Diagnostic Console. You load this Microsoft Management Console snap-in by pressing Windows Logo+R, typing **perfmon.msc**, and clicking OK. Figure 5.10 shows the console window that appears.

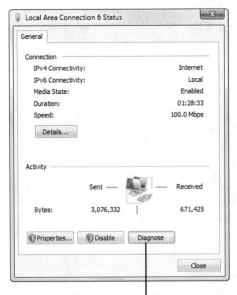

Starts the Windows Network Diagnostics Tool

FIGURE 5.9   Click Diagnose in the connection status dialog box to launch the Windows Network Diagnostics Tool.

The console root—Performance Diagnostics—displays the Resource Monitor, which is divided into six sections:

- **Resource Overview**—This section shows graphs of the data in the CPU, Disk, Network, and Memory sections.

- **CPU**—This section shows the percentage of CPU resources that your system is using. Click the downward-pointing arrow to expand the section and show the percentage of resources that each running process is using, as shown in Figure 5.11.

- **Disk**—This section shows the total hard disk I/O transfer rate (disk reads and writes in kilobytes per second). Expand the section to see the files involved in the current disk I/O operations.

- **Network**—This section shows the total network data-transfer rate (data sent and received in megabits per second). Expand the section to see the remote computers involved in the current network transfers.

- **Memory**—This section shows the average number of hard memory faults per second and the percentage of physical memory used. Expand the section to view the individual processes in memory, as well as the hard faults and memory used for each.

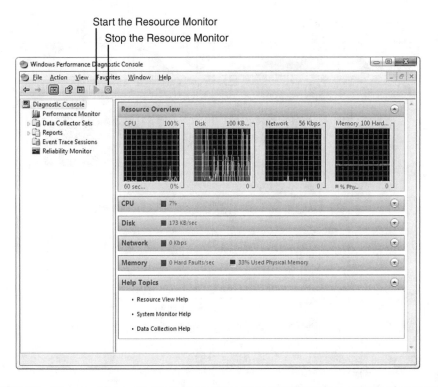

Start the Resource Monitor

Stop the Resource Monitor

FIGURE 5.10   The new Diagnostic Console enables you to monitor various aspects of your system.

> **NOTE**
>
> A memory fault does not refer to a physical problem. Instead, it means that the system could not find the data it needed in the file system cache. If it then finds the data elsewhere in memory, this is called a *soft fault*; if the system has to go to the hard disk to retrieve the data, this is called a *hard fault*.

- **Learn More**—This section contains links to the Performance Diagnostic Console help files.

The Performance Diagnostic Console tree has three branches: Monitoring Tools—which includes the Performance Monitor and the Reliability Monitor (which I discussed earlier in this chapter; see "Reliability Monitor")—Data Collector Sets, and Reports.

Start the Resource Monitor   Stop the Resource Monitor

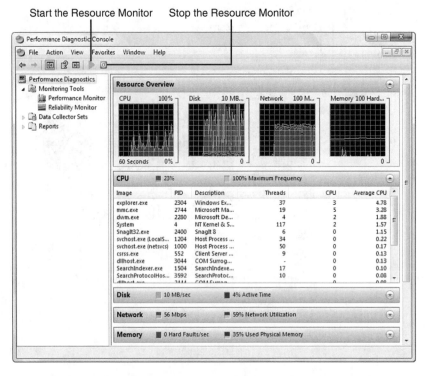

FIGURE 5.11   You can expand or collapse each Resource Monitor section to view more or less section detail.

Performance Monitor

The Performance Monitor branch displays the Performance Monitor, which provides you with real-time reports on how various system settings and components are performing (see Figure 5.12). Each item is called a *counter*, and the displayed counters are listed at the bottom of the window. Each counter is assigned a different-colored line, and that color corresponds to the colored lines shown in the graph. Note, too, that you can get specific numbers for a counter—the most recent value, the average, the minimum, and the maximum—by clicking a counter and reading the boxes just below the graphs. The idea is that you should configure Performance Monitor to show the processes you're interested in (page file size, free memory, and so on) and then keep Performance Monitor running while you perform your normal chores. By examining the Performance Monitor readouts from time to time, you gain an appreciation of what is typical on your system. Then if you run into performance problems, you can check Performance Monitor to see whether you've run into any bottlenecks or anomalies.

Performance Monitor was called System Monitor in previous versions of Windows, and it has been around for a while. However, Vista's version has a few new features that make it easier to use and a more powerful diagnostics tool:

- If you're using a counter with a significantly different scale, you can scale the output so the counter appears within the graph. For example, the graph's vertical axis runs from 0 to 100; if you're displaying a percentage counter, the Scale value is 1.0, which means the graph numbers correspond directly to the percentages (50 on the graph corresponds to 50%). If you're also showing, say, the Commit Limit counter, which shows values in bytes, the numbers can run in the billions. The Commit Limit counter's Scale value is 0.00000001, so 20 on the graph corresponds to 2 billion bytes.

- You can save the current graph as a GIF image file.

- You can toggle the display of individual counters on and off.

- You can change the duration of the sample (the number of seconds of data that appear on the chart). You can specify a value between 2 and 1,000 seconds.

- You can see individual data points by hovering the mouse over a counter. After a second or two, Performance Monitor displays the counter name, the time and date of the sample, and the counter value at that time (refer to Figure 5.12).

- The horizontal (time) axis now has labels that tell you the beginning and end times of the current sample.

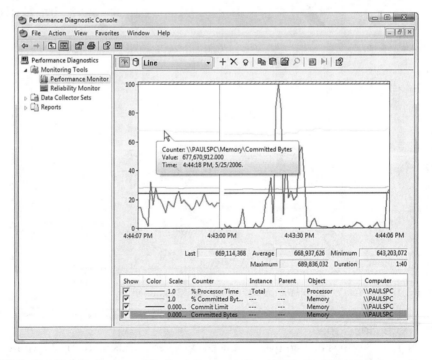

FIGURE 5.12   Use Performance Monitor to keep an eye on various system settings and components.

Data Collector Sets

A *data collector* is a custom set of performance counters, event traces, and system-configuration data that you define and save so that you can run and view the results any time you need them. You can also configure a data collector set to run for a preset length of time or until the set reaches a specified size. You can configure a data collector to run on a schedule as well. For example, you could run the data collector every hour for 15 minutes from 9 a.m. to 5 p.m. This enables you to benchmark performance and analyze the results not only intraday (say, to compare performance at different times of the day), but also interday (say, to see if performance is slowing over time).

Reports

This section holds the reports created by each data collector set. These are .blg files, and you can see the results by clicking the report and then switching to Sysmon view (click the Chart icon in the toolbar), as shown in Figure 5.13. Alternatively, open the folder that contains the report file in Windows Explorer (the default save location is %SystemDrive%\perflogs) and double-click the report file.

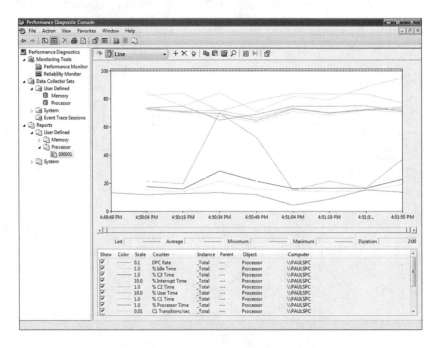

FIGURE 5.13   A data collector set report displayed in Sysmon view.

Event Trace Sessions

The Event Trace Sessions branch (part of the Data Collector Sets branch), shown in Figure 5.14, lists the defined sessions for tracing events of various types. In particular, note the sessions named EventLog-Application, EventLog-SECURITY, and EventLog-System. These sessions generate the Application, Security, and System event logs that you see in the Event Viewer (discussed in the next section).

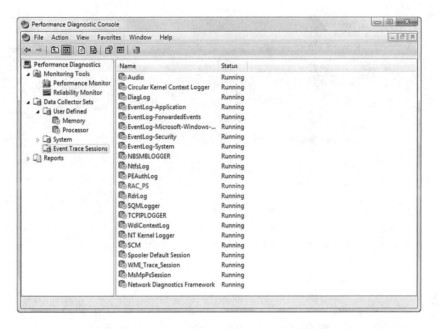

FIGURE 5.14   The Event Trace Sessions branch shows the defined sessions that Vista uses for tracing system events.

Event Viewer

Windows Vista constantly monitors your system for unusual or noteworthy occurrences. It might be a service that doesn't start, the installation of a device, or an application error. Vista tracks these occurrences, called *events*, in several different event logs. For example, the Application log stores events related to applications, including Windows XP programs and third-party applications. The System log stores events generated by Windows XP and components such as system services and device drivers.

You should scroll through the Application and System event logs regularly to look for existing problems or for warnings that could portend future problems. To examine these logs, you use the Event Viewer snap-in, which has a much-improved interface in Windows Vista. You get to the Event Viewer by using any of the following techniques:

- Select Start, right-click My Computer, click Manage, and then click Event Viewer.
- Press Windows Logo+R, type **eventvwr.msc**, and then click OK.
- Select Start, Control Panel, System and Maintenance, and then click the View Event Logs link under Administrative Tools.

Figure 5.15 shows the home page of the Event Viewer, which offers a summary of events, recent views, and available actions. (If you don't see the Action pane, click the Show/Hide Action Pane toolbar button, pointed out in Figure 5.15.)

Show/Hide Action Pane

FIGURE 5.15   The Event Viewer is much improved in Windows Vista, with a new interface and new features.

The scope pane offers three branches: Custom Views, Windows Logs, and Applications and Services Logs.

The Custom Views branch lists the event views that have been defined on your system (as described below). If you filter an event log or create a new event view, the new view is stored in the Custom Views branch.

The Windows Logs branch displays several sub-branches, four of which represent the main logs that the system tracks (see Figure 5.16):

- **Application**—Stores events related to applications, including Windows Vista programs and third-party applications

- **Security**—Stores events related to system security, including logons, user accounts, and user privileges

- **Setup**—Stores events related to Windows setup

- **System**—Stores events generated by Windows Vista and components such as system services and device drivers

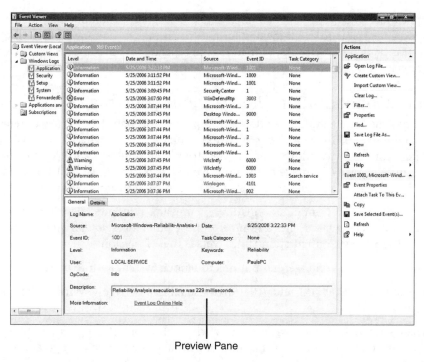

Preview Pane

FIGURE 5.16   Click a log to see a list of the events in that log.

When you select a log, the middle pane displays the available events, including the event's date, time, and source; its type (Information, Warning, or Error); and other data. Here's a summary of the major interface changes and new features that you get when viewing a log in Vista's Event Viewer:

- The Preview pane shows you the basic event data in the General tab, and more specific data in the Details tab. You can toggle the Preview pane on and off by selecting View, Preview Pane.

- Event data is now stored in XML format. To see the schema, click XML View in the Preview pane's Details tab.

- The Filter command now generates queries in XML format.

- You can click Create Custom View to create a new event view based on the event log, event type, event ID, and so on.

- You can attach tasks to events. Click the event you want to work with and then click Attach Task to This Event in the Action pane. This launches the Scheduled Tasks Wizard, which enables you to either run a program or script or have an email sent to you each time the event fires.

- You can save selected events to a file using the Event File (.elf) format.

The Applications and Services Logs branch lists the programs, components, and services that support the standard event-logging format that is new to Windows Vista. All of the items in this branch formerly stored their logs in separate text files that were unavailable in older versions of Event Viewer unless you specifically opened the log file.

System Configuration Utility Enhancements

If you're having trouble during Windows startup, or if you want to try a few different startup configurations to see whether you can eliminate startup items or improve the overall performance of Windows, don't bother trying out different startup configurations by hand. Instead, take advantage of the improved System Configuration Utility, which gives you a graphical front end that offers precise control over how Windows starts.

You launch the System Configuration Utility by pressing Windows Logo+R, typing **msconfig**, and clicking OK. Here's a summary of the differences you see in the Vista version of the System Configuration Utility versus the XP version:

- The General tab no longer has buttons to launch System Restore or expand a file.

- The tabs for SYSTEM.INI and WIN.INI (those relics of a bygone Windows era) are gone.

- There's a new Tools tab (see Figure 5.17) that lists about 15 programs and tools that you can run to troubleshoot startup problems and the system configuration.

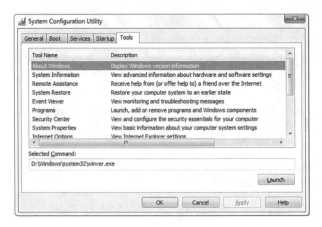

FIGURE 5.17   The System Configuration Utility's new Tools tab gives you quick access to a few useful programs.

Windows Backup

You saw in Chapter 4, "File System Improvements," that Windows Vista implements volume shadow copies and transactional NTFS, which enable you to roll back changes to a volume, folder, or file (see "Shadow Copies and Transactional NTFS"). This is a great technology that ought to get you out of a jam or two. However, shadow copies are no substitute for regular backups, which remain the best way to ensure the safety of your data.

Unfortunately, in previous versions of Windows, backing up files was never as easy as it should have been. The Microsoft Backup program from the past few versions of Windows seemed, at best, an afterthought, a token thrown in because an operating system should have *some* kind of backup program. Most users who were serious about backups immediately replaced Microsoft Backup with a more robust third-party alternative.

That might not happen in Windows Vista because the new backup program—now called Windows Backup—is quite an improvement on its predecessors:

- You can back up to a writeable optical disc, USB Flash drive, or other removable medium.

- You can back up to a network share.

- After you set up the program, backing up is completely automated, particularly if you back up to a resource that has plenty of room to hold your files (such as a hard disk or roomy network share).

- You can create a *system image backup*—which Microsoft calls a CompletePC backup—that saves the exact state of your computer and thus enables you to completely restore your system if your computer dies or is stolen.

If there's a downside to Windows Backup, it's that it's not very friendly to power users. It's completely wizard-driven, and there's no way to configure a backup manually.

As a measure of how important automated backups are in Windows Backup, when you first launch the program (select Start, All Programs, Accessories, System Tools, Backup), it displays the page shown in Figure 5.18 and prompts you to configure and start the automatic backups feature.

If you want to back up your entire system on a schedule, click the Start Automatic File Backup link. This launches the Windows Backup Wizard, which takes you through the steps of specifying the backup file types (documents, photos, music, and movies and videos), where you want to back up (such as a removable medium or a network share), what drives you want to include in the backup, and a backup schedule.

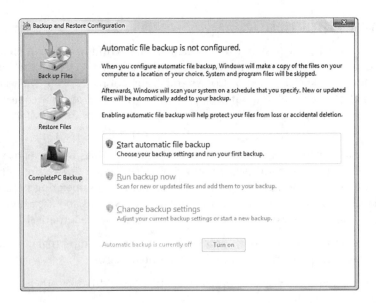

FIGURE 5.18   When you first launch Windows Backup, the program prompts you to configure and start the Automatic Backups feature.

From Here

Here are some other sections in the book where you'll find information related to the topics in this chapter:

- You can also view the Windows System Performance Rating on the Control Panel's System page. See the section "The System Rating," in Chapter 2.

- For the details on shadow copies, see the section "Shadow Copies and Transactional NTFS," in Chapter 4.

- For more information on the new Network Center window, see the section "The Network Center," in Chapter 8.

6

Security Enhancements in Windows Vista

As the Internet became more popular in the late 1990s and early 2000s, Microsoft's operating systems seemed to become less secure. It's difficult to say whether overall OS security got worse with each new release, but it's not hard to see that a perfect security storm was brewing:

- Thanks to the Internet, news of vulnerabilities spread quickly and efficiently.

- An increasing number of malicious users online worked to exploit those vulnerabilities.

- An increasing number of Windows users got online, most of whom didn't keep up with the latest security patches from Microsoft.

- An increasing number of online users had always-on broadband connections, which give malicious users more time to locate and break into poorly patched machines.

So even though it might have been the case that each new version of Windows was no less secure than it predecessors, it *appeared* that Windows was becoming increasingly vulnerable to attack.

To combat not only this perception but also the fundamental design flaws that were causing these security holes, Microsoft began its Trustworthy Computing Initiative (TCI) in 2003. The goal was to make people "as comfortable using devices powered by computers and software as they are today using a device that is powered by electricity."

How is Microsoft going about this? It's a broad initiative, but it really comes down to two things:

- Reduce the "attack surface area." This means reducing the number of places where an attacker can get a foothold on the system. For example, why run any ActiveX controls that the user or system doesn't require, particularly if that object is potentially exploitable?

- Help the user to avoid making "bad trust decisions." If the user lands on a phishing website, why not have the web browser warn the user that the site is probably not trustworthy?

Windows Vista is Microsoft's first major opportunity to put these and other TCI ideas into effect. This chapter takes you on a tour of the new and improved security features in Windows Vista.

Control Panel's Security Settings

With so many new security features, it's a good thing that Windows Vista does a better job of organizing security-related tasks than previous versions of Windows. Vista's one-stop security shop is, appropriately, the Control Panel, which has a Security icon in the Home folder that has three links:

- **Security**—Click this link to open the Security folder and see Vista's main security settings, as shown in Figure 6.1. I discuss most of these features in this chapter.

- **Check for Updates**—Click this link to open the Windows Update folder, which shows when you last checked for updates, your current Windows Update status, and a link for checking updates.

FIGURE 6.1   Click the Control Panel's Security link to see this list of Vista's main security settings.

- **Check This Computer's Security Status**—Click this link to open the Security Center. The Security Center is covered in the next section.

New Security Center Features

Windows XP Service Pack 2 introduced the world to the Security Center, which enabled you to see the status of the Windows Firewall, Automatic Updates, and virus protection. It also offered links to various security settings.

The Security Center in Windows Vista remains pretty much the same, except that it now offers two new items in the Security Essentials area, as shown in Figure 6.2:

- **Malware Protection**—This item tells you the current status of Virus Protection (*still not included in Windows*) and Spyware Protection. That latter is handled by Windows Defender (see "Thwarting Spyware with Windows Defender," later in this chapter).

> **TIP**
>
> As in XP, if you have an antivirus program installed that Windows doesn't recognize, you can tell Vista that you'll monitor the program yourself. Click the Show Me Other Available Options link, and then click I Have an Antivirus Program that I'll Monitor Myself.

- **Other Security Settings**—This item checks your Internet security and User Account Control settings. If you have Internet Explorer's Protected mode enabled, and if you have User Account Control enabled, this item's status shows as OK. If you have Protected mode disabled, or if you have User Account Protection disabled, this item's status shows as Not OK.

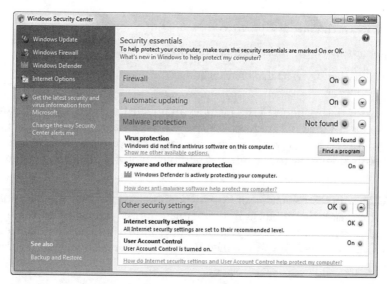

FIGURE 6.2   Windows Vista's version of the Security Center.

Windows Firewall: Bidirectional Protection

If you access the Internet using a broadband—cable modem or DSL—service, chances are, you have an always-on connection, which means there's a much greater chance that a malicious hacker could find your computer and have his way with it. You might think that with millions of people connected to the Internet at any given moment, there would be little chance of a "script kiddy" finding you in the herd. Unfortunately, one of the most common weapons in a black-hat hacker's arsenal is a program that runs through millions of IP addresses automatically, looking for live connections. The problem is compounded by the fact that many cable systems and some DSL systems use IP addresses in a narrow range, thus making it easier to find always-on connections.

When a cracker finds your address, he has many avenues with which to access your computer. Specifically, your connection uses many different ports for sending and receiving data. For example, web data and commands typically use port 80, email uses ports 25 and 110, the File Transfer Protocol (FTP) uses ports 20 and 21, the domain name system (DNS) uses port 53, and so on. In all, there are dozens of these ports, and every one is an opening through which a clever cracker can gain access to your computer.

As if that weren't enough, attackers can check your system to see whether some kind of Trojan horse virus is installed. (Malicious email attachments sometimes install these programs on your machine.) If the hacker finds one, he can effectively take control of your machine (turning it into a *zombie computer*) and either wreak havoc on its contents or use your computer to attack other systems.

Again, if you think your computer is too obscure or worthless for someone else to bother with, think again. A typical computer connected to the Internet all day long will be probed for vulnerable ports or installed Trojan horses at least a few times a day. If you want to see just how vulnerable your computer is, several good sites on the Web will test your security:

- Gibson Research (Shields Up): grc.com/default.htm
- DSL Reports: www.dslreports.com/secureme_go
- HackerWhacker: www.hackerwhacker.com

The good news is that Windows Vista includes an updated version of the Windows Firewall tool that debuted in Windows XP. This program is a personal firewall that can lock down your ports and prevent unauthorized access to your machine. In effect, your computer becomes invisible to the Internet (although you can still surf the Web and work with email normally).

The main change in Vista's version of Windows Firewall is that the program is now *bidirectional*. This means that it blocks not only unauthorized *incoming* traffic, but also unauthorized *outgoing* traffic. If your computer does have a Trojan horse installed (it might have been there before you installed Vista, or someone with physical access to your computer might have installed it), it might attempt to send data out to the Web. For example, it might attempt to contact a controlling program on another site to get instructions, or it might attempt to send sensitive data from your computer to the Trojan's owner. A bidirectional firewall can put a stop to that.

The Windows Firewall in Vista also supports the following new features:

- The IP Security (IPSec) protocol

- Environments that use only Internet Protocol version 6 (IPv6)

- Both incoming and outgoing firewall exceptions

- Exceptions applied to specific computers and users

- Exceptions applied to many different protocols (not just TCP and UDP)

- Exceptions applied to both local and remote ports

- Exceptions applied to specific interface types: location area network, remote access, or wireless

- Exceptions applied to specific Vista services

- Command-line support for controlling the firewall

From this list, you can see that Vista's firewall is a far more sophisticated tool than any of the versions that shipped with XP or its service packs. Reflecting that sophistication is a powerful new interface for working with Windows Firewall settings, exceptions, and monitoring. It's called Windows Firewall with Advanced Security (WFAS), and it's a Microsoft Management Console snap-in. To load it, press Windows Logo+R, type `wf.msc`, and click OK. Figure 6.3 shows the snap-in with all its branches opened in the Scope pane.

The home page of the snap-in presents an overview of the current firewall settings, as well as a number of links to configure and learn about WFAS. This snap-in configures the firewall by setting policies and storing them in two profiles: The Domain Profile is used when your computer is connected to a network domain; the Standard Profile is used when your computer is not connected to a domain.

The scope pane contains four main subbranches:

- **Inbound Rules**—This branch presents a list of defined rules for inbound connections. In most cases, the rules aren't enabled. To enable a rule, you right-click it and then click Enable Rule (or you can click Enable Rule in the Action pane). You can also create your own rules by right-clicking Inbound Ruless and then clicking New Rule. This launches the New Inbound Rule Wizard, shown in Figure 6.4.

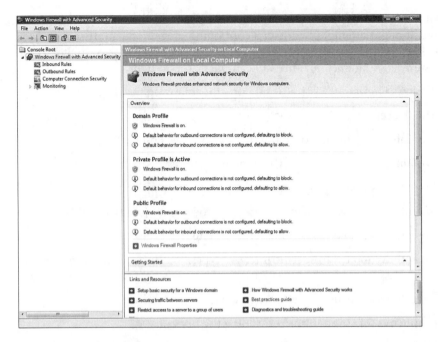

FIGURE 6.3 The new Windows Firewall with Advanced Security snap-in offers sophisticated firewall-management features.

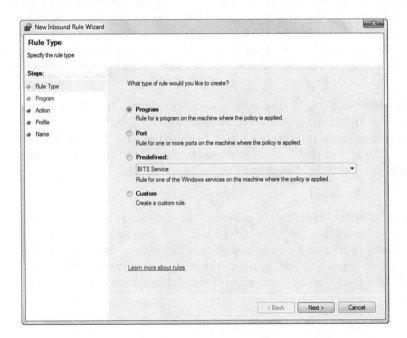

FIGURE 6.4 You can create your own firewall exceptions for inbound (shown here) and outbound traffic.

- **Outbound Rules**—This branch presents a list of defined rules for outbound connections. As with inbound connections, you can enable the rules you want to use and create your own rules. Note, too, that you can customize any rule by double-clicking it to display its property sheet (see Figure 6.5). With this property sheet you can change the program executable to which the rule is applied, allow or block a connection, set the computer and user authorization, change the ports and protocols, and specify the interface types and services.

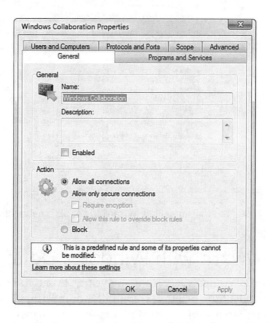

FIGURE 6.5   Use an exception's property sheet to customize all aspects of the exception.

- **Computer Connection Security**—You use this branch to create and manage *authentication rules*, which determine the restrictions and requirements that apply to connections with remote computers. Right-click Computer Connection Security and then click New Rule to launch the New Authentication Rule Wizard, shown in Figure 6.6.

- **Monitoring**—This branch shows the enabled firewall settings. For example, the Firewall subbranch shows the enabled inbound and outbound firewall rules, and the Connection Security, Rules subbranch shows the enabled authentication rules.

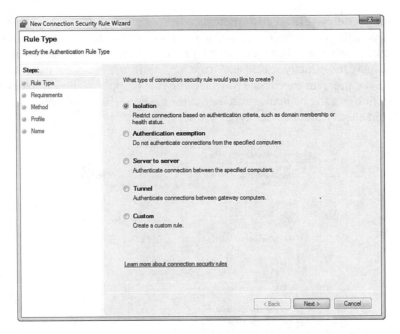

FIGURE 6.6   Use the New Authentication Rule Wizard to set up a new authentication rule.

Thwarting Spyware with Windows Defender

I've been troubleshooting Windows PCs for many years. It used to be that most problems were caused by users accidentally deleting system files or making ill-advised attempts to edit the Registry or some other important configuration file. Recent versions of Windows (particularly XP) could either prevent these kinds of PEBCAK (Problem Exists Between Chair and Keyboard) issues or recover from them without a lot of trouble. However, I think we're all too well aware of the latest menace to rise in the past few years, and it has taken over as the top cause of desperate troubleshooting calls I receive: *malware*, the generic term for malicious software such as viruses and Trojan horses. The worst malware offender by far these days is *spyware*, a plague upon the earth that threatens to deprive a significant portion of the online world of its sanity. As often happens with new concepts, the term *spyware* has become encrusted with multiple meanings as people attach similar ideas to a convenient and popular label. However, spyware is generally defined as any program that surreptitiously monitors a user's computer activities—particularly the typing of passwords, PINs, and credit card numbers—or harvests sensitive data on the user's computer, and then sends that information to an individual or a company via the user's Internet connection (the so-called *back channel*) without the user's consent.

You might think that having a robust firewall between you and the bad guys would make malware a problem of the past. Unfortunately, that's not true. These programs piggyback on other legitimate programs that users actually *want* to download, such as file-sharing programs, download managers, and screen savers. This downloading and installation of a program without the user's knowledge or consent is often called a *drive-by download*. This is closely related to a *pop-up download*, the downloading and installation of a program after the user clicks an option in a pop-up browser window, particularly when the option's intent is vaguely or misleadingly worded.

To make matters even worse, most spyware embeds itself deep into a system, and removing it is a delicate and time-consuming operation beyond the abilities of even experienced users. Some programs actually come with an Uninstall option, but it's nothing but a ruse, of course. The program appears to remove itself from the system, but what it actually does is a *covert reinstall*—it reinstalls a fresh version of itself when the computer is idle.

All this means that you need to buttress your firewall with an antispyware program that can watch out for these unwanted programs and prevent them from getting their hooks into your system. In previous versions of Windows, you needed to install a third-party program. However, Windows Vista comes with an antispyware program called Windows Defender (formerly Microsoft AntiSpyware).

You open Windows Defender using any of the following methods:

- From the Control Panel home, click Security and then Windows Defender. (If you're using Control Panel Classic, double-click the Windows Defender icon.)

- Click Start, All Programs, Windows Defender.

- Double-click the Windows Defender icon in the taskbar's notification area.

Whichever method you use, you end up at the Windows Defender Home screen, shown in Figure 6.7. This window shows you the date, time, and results of your last scan, as well as the current Windows Defender status.

Spyware Scanning

Windows Defender protects your computer from spyware in two ways: It can scan your system for evidence of installed spyware programs (and remove or disable those programs, if necessary), and it can monitor your system in real time to watch for activities that might be caused by spyware (such as a drive-by download or data being sent via a back channel).

For the scanning portion of its defenses, Windows Defender supports three different scan types:

- **Quick Scan**—This scan checks just those areas of your system where evidence of spyware is likely to be found. This scan usually takes just a couple of minutes.

- **Full System Scan**—This scan checks for evidence of spyware in system memory, all running processes, and the system drive (usually drive C:), and it performs a "deep scan" on all folders. This scan might take 30 minutes or more, depending on your system.

- **Select Drives and Folders**—This scan checks just the drives and folders that you select. The length of the scan depends on the number of locations you select and the number of objects in those locations.

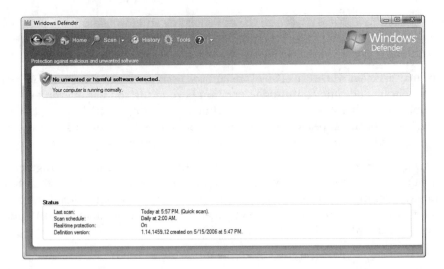

FIGURE 6.7   Windows Defender removes spyware from your system and keeps your system safe by preventing spyware installations.

The Quick scan is the default, and you can initiate one at any time by clicking the Scan link. Otherwise, pull down the Scan menu and select Quick Scan, Full Scan, or Custom Scan, the last of which displays the Select Scan Options page shown in Figure 6.8.

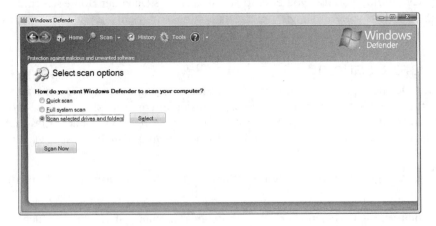

FIGURE 6.8   In the Scan menu, select Custom Scan to see the Select Scan Options page.

Windows Defender Settings

By default, Windows Defender is set up to perform a Quick scan of your system every morning at 2:00 a.m. To change this, click Tools, and then click Options to display the Options page shown in Figure 6.9. Use the controls in the Automatic Scanning section to specify the scan frequency time and type.

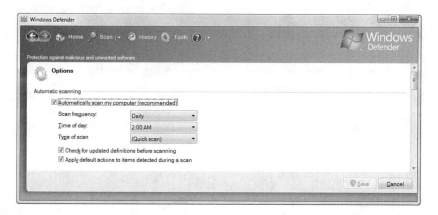

FIGURE 6.9   Use the Options page to set up a spyware scan schedule.

The rest of the Options page offers options for customizing Windows Defender. There are four more groups (most of which you can see in Figure 6.10):

- **Default Actions**—Set the action that Windows Defender should take if it finds alert items (potential spyware) in the High, Medium, and Low categories: Signature Default (Windows Defender's default action for the detected spyware), Ignore, or Remove.

- **Real-Time Protection Options**—Enables and disables real-time protection. You can also toggle security agents on and off. *Security agents* monitor Windows components that are frequent targets of spyware activity. For example, activating the Auto Start security agent tells Windows Defender to monitor the list of startup programs to ensure that spyware doesn't add itself to this list and run automatically at startup.

> **TIP**
>
> Windows Defender will often warn you that a program might be spyware and ask whether you want to allow the program to operate normally or to block it. If you accidentally allow an unsafe program, click Tools, Allowed Items; select the program in the Allowed Items list and then click Clear. Similarly, if you accidentally blocked a safe program, click Tools, Quarantined Items; select the program in the Quarantined Items list; and then click Restore.

- **Advanced Options**—Use these options to enable scanning inside compressed archives and to prevent Windows Defender from scanning specific folders.

- **Administrator Options**—This section has a check box that toggles Windows Defender on and off, and another that, when activated, allows non-Administrators to use Windows Defender.

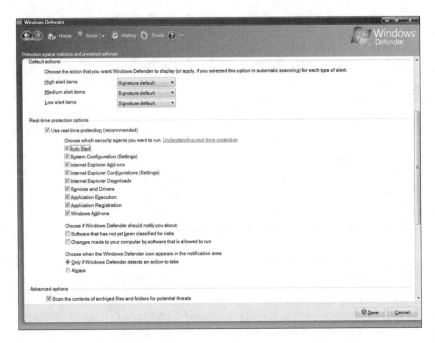

FIGURE 6.10   The rest of the General Settings page contains options for customizing various aspects of Windows Defender.

New Internet Explorer 7 Security Features

As more people, businesses, and organizations establish a presence online, the world becomes an increasingly connected place. And the more connected the world becomes, the more opportunities arise for communicating with others, doing research, sharing information, and collaborating on projects. The flip side to this new connectedness is the increased risk of connecting with a remote user whose intentions are less than honorable. It could be a fraud artist who sets up a legitimate-looking website to steal your password or credit card number, a virus programmer who sends a Trojan horse attached to a program download, or a website operator who uses web browser security holes to run malicious code on your machine.

Admittedly, online security threats are relatively rare and are no reason to swear off the online world. However, these threats *do* exist and people fall victim to them every day.

Luckily, protecting yourself from these and other e-menaces doesn't take much effort or time, particularly with the new security features built into Internet Explorer 7.

Protected Mode: Reducing Internet Explorer's Privileges

Windows Vista's antispyware initiatives aren't restricted to Windows Defender. Because spyware often leeches onto a system through a drive-by or pop-up download, it makes sense to set up the web browser as the first line of defense. Microsoft has done just that by introducing *Protected mode* for Internet Explorer (see Figure 6.11). Protected mode builds upon Vista's new User Account Control feature that I discuss later in this chapter (see "User Account Control: Smarter User Privileges"). Internet Explorer's Protected mode means that IE runs with a privilege level that's enough to surf the Web, but that's about it. Internet Explorer can't install software, modify the user's files or settings, add shortcuts to the Startup folder, or even change its own settings for the default home page and search engine. The Internet Explorer code is completely isolated from any other running application or process on your system. In fact, Internet Explorer can write data only to the Temporary Internet Files folder. If it needs to write elsewhere (during a file download, for example), it must get your permission. So any add-ons or other malware that attempt a covert install via Internet Explorer will be blocked before they can even get to Windows Defender.

> **NOTE**
>
> If you don't want to run Internet Explorer 7 in Protected mode, for some reason, you can turn it off. Select Tools, Internet Options, and then select the Security tab. Remove the checkmark from the Enable Protected Mode check box to deactivate it, and then click OK. Internet Explorer displays a message in the Information bar telling you that your security settings are putting you at risk. You can reactivate the Protected mode setting by clicking the Information bar and then clicking Fix Settings For Me. Otherwise, restart Internet Explorer to put the new setting into effect. Internet Explorer, ever persistent, will display a local SecurityRisk page that warns you about your security settings. Click the Home button to continue browsing.

Total Security: Internet Explorer Without Add-Ons

For the ultimate in browsing security, Windows Vista ships with an alternative Internet Explorer shortcut that loads the browser without any third-party add-ons, extensions, toolbars, or ActiveX controls. Select Start, All Programs, Accessories, System Tools, Internet Explorer (No Add-Ons). Internet Explorer starts and displays the Add-Ons Disabled page, shown in Figure 6.12.

Thwarting Phishers with the Phishing Filter

Phishing refers to creating a replica of an existing web page to fool a user into submitting personal, financial, or password data. The term comes from the fact that Internet scammers are using increasingly sophisticated lures as they "fish" for users' financial information and password data. The most common ploy is to copy the web page code from a major site—such as AOL or eBay—and use that code to set up a replica page that appears to be part of the company's site. (This is why phishing is also called *spoofing*.) A fake email is sent out with a link to this page, which solicits the user's credit card data or password. When the form is submitted, it sends the data to the scammer while leaving the user on an actual page from the company's site so he or she doesn't suspect a thing.

Protected mode appears in the Status bar

FIGURE 6.11   Internet Explorer 7 implements Protected mode to prevent covert spyware installs.

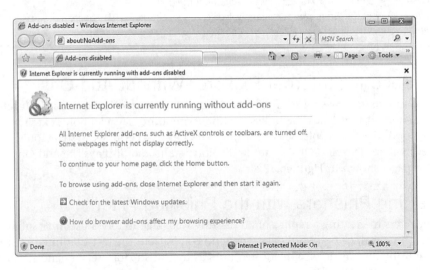

FIGURE 6.12   Select the Internet Explorer (No Add-Ons) shortcut to run Internet Explorer without third-party add-ons, extensions, toolbars, or ActiveX controls.

A phishing page looks identical to a legitimate page from the company because the phisher has simply copied the underlying source code from the original page. However, no spoof page can be a perfect replica of the original. Here are five things to look for:

- **The URL in the Address bar**—A legitimate page will have the correct domain—such as aol.com or ebay.com—while a spoofed page will have only something similar—such as aol.whatever.com or blah.com/ebay.

> **NOTE**
>
> With some exceptions (see the following discussion of domain spoofing), the URL in the Address bar is usually the easiest way to tell whether a site is trustworthy. For this reason, Internet Explorer 7 makes it impossible to hide the Address bar in all browser windows, even simple pop-ups.

- **The URLs associated with page links**—Most links on the page probably point to legitimate pages on the original site. However, some links might point to pages on the phisher's site.

- **The form-submittal address**—Almost all spoof pages contain a form into which you're supposed to type whatever sensitive data the phisher seeks from you. Select View, Source, and look at the value of the `<form>` tag's `action` attribute. This will be the address to which the form will be submitted. If the form data is clearly not being sent to the legitimate domain, you know you're dealing with a phisher.

- **Text or images that aren't associated with the trustworthy site**—Many phishing sites are housed on free web hosting services. However, many of these services place an advertisement on each page, so look for an ad or other content from the hosting provider.

- **Internet Explorer's lock icon in the status bar and Security Report area**—A legitimate site would transmit sensitive financial data only using a secure HTTPS connection, which Internet Explorer indicates by placing a lock icon in the status bar and in the Address bar's new Security Report area. If you don't see the lock icon with a page that asks for financial data, the page is almost certainly a spoof.

If you watch for these things, you'll probably never be fooled into giving up sensitive data to a phisher. However, it's often not as easy as it sounds. For example, some phishers employ easily overlooked *domain-spoofing* tricks such as replacing the lowercase letter L with the number 1, or the uppercase letter O with the number 0. Still, most experienced users don't get fooled by phishing sites, so this isn't a big problem for them.

Novice users, on the other hand, need all the help they can get. They tend to assume that everything they see on the Web is legitimate and trustworthy, and even if they're aware that scam sites exist, they don't know how to check for telltale phishing signs. To help these users, Internet Explorer 7 comes with a new tool called the Phishing Filter. This filter alerts you to potential phishing scams by doing two things each time you visit a site:

- Analyzing the site content to look for known phishing techniques (that is, to see if the site is *phishy*). The most common of these is a check for domain spoofing. This is a common scam that also goes by the names *homograph spoofing* and the *lookalike attack*. Internet Explorer 7 also supports International Domain Names (IDN), which refers to domain names written in languages other than English, and it checks for *IDN spoofing*, domain name ambiguities in the user's chosen browser language.

- Checking to see if the site is listed in a global database of known phishing sites. This database is maintained by a network of providers such as Cyota, Inc. and Internet Identity and MarkMonitor, as well as by reports from users who come upon phishing sites while surfing. According to Microsoft, this "URL reputation service" is updated several times an hour with new data.

Internet Explorer's Phishing Filter is an opt-in tool because not all users need a helping hand when it comes to avoiding phishing scams. You have to activate it yourself, but that's not hard because as soon as you navigate to your first website in Internet Explorer 7, the Microsoft Phishing Filter dialog box appears, as shown in Figure 6.13. If you want to use the Phishing Filter, leave the Turn On Automatic Phishing Filter option activated and click OK.

> **NOTE**
>
> If you turn off the automatic Phishing Filter checks, you can still check for phishing site by site. After you navigate to a site that you want to check, select Tools, Phishing Filter, Check This Website.

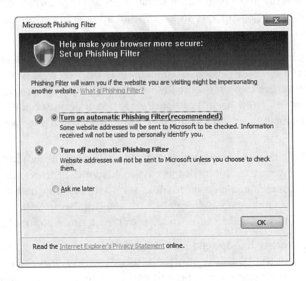

FIGURE 6.13   Internet Explorer 7 immediately asks whether you want to turn on the Phishing Filter.

Here's how the Phishing Filter works:

- If you come upon a site that Internet Explorer knows is a phishing scam, it changes the background color of the Address bar to red and displays a "Phishing Website" message in the Security Report area. It also blocks navigation to the site by displaying a separate page that tells you the site is a known phishing scam. A link is provided to navigate to the site, if you so choose.

> **NOTE**
>
> The Security Report area is another Internet Explorer 7 security innovation. Clicking whatever text or icon appears in this area produces a report on the security of the site. For example, if you navigate to a secure site, you see the lock icon in this area. Click the lock to see a report that shows the site's digital certificate information.

- If you come upon a site that Internet Explorer thinks is a potential phishing scam, it changes the background color of the Address bar to yellow and displays a "Suspicious Website" message in the Security Report area

Figure 6.14 shows Internet Explorer 7 displaying a warning about a known phishing site.

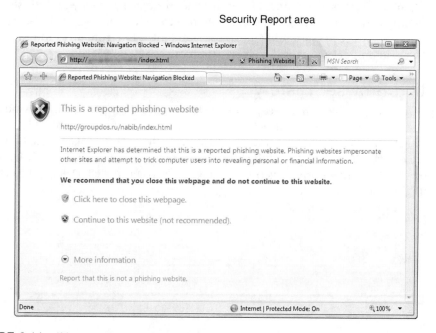

FIGURE 6.14   If Internet Explorer 7 detects a known phishing site, it displays "Phishing Website" in the Security Report area and blocks access to the site.

Click the "Suspicious Website" text, and Internet Explorer displays the security report shown in Figure 6.15. If you're sure this is a scam site, be sure to report it to help improve the database of phishing sites and prevent others from giving up sensitive data. To report a site, either clicking the Report link in the security report or select Tools, Phishing Filter, Report This Website. This opens the Phishing Filter Feedback page.

FIGURE 6.15   This report appears when you click the "Suspicious Website" warning.

Easier Add-On Management

Internet Explorer 7 gives you a much better interface for managing all your browser add-ons, including ActiveX controls, toolbars, helper objects, and more. Select Tools, Manage Add-Ons to display the Manage Add-Ons dialog box shown in Figure 6.16. You can enable and disable add-ons, delete ActiveX control, and more.

Deleting Browser History

Internet Explorer 7 makes it much easier to delete your browsing history. In previous versions, you had to make separate deletions for cache files, cookies, visited URLs, saved form data, and saved passwords. In Internet Explorer 7, you select Tools, Delete Browsing History to display the Delete Browsing History dialog box shown in Figure 6.17. From here, you can delete the browser history by category, or you can click Delete All to erase everything in one shot.

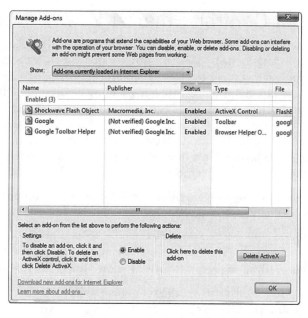

FIGURE 6.16   Use the Manage Add-Ons dialog box to view, enable, disable, and delete Internet Explorer add-ons.

FIGURE 6.17   Use the Delete Browsing History dialog box to delete some or all of your Internet Explorer 7 browsing history.

User Account Control: Smarter User Privileges

Most (I'm actually tempted to say the vast majority) of the security-related problems in recent versions of Windows boiled down to a single root cause: Most users were running Windows with administrator-level permissions. Administrators can do *anything* to a Windows machine, including installing programs, adding devices, updating drivers, installing updates and patches, changing Registry settings, running administrative tools, and creating and modifying user accounts. This is convenient, but it leads to a huge problem: Any malware that insinuates itself onto your system will also be capable of operating with administrative permissions, thus enabling the program to wreak havoc on the computer and just about anything connected to it.

Windows XP tried to solve the problem by creating a second-tier account level called the *limited user*, which had only very basic permissions. Unfortunately, there were three gaping holes in this "solution":

- XP prompted you to create one or more user accounts during setup, but it didn't force you to create one. If you skipped this part, XP started under the Administrator account.

- Even if you elected to create users, the setup program didn't give you an option for setting the account security level. Therefore, any account you created during setup was automatically added to the Administrators group.

- If you created a limited user account, you probably didn't keep it for long because XP hobbled the account so badly that you couldn't use it to do anything but the most basic computer tasks. You couldn't even install most programs because they generally require write permission for the %SystemRoot% folder and the Registry, and limited users lacked that permission.

Windows Vista tries once again to solve this problem. The new solution is called User Account Control and it uses a principle called the *least-privileged user*. The idea behind this is to create an account level that has no more permissions than it requires. Again, such accounts are prevented from editing the Registry and performing other administrative tasks. However, these users can perform other day-to-day tasks:

- Install programs and updates

- Add printer drivers

- Change wireless security options (such as adding a WEP or WPA key)

In Windows Vista, the least-privileged user concept arrives in the form of a new account type called the standard user. This means that Vista has three basic account levels:

- **Administrator account**—This account can do anything to the computer.

- **Administrators group**—Members of this group (except the Administrator account) run as standard users but are able to elevate their privileges when required just by clicking a button in a dialog box (see the next section).

- **Standard users group**—These are the least-privileged users, although they, too, can elevate their privileges when needed; however, they require access to an administrator password to do so.

Elevating Privileges

This idea of *elevating privileges* is at the heart of Vista's new security model. In Windows XP, you could use the Run As command to run a task as a different user (that is, one with higher privileges). In Vista, you usually don't need to do this because Vista prompts you for the elevation automatically.

If you're a member of the Administrators group, you run with the privileges of a standard user for extra security. When you attempt a task that requires administrative privileges, Vista prompts for your consent by displaying a User Account Control dialog box similar to the one shown in Figure 6.18. Click Control to permit the task to proceed. If this dialog box appears unexpectedly, it's possible that a malware program is trying to perform some task that requires administrative privileges; you can thwart that task by clicking Cancel instead.

FIGURE 6.18   When an administrator launches a task that requires administrative privileges, Windows Vista displays this dialog box to ask for consent.

If you're running as a standard user and attempt a task that requires administrative privileges, Vista uses an extra level of protection. That is, instead of just prompting you for consent, it prompts you for the credentials of an administrator, as shown in Figure 6.19. If your system has multiple administrator accounts, each one is shown in this dialog box. Type the password for any administrator account shown, and then click Submit. Again, if this dialog box shows up unexpectedly, it might be malware, so you should click Cancel to prevent the task from going through.

Note, too, that in both cases Windows Vista switches to *secure desktop* mode, which means you can't do anything else with Vista until you give your consent or credentials or cancel the operation. Vista indicates the secure desktop by darkening everything on the screen except the User Account Control dialog box.

NOTE

User Account Control seems sensible on the surface, but Microsoft has not always implemented it in a sensible way. For example, sometimes you are prompted for elevation during simple tasks such as file deletions and renames, or when you change the system date or time. This has led to a backlash against User Account Control in some circles, and I'm sympathetic to a point (so is Microsoft, who has promised to tweak User Account Control before shipping the final Vista code). However, all the people who are complaining about User Account Control are beta testers who, by definition, are tweaking settings, installing drivers and programs, and generally pushing Vista to its limits. Of course you're going to get hit with lots of UAC dialog boxes under those conditions. However, the average user really doesn't tweak their system all that often, so I think UAC will be much less of a problem than its critics suggest.

It's also possible to elevate your privileges for any individual program. You do this by right-clicking the program file or shortcut and then clicking Run as Administrator. This displays either the consent dialog box shown in Figure 6.18 (if you're an administrator) or the credentials dialog box shown in Figure 6.19 (if you're a standard user).

FIGURE 6.19   When a standard user launches a task that requires administrative privileges, Windows Vista displays this dialog box to ask for administrative credentials.

NOTE

You might have older programs that simply won't run under Vista's User Account Control security model because they require administrative privileges. If you don't want to give a standard user an administrator's password, you can still enable the user to run the program. Find the program's executable file, right-click it, and then click Properties. In the property sheet that appears, display the Compatibility tab, activate the Run This Program as an Administrator check box, and then click OK. (You can also do this with any shortcut to the executable. Vista assigns the elevated privilege to the executable and all its shortcuts.) Vista then runs a diagnostic test on the program to see the administrative privileges it requires. This is a security feature that ensures that the program gets only the minimum number of privileges that it requires to function properly.

File and Registry Virtualization

You might be wondering how secure Windows Vista really is if a standard user can install programs. Doesn't that mean that malware can install as well? No—Vista implements a new model for installation security. In Vista, you need administrative privileges to write anything to the %SystemRoot% folder (usually C:\Windows), the %ProgramFiles% folder (usually C:\Program Files), and the Registry. Vista handles this for standard users in two ways:

- During a program installation, Vista first prompts the user for credentials (that is, Vista displays one of the Windows Security dialog boxes shown earlier in Figures 6.18 and 6.19). If they are provided, Vista gives permission to the program installer to write to %SystemRoot%, %ProgramFiles%, and the Registry.

- If the user cannot provide credentials, Vista uses a technique called *file and Registry virtualization*, which creates virtual %SystemRoot% and %ProgramFiles% folders, and a virtual HKEY_LOCAL_MACHINE Registry key, all of which are stored with the user's files. This enables the installer to proceed without jeopardizing actual system files.

User Account Control Policies

You can customize User Account Control to a certain extent by using group policies. In the Local Security Settings snap-in (press Windows Logo+R, type **secpol.msc**, and click OK), open the Security Settings, Local Policies, Security Options branch. Here you'll find six policies related to User Account Control (as shown in Figure 6.20):

- **User Account Control: Admin Approval Mode for the Built-In Administrator Account**—This policy controls whether the Administrator account falls under User Account Control. If you enable this policy, the Administrator account is treated like any other account in the Administrators group and you must click Continue in the consent dialog box when Windows Vista requires approval for an action.

- **User Account Control: Behavior of the Elevation Prompt for Administrators in Admin Approval Mode**—This policy controls the prompt that appears when an administrator requires elevated privileges. The default setting is Prompt for Consent, where the user clicks either Continue or Cancel. You can also choose Prompt for Credentials to force the user to type his or her password. If you choose No Prompt, administrators cannot elevate their privileges.

- **User Account Control: Behavior of the Elevation Prompt for Standard Users**—This policy controls the prompt that appears when a standard user requires elevated privileges. The default setting is Prompt for Credentials, to force the user to type an administrator password. You can also choose No Prompt to prevent standard users from elevating their privileges.

- **User Account Control: Delete Application Installs and Prompt for Elevation**—Use this policy to enable or disable automatic privilege elevation while installing programs.

- **User Account Control: Run All Administrators in Admin Approval Mode Users**— Use this policy to enable or disable running administrators (excluding the Administrator account) as standard users.

- **User Account Control: Only Elevate Executables That Are Signed and Validated**—Use this policy to enable or disable whether Vista checks the security signature of any program that asks for elevated privileges.

- **User Account Control: Switch to the Secure Desktop When Prompting for Elevation**—Use this policy to enable or disable whether Vista switches to the secure desktop when the elevation prompts appear.

- **User Account Control: Virtualize File and Registry Write Failures to Per-User Locations**—Use this policy to enable or disable file and Registry virtualization for standard users.

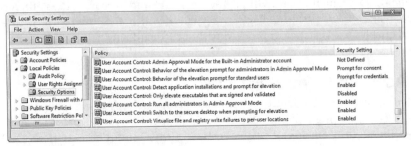

FIGURE 6.20   Vista policies related to User Account Control.

More New Security Features

The security features you've seen so far are certainly worth the price of admission and should be enough to make Vista the most secure Windows OS yet. But Microsoft has more security tricks up its sleeve. The next few sections take you on a quick tour of the most important or interesting of the rest of Vista's new security innovations.

Preventing Rogue Services with Windows Service Hardening

If you could map out the Windows attack surface, the biggest feature in the resulting landscape would be, by far, the system and third-party services that run in the background. Services are a tempting malware target for two reasons. First, most services are "always on," in the sense that they start when Windows loads and then remain running until you shut down the system. Second, most services run with a high privilege level that gives them full access to the system. Malware that manages to get into a computer can use the system services to perform almost any task, from installing a Trojan horse to formatting the hard drive.

To reduce the chance that a malware program could turn a system's services on itself, Windows Vista implements a new service security technology called Windows Service Hardening. This technology doesn't prevent malware from infecting a service. (That's the job of Windows Firewall and Windows Defender.) Instead, Windows Service Hardening is designed to limit the damage that a compromised service can wreak upon a system by implementing the following security techniques:

- All services run in a lower privilege level.

- All services have been stripped of permissions that they don't require.

- All services are assigned a *security identifier* (SID) that uniquely identifies each service. This enables a system resource to create its own *access control list* (ACL) that specifies exactly which SIDs can access the resource. If a service that's not on the ACL tries to access the resource, Vista blocks the service.

- A system resource can restrict which services are allowed write permission to the resource.

- All services come with network restrictions that prevent services from accessing the network in ways not defined by the service's normal operating parameters.

System Drive Encryption with BitLocker

Take new Vista technologies such as the bidirectional Windows Firewall, Windows Defender, and Windows Service Hardening; throw in good patch-management policies (that is, applying security patches as soon as they're available); and add a dash of common sense, and your computer should never be compromised by malware while Vista is running.

However, what about when Vista is *not* running? If your computer is stolen or if an attacker breaks into your home or office, your machine can be compromised in a couple of different ways:

- By booting to a floppy disk and using command-line utilities to reset the Administrator password.

- By using a CD-based operating system to access your hard disk and reset folder and file permissions.

Either exploit gives the attacker access to the contents of your computer. If you have sensitive data on your machine—financial data, company secrets, and so on—the results could be disastrous.

To help you prevent a malicious user from accessing your sensitive data, Windows Vista comes with a new technology called BitLocker that encrypts the entire system drive. That way, even if a malicious user gains physical access to your computer, he or she won't be able to read the system drive contents. BitLocker works by storing the keys that encrypt and decrypt the sectors on a system drive in a Trusted Platform Module (TPM) 1.2 chip, which is a hardware component available on many newer machines.

To enable BitLocker—which is available only in the Enterprise and Ultimate editions of Windows Vista—open the Control Panel and select Security, BitLocker Drive Encryption (or just open the BitLocker Drive Encryption icon directly if you're using Classic view). In the BitLocker Drive Encryption window, shown in Figure 6.21, click Turn On BitLocker.

FIGURE 6.21   Use the Control Panel BitLocker Drive Encryption window to turn BitLocker on and off.

This launches the Turn On BitLocker Drive Encryption Wizard, which takes you through the following tasks:

- Save a startup key on a removable USB device (see Figure 6.22). You need to insert this device each time you start your computer to decrypt the system drive.

- Creating, displaying, printing, or saving the recovery password. You need this password if BitLocker blocks access to your computer. (BitLocker blocks access if it detects that one or more system files have been tampered with.) You can either enter the 48-digit(!) password by hand or use the recovery key you save to a USB device in the next step.

- Encrypt the system volume. After this is done, you must insert the device with the startup key each time you want to load Vista.

> **NOTE**
>
> You can also use the Trusted Platform Module (TPM) Management snap-in to work with the TPM chip on your computer. Press Windows Logo+R, type `tpm.msc`, and click OK. This snap-in enables you to view the current status of the TPM chip, view information about the chip manufacturer, and perform chip-management functions.

FIGURE 6.22   The Turn On BitLocker Drive Encryption Wizard takes you through the process of preparing and encrypting your system drive.

Avoiding Overflows with Support for the NX Bit

One common cause of system crashes, and a common technique used by makers of malicious software, is the *buffer overflow*. A buffer is a memory area set aside to hold data. The buffer has a fixed size, which means it can't handle data larger than that size. A well-programmed system includes checks to ensure that only data of the correct size (or less) gets written to the buffer.

In practice, however, the desire for faster code or sheer sloppiness by the programmer can occasionally result in unprotected memory buffers. When buffer overflow occurs, either by accident or by design, the extra data is written to memory areas that are adjacent to the buffer. If these adjacent areas just hold more data, nothing terrible happens. However, if the adjacent areas contain core operating system code, the system can crash; even worse, if the adjacent areas are designed to run system control code, a clever hacker can take advantage of that to run whatever code he or she wants, usually with disastrous results.

To help prevent these nasty aspects of buffer overflow, recent CPUs have implemented the NX (No eXecute) attribute, which can brand certain memory areas as nonexecutable. This means that even if a buffer overflows into a code area, no malicious code can run because that area is marked with the NX attribute.

Windows Vista fully supports the NX bit, allowing it to brand core system areas such as the stack and the head as nonexecutable.

Thwarting Malware Randomly with ASLR

Microsoft isn't assuming that users' machines will never be subject to malware attacks. To that end, Windows Vista implements not only support for the NX bit and continued support for Data Execution Prevention (which prevents malicious code from running in protected memory locations). Vista also implements an open-source security feature called Address Space Layout Randomization (ASLR). This feature is aimed at thwarting some common attacks that attempt to run system code. In previous versions of Windows, certain system DLLs and executables were always loaded into memory using the same addresses each time, so attackers could launch one of those processes because they knew the function's entry point. With ASLR, Vista loads these system functions randomly into one of 256 memory locations, so attackers can't be certain where a particular bit of system code resides in memory.

Using Parental Controls to Restrict Computer Usage

If you have children who share your computer, or if you're setting up a computer for the kids' use, it's wise to take precautions regarding the content and programs that they can access. Locally, this might take the form of blocking access to certain programs (such as your financial software), using ratings to control which games they can play, and setting time limits on when the computer is used. If the computer has Internet access, you might also want to allow (or block) specific sites, block certain types of content, and prevent file downloads.

All this sounds daunting, but Windows Vista's new Parental Controls make things a bit easier by offering an easy-to-use interface that lets you set all of the afore-mentioned options and lots more. (You get Parental Controls in the Home Basic, Home Premium, and Ultimate editions of Windows Vista.)

Before you begin, be sure to create a standard user account for each child that uses the computer. When that's done, you get to Parental Controls by opening Control Panel and selecting the Set Up User Account link (or by launching the Parental Controls icon directly if you're using Classic view). Click the user you want to work with to get to the User Controls window. You should activate two options here:

- **Parental Controls**—Click On, Enforce Current Settings. This enables the Windows Vista Web Filter, and the Time Limits, Games, and Allow and Block Specific Programs links in the Settings area.

- **Activity Reporting**—Click On, Collect Information About Computer Usage. This tells Vista to track system events such as blocked logon attempts and attempted changes to user accounts, the system date and time, and system settings. Activating this option also enables the Activity Reports link in the Settings area, as shown in Figure 6.23.

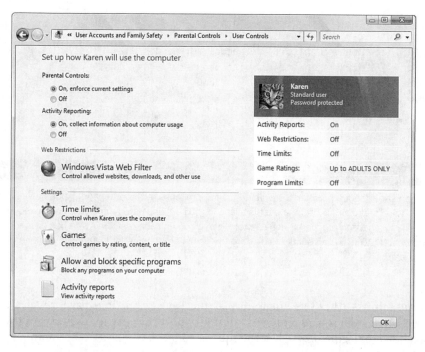

FIGURE 6.23   The User Controls page enables you to set up web, time, game, and program restrictions for the selected user.

The User Controls window gives you four links to use when setting up the controls for this user:

- **Windows Vista Web Filter**—Click this link to display the Web Restrictions page. Here you can allow or block specific websites, set up general site restrictions (such as Kids Websites Only), block content categories (such as Pornography, Mature Content, and Bomb Making), and block file downloads.

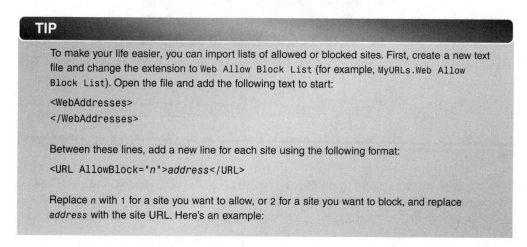

TIP

To make your life easier, you can import lists of allowed or blocked sites. First, create a new text file and change the extension to `Web Allow Block List` (for example, `MyURLs.Web Allow Block List`). Open the file and add the following text to start:

```
<WebAddresses>
</WebAddresses>
```

Between these lines, add a new line for each site using the following format:

```
<URL AllowBlock="n">address</URL>
```

Replace *n* with 1 for a site you want to allow, or 2 for a site you want to block, and replace *address* with the site URL. Here's an example:

```
<WebAddresses>
<URL AllowBlock="1">http://www.goodcleanfun.com</URL>
<URL AllowBlock="1">http://www.wholesomestuff.com</URL>
<URL AllowBlock="2">http://www.smut.com</URL>
<URL AllowBlock="2">http://www.depravity.com</URL>
</WebAddresses>
```

NOTE

If the user is logged on when a restricted time approaches, an icon appears in the notification area to let that user know. If the user is stilled logged on when the restricted time occurs, the user is immediately logged off and cannot log back on until the restricted time has passed. Fortunately, Vista is kind enough to restore the user's programs and documents when he or she logs back on.

- **Time Limits**—Click this link to display the Time Restrictions page, which shows a grid where each square represents an hour during the day for each day of the week, as shown in Figure 6.24. Click the squares to block computer usage during the selected times.

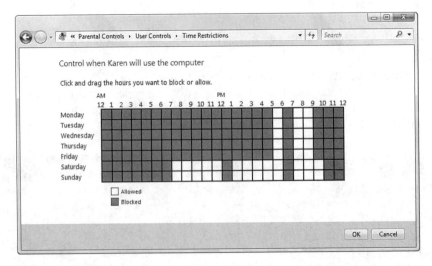

FIGURE 6.24 Use the grid on the Time Restrictions page to block computer access during specified hours.

- **Games**—Click this link to display the Game Controls page. Here you can allow or disallow all games, restrict games based on ratings and contents, and block or allow specific games. For the details, see "Parental Controls for Games" in Chapter 10.

- **Allow and Block Specific Programs**—Click this link to display the Application Restrictions page, which displays a list of the programs on your computer. Click the check boxes for the programs you want to allow the person to use.

Network Access Protection

Over the past few years, we've all heard too many reports of viruses and other malware spreading around the globe in the electronic equivalent of a wildfire. One of the reasons these plagues spread so quickly is that they often start on computers connected to local area networks. The malware takes over the hapless network client and soon begins moving through the network, taking down clients and servers as it goes.

A client computer that allows a malware infection to spread to the network is an IT professional's worst nightmare, but Windows Vista has a solution. It's called Network Access Protection (NAP), and the idea behind it is simple: If a client computer is compromised—even if it's only theoretically possible that it might be compromised—don't let it connect to the network. (NAP comes with the Business, Enterprise, and Ultimate editions of Windows Vista.)

The way NAP works is that Vista runs a service called the Network Access Protection Agent. This service checks the *health status* of the computer: its installed security patches, downloaded virus signatures, security settings, and more. Before the network logon—either via the local area network or via a remote connection—the agent reports the computer's health status to a NAP enforcement service running on the server. (This enforcement service is part of Windows Server "Longhorn.") If any of the health items are not completely up-to-date or within the network guidelines, the NAP enforcement service either doesn't let the computer log on to the network, or it shuttles the computer off to a restricted area of the network. You can also set up the server's NAP process to automatically update the client computer with the latest patches, virus signatures, security settings, and so on.

Thwarting Spam with Windows Mail's Junk Filter

Spam—unsolicited commercial messages—has become a plague upon the earth. Unless you've done a masterful job at keeping your address secret, you probably receive at least a few spam emails every day, and it's more likely that you receive a few dozen. The bad news is that most experts agree that it's only going to get worse. And why not? Spam is one of the few advertising media for which the costs are substantially borne by the users, not the advertisers.

The best way to avoid spam is to not get on a spammer's list of addresses in the first place. That's hard to do these days, but there are some steps you can take:

- Never use your actual email address in a newsgroup account. The most common method that spammers use to gather addresses is to harvest them from newsgroup posts. One common tactic you can use is to alter your email address by adding text that invalidates the address but is still obvious for other people to figure out:

```
user@myisp.remove_this_to_email_me.com
```

- When you sign up for something online, use a fake address, if possible. If you need or want to receive email from the company and so must use your real address, make sure you deactivate any options that ask if you want to receive promotional offers. Alternatively, enter the address from an easily disposable free web-based account (such as a Hotmail account) so that any spam you receive will go there instead of to your main address. If your free email account gets too overrun with junk mail, remove it and create a new one. (You can also do this through your ISP if it allows you to create multiple email accounts.)

- Never open suspected spam messages because doing so can sometimes notify the spammer that you've opened the message, thus confirming that your address is legit. For the same reason, you should never display a spam message in the Windows Mail Preview pane. Shut off the Reading pane (select View, Layout, deactivate Show Preview Pane, and click OK) before selecting any spam messages that you want to delete.

- Never—I repeat, *never*—respond to spam, even to an address within the spam that claims to be a "removal" address. By responding to the spam, all you're doing is proving that your address is legitimate, so you'll just end up getting *more* spam.

If you do get spam despite these precautions, the good news is that Windows Mail comes with a Junk Email feature that can help you cope. Junk Email is a *spam filter*, which means that it examines each incoming message and applies sophisticated tests to determine whether the message is spam. If the tests determine that the message is probably spam, the email is exiled to a separate Junk E-mail folder. The Windows Mail spam filter is based on the much-admired filter that comes with Outlook 2003, which was voted best spam filter by Consumer Reports in September 2005. It's not perfect (no spam filter is), but with a bit of fine-tuning as described in the next few sections, it can be a very useful antispam weapon.

Setting the Junk Email Protection Level

Filtering spam is always a trade-off between protection and convenience. That is, the stronger the protection you use, the less convenient the filter becomes, and vice versa. This inverse relationship is caused by a filter phenomenon called the *false positive*. This is a legitimate message that the filter has pegged as spam and so (in Windows Mail's case) moved the message to the Junk E-mail folder. The stronger the protection level, the more likely it is that false positives will occur, so the more time you must spend checking the Junk E-mail folder for legitimate messages that need to be rescued. Fortunately, Windows Mail gives you several Junk Email levels to choose from so you can choose a level that gives the blend of protection and convenience that suits you.

To set the Junk Email level, select Tools, Junk E-mail Options. Windows Mail displays the Junk E-mail Options dialog box. The Options tab, shown in Figure 6.25, gives you four options for the Junk Email protection level:

- **No Automatic Filtering**—This option turns off the Junk Email filter. However, Windows Mail still moves messages from blocked senders to the Junk E-mail folder (see "Blocking Senders," later in this chapter.) Choose this option only if you use a third-party spam filter or if you handle spam using your own message rules.

- **Low**—This is the default protection level, and it's designed to move only messages with obvious spam content to the Junk E-mail folder. This is a good level to start with—particularly if you get only a few spams a day—because it catches most spam and has only a minimal risk of false positives.

- **High**—This level handles spam aggressively and so only rarely misses a junk message. On the downside, the High level also catches the occasional legitimate message in its nets, so you need to check the Junk E-mail folder regularly to look for false positives. Use this level if you get a lot of spam—a few dozen messages or more each day.

> **NOTE**
>
> If you get a false positive in your Junk E-mail folder, click the message and then select Message, Junk E-mail, Mark as Not Junk.

- **Safe Lists Only**—This level treats all incoming messages as spam, except for those messages that come from people or domains in your Safe Senders list (see "Specifying Safe Senders," later in this chapter) or that are sent to addresses in your Safe Recipients list. Use this level if your spam problem is out of control (a hundred or more spams each day) and if most of your nonspam email comes from people you know or from mailing lists you subscribe to.

If you hate spam so much that you never want to even *see* it, much less deal with it, activate the Permanently Delete Suspected Junk E-mail check box.

> **CAUTION**
>
> Spam is so hair-pullingly frustrating that you might be tempted to activate the Permanently Delete Suspected Junk E-mail check box out of sheer spite. I don't recommend this, however. The danger of false positives is just too great, even with the Low level, and it's not worth missing a crucial message.

Fine-Tuning the Spam Filter

You can improve the performance of the Junk Email filter by giving Windows Mail a bit more information. Specifically, you can specify safe senders and you can block senders and countries.

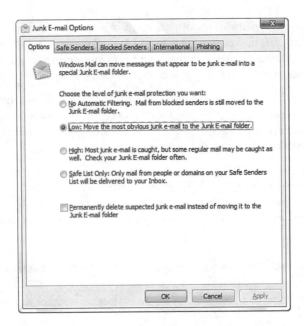

FIGURE 6.25   Use the Options tab to set the Junk Email protection level that you prefer.

Specifying Safe Senders

If you use the Low or High Junk Email protection level, you can reduce the number of false positives by letting Windows Mail know about the people or institutions that regularly send you mail. By designating these addresses as Safe Senders, you tell Windows Mail to automatically leave their incoming messages in your Inbox and never to redirect them to the Junk E-mail folder. And certainly if you use the Safe Lists Only protection level, you must specify some Safe Senders because Windows Mail treats everyone else as a spammer (unless someone sends mail to an address in your Safe Recipients list—see the next section).

Your Safe Senders list can consist of three types of addresses:

- Individual email addresses of the form *someone@somewhere.com*. All messages from these individual addresses will not be treated as spam.

- Domain names of the form *@somewhere.com*. All messages from any address within that domain will not be treated as spam.

- Your Contacts list. You can tell Windows Mail to treat everyone in your Contacts list as a Safe Sender, which makes sense because you're unlikely to be spammed by someone you know.

You can specify a Safe Sender either by entering the address by hand (using the Safe Senders tab in the Junk E-mail Options dialog box) or by using an existing message from the sender (click the message; select Message, Junk E-mail; and then select either Add Sender to Safe Senders List or Add Sender's Domain [@example.com] to Safe Sender's List).

Blocking Senders

If you notice that a particular address is the source of much spam or other annoying email, the easiest way to block the spam is to block all incoming messages from that address. You can do this using the Blocked Senders list, which watches for messages from a specific address and relegates them to the Junk E-mail folder.

As with Safe Senders, you can specify a Blocked Sender either by entering the address by hand (using the Blocked Senders tab in the Junk E-mail Options dialog box) or by using an existing message from the sender (select the message you want to work with and then select Message, Junk E-mail, Add Sender to Blocked Senders List).

Blocking Countries and Languages

Windows Mail also has two features that enable you to handle spam with an international flavor:

- **Spam that comes from a particular country or region**—If you receive no legitimate messages from that country or region, you can treat all messages from that location as spam. Windows Mail does this by using the *top-level domain* (TLD), which is the final suffix that appears in a domain name. There are two types: a *generic top-level domain* (gTLD), such as com, edu, and net; and a *country code top-level domain* (ccTLD), such as ca (Canada) and fr (France). Windows Mail uses the latter to filter spam that comes from certain countries.

- **Spam that comes in a foreign language**—If you don't understand that language, you can safely treat all messages that appear in that language as spam. The character set of a foreign language always appears using a special *encoding* unique to that language. (An encoding is a set of rules that establishes a relationship between the characters and their representations.) Windows Mail uses this encoding to filter spam that appears in a specified language.

In the Junk E-mail Options dialog box, display the International tab and use the following techniques:

- To filter spam based on one or more countries, click Blocked Top-Level Domain List, activate the check box beside each of the countries you want to filter, and then click OK.

- To filter spam based on one or more languages, click Blocked Encodings List, activate the check box beside each of the languages you want to filter, and then click OK.

Email Phishing Protection

Internet Explorer Phishing Filter works well if you stumble upon a phishing site while surfing the Web. However, most phishing "lures" are email messages that appear to be from legitimate businesses, and they include links that send you to phishing sites where they hope to dupe you into giving up confidential information. To help prevent you from falling into that trap, Windows Mail includes an anti-phishing feature of its own: If it detects a potential phishing email, it blocks that message from appearing. This feature is controlled by the Phishing tab in the Junk E-mail Options dialog box, shown in Figure 6.26. Note, too, that you can also redirect potential phishing messages to the Junk E-mail folder by activating the Move Phishing E-mail to the Junk Mail Folder check box.

FIGURE 6.26   Use the Phishing tab to block potential phishing messages.

From Here

Here are some other sections in the book where you'll find information related to the topics in this chapter:

- To learn how Vista keeps your documents secure, see the section "Shadow Copies and Transactional NTFS," in Chapter 4.

- To learn about Vista's version of MMC, see the section "Windows Performance Diagnostic Control," in Chapter 5.

- I talk about running games in Windows Vista in detail in the section "The Game Explorer," in Chapter 10.

Mobile Computing in Windows Vista

Notebook computers used to occupy very specific and unalterable niches in the computing ecology. Sales professionals didn't leave home without them, executives on business trips routinely packed their portables, and corporate employees without a personal machine lugged a laptop home to do some extra work. In each case, though, the notebook computer—with its cramped keyboard, hard-to-read LCD display, and minuscule hard disk—was always considered a poor substitute for a desktop machine.

For many years, it seemed that notebooks were doomed to remain among the lower castes in the social hierarchy of personal computers. But recent developments have caused notebooks to shed their inferiority complex. Today's luggables have impressive 1024×768 (or better) displays, tens of gigabytes of hard disk real estate, and built-in wireless capabilities. Add a couple of PC card slots, connectors for full-size keyboards and monitors, and maybe even a docking station, and suddenly your desktop system doesn't look so superior.

The notebook community's bid for respectability wasn't lost on the designers of Windows Vista. They've incorporated many new notebook PC features into the operating system, including improved power management, the Mobility Center, Presentation Settings, and Windows SideShow. Vista supports Tablet PCs in a big way with many more options and settings, a revamped Input Panel, new gestures, and extensive tools for improving handwriting recognition. This chapter takes you through all of these new features.

The Mobile PC Control Panel

Most Windows Vista mobility enhancements are designed with a single purpose in mind: to give you easier access to the notebook-related features that you use most. That makes sense because when you're using a notebook on the go, you might have only a limited amount of battery power, and you don't want to waste it trying to locate some obscure configuration option. And it's still true that most notebook keyboards and pointing devices are harder to use than their full-size desktop counterparts, so the fewer keystrokes and mouse clicks required to perform Windows tasks, the better.

Your first indication that Vista wants to make your mobile computing life easier is the new Mobile PC Control Panel page, shown in Figure 7.1 (in the Control Panel, select the Mobile PC link). The idea behind the Mobile PC page is to consolidate in a single spot all the Vista configuration options that are directly or indirectly related to notebooks. Whether you want to change the screen orientation on your Tablet PC, adjust settings before a presentation, or change power options, it's all just a mouse click or two away.

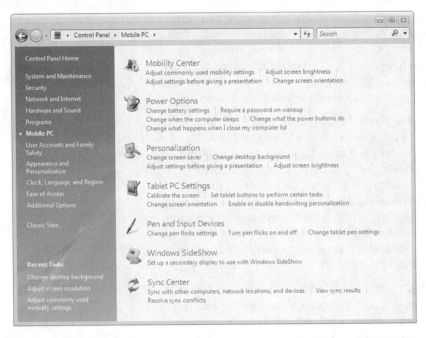

FIGURE 7.1   The Mobile PC Control Panel gives you quick access to most notebook-related configuration options.

The Windows Mobility Center

The Mobile PC Control Panel offers links to a fairly broad range of notebook features. A more targeted approach is found in the new Vista Windows Mobility Center, which you start by clicking the Mobility Center link in the Mobile PC Control Panel. Figure 7.2

shows the Windows Mobility Center window that appears. (Note that you see the full Mobility Center only in the Business, Enterprise, and Ultimate editions of Vista.)

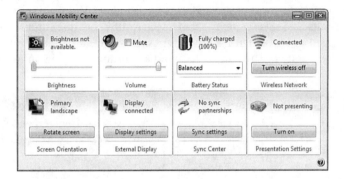

FIGURE 7.2   The new Mobility Center offers a selection of information and controls for notebook-related features.

The Mobility Center offers information on eight key notebook areas, as well as controls to adjust these features:

- **Brightness**—The current brightness setting of your notebook screen (if your machine supports this features). Use the slider to adjust the brightness.

- **Volume**—The current notebook speaker volume. Use the slider to adjust the volume, or click Mute to toggle sound off and on.

- **Battery Status**—The current charge level of the notebook battery. Use the drop-down list to select one of three power plans: Balanced, Power Saver, or High Performance or (I discuss these plans later; see "Power Management in Vista").

- **Wireless Network**—The wireless connection status (Connected or Disconnected), and the signal strength, if connected.

- **Screen Orientation**—The current orientation of the Tablet PC screen. Click Rotate Screen to rotate the screen by 90° counterclockwise.

- **External Display**—The current status of the external monitor connected to your notebook or docking station.

- **Sync Center**—The current synchronization status of your offline files. Click the Sync button to synchronization your notebook's offline files. For more information, see "The Sync Center," in Chapter 8, "New Networking Features."

- **Presentation Settings**—The current status of your presentation settings. Click Turn On to activate you presentation settings (see "Presentation Settings," later in this chapter).

Note, too, that Microsoft is giving PC manufacturers access to the Mobility Center, so we'll likely see the Mobility Center window customized with features that are specific to particular notebooks.

Power Management in Vista

If you're forced to run your notebook without AC (on an airplane, for example), maximizing battery life is crucial. Like most of its predecessors, Windows Vista supports various power schemes—Vista calls them *power plans*—that specify different time intervals for when the notebook is plugged in and when it's on batteries. However, it's equally important to monitor the current state of the battery to avoid a shutdown while you're working.

> **NOTE**
>
> One way in which Windows Vista helps preserve battery power is through its new ReadyDrive technology, which takes advantage of a new storage medium called the *hybrid hard drive*. This is a hard drive that also comes a with non-volatile flash memory chip, typically with a capacity of 1GB. The size of the flash memory means that ReadyDrive can write most data to and from the flash memory, which means much less work for the hard drive and less of a drain on the battery. ReadyDrive also enables Vista to enter into and resume from Sleep mode faster because it can write and restore the notebook's current state more quickly by using the flash memory.

Monitoring Battery Life

To help you monitor battery life, Windows Vista displays the Power icon in the notification area. When you're running on AC power, the Power icon also includes a plug, as shown in Figure 7.3. When you're on batteries, the Power icon displays without the plug, as shown in Figure 7.4, and is completely green. As your notebook uses up battery power, the amount of green decreases accordingly.

Power icon on AC power

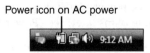

FIGURE 7.3   On AC power, the Power icon includes a plug.

Power icon on battery power

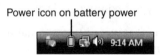

FIGURE 7.4   On batteries, the amount of green in the Power icon tells you how much battery power is left.

To see the exact level of battery power remaining, you have three choices:

- Open the Mobility Center (as described in the previous section) and examine the Battery Status display.

- Hover the mouse pointer over the Power icon. After a second or two, Windows Vista displays a fly-out (see Figure 7.5) that tells you the approximate time left on battery power and percentage of battery life remaining.

FIGURE 7.5   Hover the mouse pointer over the Power icon to see this fly-out.

- Click the Power icon. Windows Vista displays a larger fly-out (see Figure 7.6) that not only shows you the approximate time left on battery power and percentage of battery life remaining, but also enables you to change the current power plan (Balanced, Power Saver, or High Performance).

FIGURE 7.6   Click the Power icon to see this fly-out.

Specifying a Power Plan

Windows Vista shuts down some system components in an effort to keep your battery running longer. This is controlled by your current *power plan*, a power-management configuration that specifies which components get shut down and when Windows Vista shuts them down. Windows Vista has three power plans:

- **Power Saver**—Devices such as the screen and hard disk are powered down after a short idle interval. For example, on battery power, Windows Vista turns off the notebook screen after 3 minutes and the hard disk after 5 minutes.

- **High Performance**—Devices are powered down only after a longer idle interval, which improves performance because you're less likely to have to wait for them to start up again. For example, on battery power, Windows Vista turns off the notebook screen and hard disk after 20 minutes.

- **Balanced**—This is the middle road (more or less) between the Power Saver and High Performance plans. For example, on battery power, Windows Vista turns off the notebook screen after 5 minutes and the hard disk after 10 minutes.

The default power plan is Balanced, but Windows Vista gives you three methods to change it:

- **Using the Mobility Center**—In the Battery Status section, use the drop-down list to select a power plan.

- **Using the Power icon**—Click the Power icon to see the banner shown in Figure 7.6, and then click the power plan you prefer.

- **Using the Power Options window**—Double-click the Power icon to display the Power Options window shown in Figure 7.7; then click a power plan option.

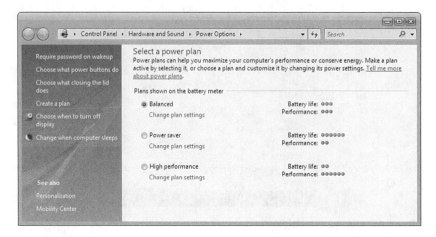

FIGURE 7.7   Double-click the Power icon to display the Power Options window.

Creating a Custom Power Plan

Vista's preset power plans are probably fine for most uses, but you might want to tweak some plan characteristics. For example, you might want a plan that never turns off the hard disk or that waits longer before turning off the display when the notebook is on AC power. For these and other custom plan settings, Vista gives you two choices:

- **Create your own plan**—You can set up a new plan that specifies the intervals when Vista turns off the display and puts the computer to sleep both on battery and while plugged in. In the Power Options window, click Create a Plan to get started.

- **Customize an existing plan**—This method gives you much more choice for your custom power plan configuration. In the Power Options window, click the Change Plan Settings link under the plan you want to customize. The Edit Plan Settings window enables you to change the intervals when the display is turned off and when the notebook goes into sleep mode. For more options, click the Change Advanced Power Settings link. This displays the Advanced Settings tab, shown in Figure 7.8, which offers a wide range of power-management settings.

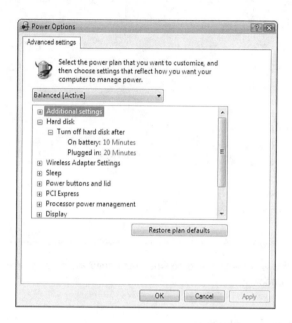

FIGURE 7.8   Customizing an existing power plan gives you a much wide range of power-management options.

Configuring Your Notebook's Power Buttons

Most newer notebooks enable you to configure three "power buttons": closing the lid, using the on/off button, and using the sleep button. When you activate these buttons, they put your system into sleep or hibernate mode, or turn it off altogether. On some notebooks, there isn't a separate sleep button; you simply tap the on/off button quickly.

To configure these buttons for power management in Vista, open the Power Options window and click the Choose What Power Buttons Do link to see the System Settings window, shown in Figure 7.9. Use the lists to configure the power button, sleep button, and lid switch for battery power and AC power.

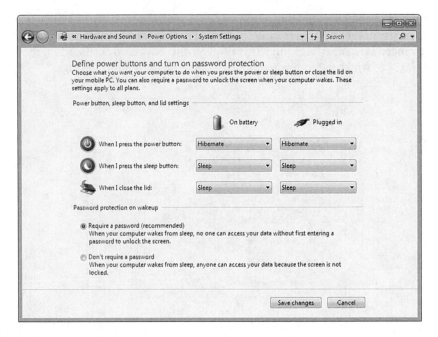

FIGURE 7.9 Use this window to configure what Vista does when you press the power or sleep button or close the notebook lid.

Presentation Settings

The portability of a notebook or other mobile computer means that these machines are now the first choice as the source of content for presentations, from the boardroom to the conference room. That's the good news. The bad news is that you always need to (or should) tend to a few chores before starting your presentation:

- Turn off your screen saver. The last thing you want is your screen saver kicking in while you're spending some extra time explaining a point.

- Turn off system notifications, including alerts for incoming email messages and instant-messaging posts. Your viewers don't want to be interrupted by these distractions.

- Adjust the speaker volume to an acceptable level.

- Select an appropriate desktop wallpaper image. Your desktop could be visible before or after the presentation, if only briefly. Even so, you probably want a wallpaper that invokes a professional image, or you might prefer a blank desktop.

If you're a regular presenter, changing all these settings before each presentation and reversing them afterward is a time-consuming chore. However, Windows Vista comes with a new feature called Presentation Settings that promises to take most of the drudgery out of this part of presenting. The Presentation Settings feature is a collection of configuration options, including screen blanking, system notifications, speaker volume, and desktop wallpaper. You use Presentation Settings to specify the configuration options you want to use during a presentation. After you've done that once, you can use Presentation Settings to turn those options on (and off) with just a few mouse clicks. (Presentation Settings is available for all versions of Vista except Home Basic.)

To configure the Presentation Settings, follow these steps:

1. Select Start, Control Panel, Mobile PC.

2. Click Adjust Settings Before Giving a Presentation. Windows Vista displays the Presentation Settings dialog box shown in Figure 7.10.

FIGURE 7.10   Use the Presentation Settings dialog box to configure the Vista settings you want to use while you give a presentation.

3. Use the following controls to set up your notebook for presentations:

   • **Turn Off the Screen Saver**—Activate this check box to prevent the screen saver from kicking in.

   • **Set the Volume To**—Activate this check box and then use this slider to set the volume level you want.

   • **Show this Background**—Activate this check box and then select a background or (None).

4. Click OK.

When it's time to make your presentation, you have two ways to switch over to your saved settings:

- Open the Mobility Center and select Turn On in the Presentation Settings section. (Select Turn Off when you're done.)

- Open the Presentation Settings dialog box, activate the I Am Currently Giving a Presentation check box, and click OK. (Deactivate this checkbox when you're done.)

> **NOTE**
>
> Another new presentation-related feature in Vista is Network Projection, which enables you run a presentation on a projector connected to a network. Select Start, All Programs, Accessories, Connect to a Network Projector. Then click either Choose from Available Network Projectors (to see a list of projectors) or Enter the Projector Address (to type the address of a specific projector). This feature is not available if you're running Vista Home Basic.

Windows SideShow

Here's a scenario that's all too familiar for a lot of us: You're on your way to an offsite meeting, and when you arrive at the building, you forget which conference room you're supposed to go to. You have the information with you, but it's stored in your calendaring program on your notebook. You have no choice but to boot your computer, load your calendar, get the info you need, and then shut everything down again.

No one likes to power up a computer just to check a quick fact—it wastes both time and battery power. To avoid this, many people simply write whatever important information they need on a sticky note and attach it to the outside of the notebook, but how low-tech can you get?

Here's another scenario: You're waiting in an airport lounge and want to listen to music or catch up on some podcasts, but there's no AC outlet available. How do you listen to the audio without draining your battery entirely? One solution is to configure Windows to not go into sleep mode when you shut the notebook lid. The computer remains running, but the screen turns off automatically when you close the lid, so you save quite a bit of power. However, to control the media playback, you have to open the lid anyway.

One of the most intriguing innovations in Windows Vista is a feature that lets you view information without starting up your computer or resorting to sticky notes, and lets you manipulate a program such as Windows Media Player without having to open the notebook lid. It's called Windows SideShow and it's a new technology that does two things:

- It enables a notebook manufacturer to add a small display—called a *secondary display* or an *auxiliary display*—to the outside of a notebook case.

- It enables Windows Vista to display information on the secondary display no matter what power state the notebook is in: on, off, or sleep.

If you use a clamshell-style cellphone, you've seen a similar idea: when the phone is closed, a screen on the outside of the phone shows you the current time, battery state, and other data.

With Windows SideShow, however, you get a much more powerful interface that can display a wider variety of content:

- Developers of existing programs can choose to send data to the secondary display.

- Developers can build new gadgets designed for SideShow (see "Gadgets and the Windows Sidebar" in Chapter 3, "The Windows Vista Interface").

Microsoft created an application programming interface for SideShow, so third-party developers should create a lot of programs and gadgets that you can add to your SideShow menu.

Using the Windows SideShow Control Panel (see Figure 7.11), you decide which programs or gadgets you want to appear in the SideShow secondary display. The list of possible gadgets was not finalized as I wrote this, but examples include a calendar (for example, Windows Calendar or the Outlook Calendar), email (such as Windows Mail or the Outlook Inbox), and Windows Media Player. Depending on the layout of the secondary display, you then choose which program or gadget you want to work with.

> **NOTE**
>
> Windows SideShow isn't strictly for notebooks. Microsoft has shown images of secondary displays running on keyboards, remote controls, and cellphones. Basically, any device that can wirelessly connect to a Vista machine can be transformed into a SideShow-ready device with the addition of a secondary display.

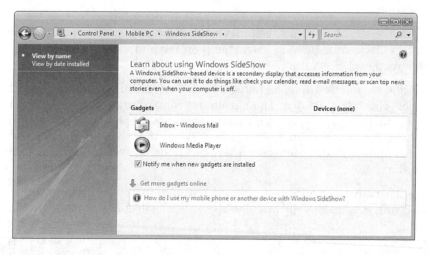

FIGURE 7.11   Use the SideShow Control Panel to decide which programs and gadgets you want to appear in the SideShow secondary display.

New Vista Tablet PC Features

In the "old days," working on a document usually meant pulling out a blank sheet of paper, taking up a pen (or some other writing instrument), and then writing out your thoughts in longhand. Nowadays, of course, this pen-and-paper approach has been almost entirely superseded by electronic document editing. However, there are still plenty of situations in which people still write things out in longhand:

- Jotting down an address or other data while on the phone

- Taking notes at a meeting

- Recording a list of things to do while visiting a client

- Creating a quick map or message to be faxed

- Sketching out ideas or blueprints in a brainstorming session

Unfortunately, for all but the most trivial notes, writing on paper is inefficient because, in most cases, you eventually have to put the writing into electronic form, either by entering the text by hand or by scanning the document.

What the world has needed for a long time is a way to bridge the gap between purely digital and purely analog writing. We've needed a way to combine the convenience of the electronic format with the simplicity of pen-based writing. After several aborted attempts (think: the Apple Newton), that bridge was built in recent years: the Tablet PC. At first glance, many Tablet PCs look just like a small notebook computer, and it certainly can be used just like any notebook. However, a Tablet PC boasts three hardware innovations that make it unique:

- A pressure-sensitive touch screen that replaces the usual notebook LCD screen. Some Tablet PC screens respond to touch, but most respond to only a specific type of pen (discussed next).

- A *digital pen* that acts as an all-purpose input device: You can use the pen to click, double-click, click-and-drag, and tap out individual characters using an onscreen keyboard. In certain applications, you can also use the pen to "write" directly on the screen, just as though it was a piece of paper, thus enabling you to jot notes, sketch diagrams, add proofreader marks, or just doodle your way through a boring meeting.

- The capability to physically reorient the screen so that it lies flat on top of the keyboard, thus making the machine appear like a tablet or pad of paper.

NOTE

Some Tablet PCs come with a screen that's sensitive to finger touches. Windows Vista supports these screens.

The first Tablet PCs came with their own unique operating system, Windows XP Tablet PC Edition. With Windows Vista, the Tablet PC–specific features are now built into the regular operating system, although they are activated only when Vista is installed on a Tablet PC (and you're running any Vista edition except Home Basic).

Before moving on to the new Tablet PC, I should note that Vista comes with a couple of tools that were also part of the XP version: Windows Journal and Sticky Notes. These programs are identical to the XP versions.

Changing the Screen Orientation

The first Tablet PC feature to mention is one that you've already seen. The new Mobility Center comes with a Screen Orientation section that tells you the current screen orientation (see Figure 7.2, earlier in this chapter). There are four settings in all:

- **Primary landscape**—This is the default orientation, with the taskbar at the bottom of the display and the top edge of the desktop at the top of the display.

- **Secondary portrait**—This orientation places the taskbar at the right edge of the display, and the top edge of the desktop at the left of the display.

- **Secondary landscape**—This orientation places the taskbar at the top of the display, and the top edge of the desktop at the bottom of the display.

- **Primary portrait**—This orientation places the taskbar at the left edge of the display, and the top edge of the desktop at the right of the display.

Tablet PC Settings

Before you start inking with Vista, you'll probably want to configure a few settings, and Vista offers quite a few more than XP. Your starting point is the Control Panel's Mobile PC window—specifically, the renamed Tablet PC Settings icon (formerly Tablet and Pen Settings). In the Tablet PC Settings dialog box that appears, the General tab is basically the same as the old Settings tab, and the Display tab is identical to its predecessor. However, there is a new Handwriting Recognition tab, shown in Figure 7.12, that has two sections:

- **Personalization**—Later in this chapter (see "Personalizing Handwriting Recognition"), you'll see that you can provide Vista with samples of your handwriting. This increases the accuracy of the *handwriting recognizer* (the feature that converts handwritten text into typed text), but only when the Use the Personalized Recognizer check box is activated.

- **Automatic Learning**—This feature collects information about your writing, including the words you write and the style in which you write them. Note that this applies not only to your handwriting—the ink you write in the Input Panel, the recognized text, and the corrected text—but also to your typing, including email messages and web addresses typed into Internet Explorer. To use this feature, activate the Use Automatic Learning option.

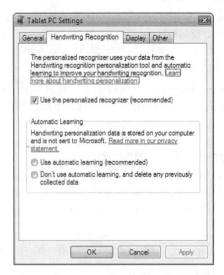

FIGURE 7.12   Use the Handwriting tab to activate new Vista features for improving handwriting recognition.

> **CAUTION**
>
> It's understandable that some people have privacy concerns about the Automatic Learning feature because it is sure to collect proprietary and sensitive data typed into email messages. However, Microsoft notes that the information stays on your computer and is stored in a proprietary format that can't be read in a text editor or word processor. It seems likely that someone will hack this new format, however, so if you do not want sensitive data stored via Automatic Learning, you should turn off this feature.

Tablet PC Input Panel

As with XP Tablet PC Edition, Windows Vista comes with a tool called the Tablet PC Input Panel that you use to enter text and other symbols with the digital pen instead of the keyboard. You have two ways to display the Input Panel:

- In Vista, an icon for the Input Panel appears in a small tab docked on the left edge of the screen. Hover the mouse pointer over the tab to display it, and then click the icon or any part of the tab.

- Move the pen over any area in which you can enter text (such as a text box). In most cases, the Input Panel icon appears near the text entry area. Click the icon when it appears.

Figure 7.13 shows the Input Panel.

FIGURE 7.13   Use the Writing Pad to hand-write words or short phrases.

TIP

You can also add an icon for the Input Panel to the Vista taskbar. Right-click the taskbar, and then click Toolbars, Tablet PC Input Panel.

The layout of the Input Panel is slightly different than in the XP version, with the icons for the writing pad, character pad, and onscreen Keyboard, and the Options button along the top. The minikeyboard that appears with the writing pad and character pad is slightly different as well, with the notable difference being the addition of the Web key full time. (In XP Tablet PC Edition, it appeared only when you were entering a web address.) This makes sense because users often need to write URLs in email messages and other correspondence.

The Vista Input Panel also comes with quite a few more options than its predecessor. Click Tools and then click Options in the menu that appears. Here's a list of some of the more significant new settings:

- **AutoComplete** (Settings tab)—When this check box is activated, the Input Panel will automatically complete your handwriting if it recognizes the first few characters. For example, if you're writing an email address that you've entered (via handwriting or typing) in the past, Input Panel recognizes it after a character or two and displays a banner with the completed entry. You need only click the completed entry to insert it. This also works with web addresses and filenames.

- **Show the Input Panel Tab** (Opening tab)—Use this check box to toggle the Input Panel tab on and off. (For example, if you display the Tablet PC Input Panel toolbar in the taskbar, you might prefer to turn off the Input Panel tab.)

- **You Can Choose Where the Input Panel Tab Appears** (Opening tab)—Choose either On the Left Edge of the Screen (the default) or On the Right Edge of the Screen.

- **New Writing Line** (Writing Pad tab)—Use this slider to specify how close to the end of the writing line you want to write to before starting a new line automatically.

- **Gestures** (Gestures tab)—In XP Tablet PC Edition, you could delete handwritten text by "scratching it out" using a Z-shape gesture. Many people found this hard to master and a bit unnatural, so Vista offers several new scratch-out gestures, which you turn on by activating the All Scratch-Out and Strikethrough Gestures option.

> **NOTE**
>
> Vista offers four new scratch-out gestures:
>
> **Strikethrough**—A horizontal line (straight or wavy) through the text.
>
> **Vertical scratch-out**—An M- or W-shape gesture through the text.
>
> **Circular scratch-out**—A circle or oval around the text.
>
> **Angled scratch-out**—An angled line (straight or wavy) through the text. The angle can be from top left to bottom right, or from bottom left to top right.

- **Password Security** (Advanced tab)—This slider (see Figure 7.14) controls the security features that Vista uses when you use the pen to enter a password into a password text box. At the High setting, Vista automatically switches to the onscreen keyboard (and doesn't allow you to switch to the writing pad or character pad) and doesn't show the pen pointer or highlight the keys that you tap while entering the password.

FIGURE 7.14   The Input Panel Options dialog box offers many new features, including security settings that protect password entries.

Using Pen Flicks

The Input Panel onscreen keyboard has keys that you can tap with your pen to navigate a document and enter program shortcut keys. However, if you just want to scroll through a document or navigate web pages, having the keyboard onscreen is a hassle because it takes up so much room. An alternative is to tap-and-drag the vertical or horizontal scroll box, or tap the program's built-in navigation features (such as the Back and Forward buttons in Internet Explorer).

Vista gives you a third choice for navigating a document: *pen flicks*. These are gestures that you can use in any application to scroll up and down in a document, or to navigate backward or forward in Internet Explorer or Windows Explorer:

- **Scroll up** (about one screenful)—Move the pen up in a straight line.
- **Scroll down** (about one screenful)—Move the pen down in a straight line.
- **Navigate back**—Move the pen to the left in a straight line.
- **Navigate forward**—Move the pen right in a straight line.

> **TIP**
>
> For a pen flick to work, you need to follow these techniques:
> - Move the pen across the screen for about half an inch (at least 10mm).
> - Move the pen very quickly.
> - Move the pen in a straight line.
> - Lift your pen off the screen quickly at the end of the flick.

You can also set up pen flicks for other program features:

- **Copy**—Move the pen up and to the left in a straight line.
- **Paste**—Move the pen up and to the right in a straight line.
- **Delete**—Move the pen down and to the right in a straight line.
- **Undo**—Move the pen down and to the left in a straight line.

To activate flicks, open the Control Panel Pen and Input Devices icon, and then display the Flicks tab (see Figure 7.15). Activate the Use Flicks to Perform Common Actions Quickly and Easily check box, and then select the flicks you want to use:

- **Navigational Flicks**—Activate this option to use the Scroll Up, Scroll Down, Back, and Forward flicks.
- **Navigational Flicks and Editing Flicks**—Activate this option to also use the Copy, Paste, Delete, and Undo flicks in any program.

If you activate the Navigational Flicks and Editing Flicks option, the Customize button becomes enabled. Click this button to display the Customize Flicks dialog box shown in Figure 7.16. You use this dialog box to apply one of Vista's built-in actions (such as Cut, Open, Print, or Redo) to a flick. Alternatively, click (add) to create a custom action by specifying a key or key combination to apply to the flick.

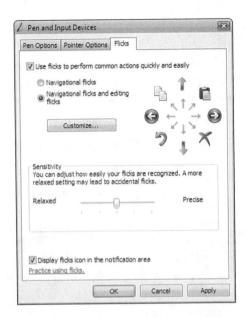

FIGURE 7.15   Use the Flicks tab to activate and configure pen flicks.

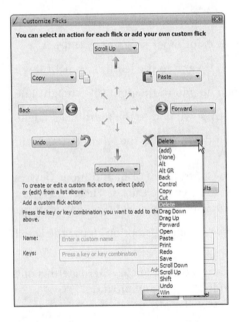

FIGURE 7.16   Use the Customize Flicks dialog box to apply different actions or key combinations to a flick gesture.

TIP

If you forget which flick does which action, you can easily find out by clicking the Pen Flicks icon in the taskbar's notification area. This displays a Pen Flick Gestures fly-out that shows your current flick settings.

Pointer Options

While we're in the Pen and Input Devices dialog box, I should also point out the new Pointer Options tab, shown in Figure 7.17. By default, Vista provides you with visual feedback when you single-tap and double-tap the pen, and when you press the pen button. I find that this visual feedback helps when I'm using the pen for mouselike actions. If you don't, you can turn them off by deactivating the check boxes.

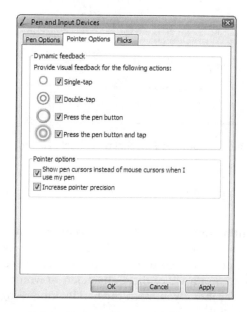

FIGURE 7.17   Use the new Pointer Options tab to toggle Vista's visual feedback for pen actions such as tapping and double-tapping.

Personalizing Handwriting Recognition

When you use a Tablet PC's digital pen as an input device, there will often be times when you don't want to convert the writing into typed text. A quick sticky note or journal item might be all you need for a given situation. However, in plenty of situations you need your handwriting converted into typed text. Certainly, when you're using the Input Panel, you always want the handwriting converted to text. However, the convenience and usefulness of handwritten text is directly related to how well the handwriting recognizer does its job. If it misinterprets too many characters, you'll spend too much time either correcting the errors or scratching out chunks of text and starting again.

Rather than just throwing up their hands and saying "That's life with a Tablet PC," Microsoft's developers are doing something to ensure that you get the most out of the handwriting recognizer. Windows Vista comes with a new tool called Handwriting Personalization (select Start, All Programs, Tablet PC, Personalize Handwriting Recognition), shown in Figure 7.18.

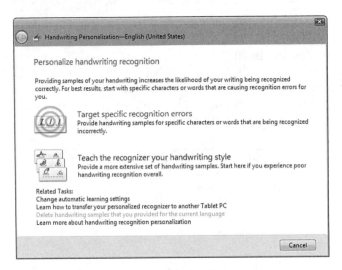

FIGURE 7.18   Use the new Handwriting Personalization tool to improve the Tablet PC's capability to recognize your handwriting.

This feature gives you two methods that improve the Tablet PC's capability to recognize your handwriting:

- Teach the handwriting recognizer to handle specific recognition errors. This is the method to use if you find that the Tablet PC does a pretty good job of recognizing your handwriting but often incorrectly recognizes certain characters or words. By providing handwritten samples of those characters or words and specifying the correct conversion for them, you teach the handwriting recognizer to avoid those errors in the future.

- Teach the handwriting recognizer to handle your handwriting style. This is the method to use if you find that the Tablet PC does a poor job of recognizing your handwriting in general. In this case, you provide a more comprehensive set of handwritten samples to give the handwriting recognizer an overall picture of your writing style.

If you select Target Specific Recognition Errors, you next get a choice of two wizards:

- **Character or Word You Specify**—Run this wizard if a character or word is consistently being recognized incorrectly. For a character, you type the character and then provide several samples of the character in handwritten form, as shown in Figure 7.19 (for the lowercase letter u, in this case). The wizard then asks you to provide handwritten samples for a few characters that are similarly shaped. Finally, the wizard asks for handwritten samples of words that contain the character. For a word, the wizard asks you to type the word; then it asks you to hand-write two samples of the word.

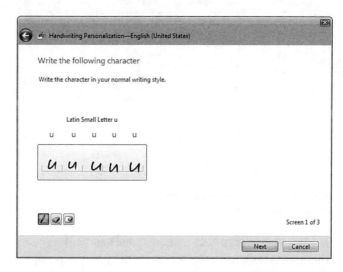

FIGURE 7.19   The wizard asks you to provide several handwritten samples of the character that is being recognized incorrectly.

- **Characters with Similar Shapes**—Run this wizard if a particular group of similarly shaped characters is causing you trouble. The wizard gives you a list of the six sets of characters that most commonly cause recognition problems, as shown in Figure 7.20. After you choose a set, the wizard goes through each character and asks you to hand-write several samples of the character and to hand-write the character in context.

If you select Teach the Recognizer Your Handwriting Style, you next get a choice of two wizards:

- **Sentences**—This wizard displays a series of sentences, and you provide a handwritten sample for each. Note that there are 50 (!) sentences in all, so wait until you have a lot of spare time before using this wizard. (The wizard does come with a Save for Later button that you can click at any time to stop the wizard and still preserve your work.)

- **Numbers, Symbols, and Letters**—This wizard consists of eight screens that take you through the numbers 0 to 9; common symbols such as !, ?, @, $, &, +, #, <, and >; and all the uppercase and lowercase letters. You provide a handwritten sample for each number, symbol, and letter.

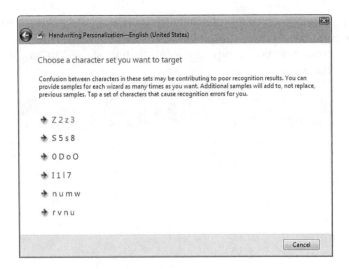

FIGURE 7.20   The wizard asks you to choose from a list of six sets of characters that are commonly confused when handwritten.

When you're done, click Update and Exit to apply your handwriting samples to the recognizer. Note that this takes a few minutes, depending on the number of samples you provided.

The Snipping Tool

Windows Vista includes a new feature called the Snipping Tool that enables you to use your pen to capture ("snip") part of the screen and save it as an image or HTML file. Start the Snipping Tool by selecting Start, All Programs, Accessories, Snipping Tool. Vista washes out the screen to indicate that you're in snipping mode and displays the Snipping Tool window. You then use your pen to draw a freehand circle (or box) around the screen area you want to capture. The snipped area then appears in the Snipping Tool window, as shown in Figure 7.21. From here, you save the snip as an HTML file or a GIF, JPEG, or PNG graphics file.

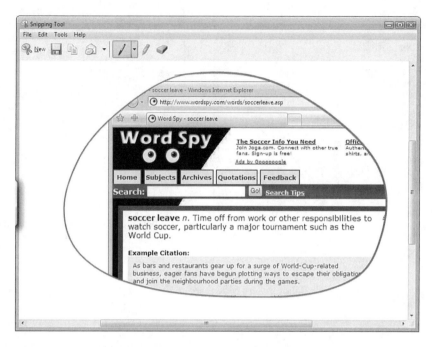

FIGURE 7.21   Use the new Snipping Tool to use your pen to capture part of the screen.

From Here

Here are some other sections in the book where you'll find information related to the topics in this chapter:

- For more about gadgets, see the section "Gadgets and the Windows Sidebar," in Chapter 3.

- For more information about synchronizing files between your notebook and another PC, see the section "The Sync Center," in Chapter 8.

- For details on running a presentation, see the section "Windows Collaboration," in Chapter 8.

New Networking Features

For many years, networking was the private playground of IT panjandrums. Its obscure lingo and arcane hardware were familiar to only this small coterie of computer cognoscenti. Workers who needed access to network resources had to pay obeisance to these powers-that-be, genuflecting in just the right way, tossing in the odd *salaam* or two.

Lately, however, we've seen a democratization of networking. Thanks to the trend away from mainframes and toward client/server setups, thanks to the migration from dumb terminals to smarter PCs, and thanks to the advent of easy peer-to-peer setups, networking is no longer the sole province of the elite. Getting connected to an existing network, or setting up your own network in a small office or home office, has never been easier.

This is particularly true with Windows Vista, which comes with a completely revamped network architecture that's designed to make networking with Vista easier and more robust. This chapter takes you through the new Vista networking interface. You'll learn about the Network Center, the Network Map, Windows Collaboration, and the Sync Center.

The Network Center

Windows Vista always displays a Network icon in the taskbar's notification area. The version of the icon you see depends on the current network status. When Vista is connected to a network with Internet access, it displays the version of the Network icon shown in Figure 8.1. For a network without Internet access, the Network icon appears without the globe, shown in Figure 8.2. Finally, if Vista cannot make a connection to any network, you see the Network icon shown in Figure 8.3.

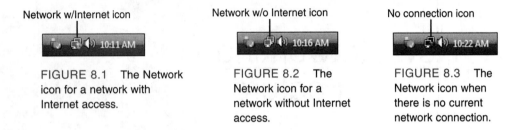

FIGURE 8.1   The Network icon for a network with Internet access.

FIGURE 8.2   The Network icon for a network without Internet access.

FIGURE 8.3   The Network icon when there is no current network connection.

Whichever icon you see in the notification area, if you double-click the icon, Vista displays the new Network Center window, as shown in Figure 8.4. You can also get to the Network Center by opening the Control Panel and clicking the View Network Status and Tasks link or, if you're using Classic view, double-clicking the Network Center icon.

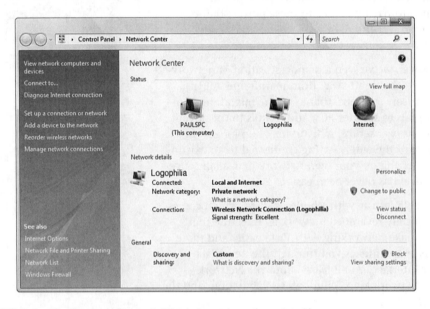

FIGURE 8.4   The Network Center is Vista's home base for networking.

Network Center is the Windows Vista networking hub that shows you the current status of your connection and gives you quick access to many networking tasks. The window is divided into four areas:

- **Status**—This section gives you a mini version of the network map: a visual display of the current connection. See the "Network Map" section, later in this chapter.

- **Network Details**—This section tells you the name of the network to which you're connected, the network category (private or public), whether you have Internet access via that connection, and which of your computer connections is in use (this will usually be either Local Area Connection for a wired connection or Wireless Network Connection). If you're connected to multiple networks or have multiple connections to a single network (wired and wireless, for example), all the connections appear here.

- **General**—This area shows the current network detection and sharing settings.

- **Tasks**—This pane on the left side of the Network Center window gives you one-click access to the most common network tasks. See the "Common Network Tasks" section, later in this chapter.

Connecting to a Network

If you don't have a current connection, the Network Center window doesn't show a network icon, the network map shows a red X through the connection line, and the status in Network Details is Not Connected. To get connected, you have three ways to get started:

- Select Start, Connect To.

- Right-click the Network icon in the notification area and then select Connect To.

- In the Network Center, click the Connect To link in the tasks pane.

Vista displays a list of available networks. For example, Figure 8.5 shows a list of wireless networks. Click the network you want to join and then click Connect.

If it's a wireless network that requires a WEP (Wired Equivalent Privacy) or WPA (Wi-Fi Protected Access) security key, you see the dialog box shown in Figure 8.6. Type the key and click Connect.

TIP

Some security keys are quite long (for example, a 128-bit WEP key has 26 hex digits). To ensure that you enter these long keys correctly, activate the Display Characters check box to enter the key in plain text. Just make sure no one in the vicinity is "shoulder surfing"—looking over your shoulder to see the key.

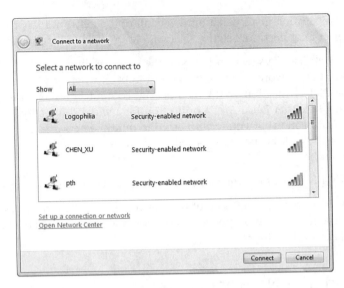

FIGURE 8.5   Select the network you want to join.

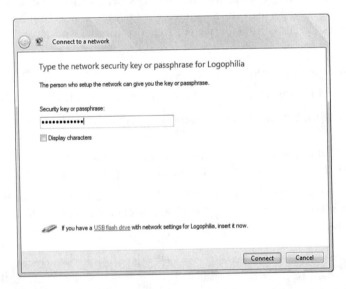

FIGURE 8.6   Most wireless networks require you to enter a security key before you can connect.

If all goes well, the connection succeeds and Vista displays a dialog box like the one shown in Figure 8.7. Note that you have two connection options for wireless networks:

- **Save This Network**—Leave this check box activated to tell Vista to always connect to it when you're within range. If you deactivate this check box instead, you'll need to manually connect each time. This might be what you want if you have the choice of several networks to connect to.

- **Make This Network Available to Anyone Using This Computer**—Leave this check box deactivated if this is a secure network that you do not want other people who use your computer to access. If you activate this check box instead, every user will be able to connect to the network.

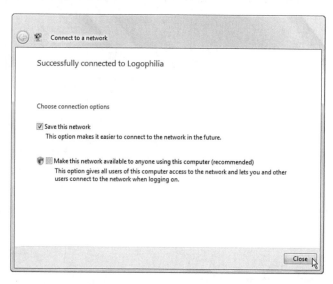

FIGURE 8.7   You see this dialog box if your connection to the network was successful.

Creating a Manual Wireless Network Connection

As a security precaution, some wireless networks are set up with SSID—Service Set Identifier, which is the network name—broadcasting disabled. This means that when you display the list of networks within range (refer to Figure 8.5), networks that don't broadcast their SSID don't appear in the list.

If you know that a network is within range but it doesn't appear in the list of available networks, you can still add the network manually. Click the Set Up a Connection or Network link, click Manually Connect to a Wireless Network, and then click Next. Vista displays the dialog box shown in Figure 8.8. You use this dialog box to enter the network particulars, including the SSID (the Network Name), Security Type, Encryption Type, and Security Key (if required). Click Next to connect.

Creating an Ad Hoc Wireless Network Connection

If you don't have a wireless access point, Vista enables you to set up a temporary network between two or more computers. This is called an *ad hoc connection*. In the list of available networks, click the Set Up a Connection or Network link, click Create an Ad Hoc (Computer-to-Computer) Network, click Next, and then click Next again. Vista displays the dialog box shown in Figure 8.9. You use this dialog box to enter the Network Name, choose the Security Type, and specify the Security key (if required). Click Next, select a file and printer sharing option, and click Next to create the network.

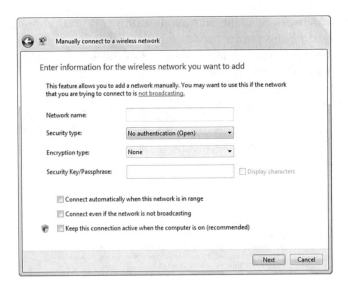

FIGURE 8.8   If a network is not broadcasting its SSID, you need to enter the network name manually.

FIGURE 8.9   Vista enables you to create a temporary connection between two or more computers.

When that's done, other people within 30 feet of your computer will see your ad hoc network in their list of available networks, as shown in Figure 8.10. Note that the network remains available as long as at least one computer is connected to it, including the computer that created the network. The network is discarded when all computers have disconnected from it.

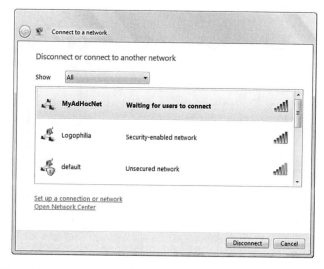

FIGURE 8.10   The ad hoc network is available to computers that are within 30 feet of the original computer.

Personalizing the Network

When you first open the Network Center, in most cases, you won't have a profile set up for the network, so Vista displays a default network name in either the Network Map or Network Details sections—usually either Network or the SSID of the wireless network. To fix this, click Personalize to display the Personalize Settings dialog box shown in Figure 8.11. Type a name in the Network text box, and then click OK. Vista updates the Network Center window with the new profile name.

> **NOTE**
>
> The Personalize Settings dialog box also enables you to perform two other personalization tasks. To specify a different icon for the network, click the Change link, click the icon you want in the Change Network Icon dialog box, and click OK. To toggle the network category between public and private, click Switch Category.

> **NOTE**
>
> Windows Vista supports three types of network categories: private, public, and domain. Private networks are usually home or small office networks where you need to work with a few nearby computers. To that end, Windows Vista turns on Network Discovery—a new feature that enables you to see other computers and devices on your network—and file and printer sharing. Public networks are usually wireless "hot spot" connections in airports, coffee shops, hotels, and other public places. When you designate a network as public, Vista turns off Network Discovery and file and printer sharing. The domain category applies to networks that are part of a corporate domain.

FIGURE 8.11   Click Personalize to display the dialog box so you can supply a profile name for your network connection.

Network Map

The new Network Map feature gives you a visual display of everything your computer is connected to: network connections (wired and wireless), ad hoc (computer-to-computer) connections, and Internet connections. Network Map also gives you a visual display of the connection status so you can easily spot problems.

In the Network Center, the Status group displays your local portion of the network map, and the layout depends on your current connections, of course. You always see an icon for your computer on the left. If your computer is connected to a network (as shown earlier in Figure 8.4), a green line joins the computer icon and a generic network icon. If the network is connected to the Internet, then another green line joins the network icon and the Internet icon on the right. If there is no connection, you see a red X through the connection line.

Windows Vista also comes with a more detailed version of Network Map. To view it, you have two choices:

- In the Network Center, click the View Full Map link.

- In the Control Panel, open the Network Map icon.

Figure 8.12 shows an example of the full Network Map.

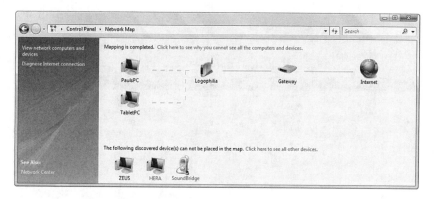

FIGURE 8.12   The full version of the Network Map.

Common Network Tasks

You saw earlier that the Network Center comes with a tasks pane that offers links to several of the most common networking tasks. The next few sections give you an overview of these tasks to give you a taste of how networking works in Windows Vista.

View Network Computers and Devices

When you're connected, you most likely want to check out what's on the network and access its resources. Vista gives you two ways to get started:

- In the Network Center tasks pane, click View Network Computers and Devices.

- Select Start, Network.

Either way, you see the Network Explorer, which lists the main network resources, such as the computers and media devices in your workgroup. As you can see in Figure 8.13, Details view shows you the resource name, category, workgroup or domain name, and the name of the network profile.

Double-click a resource to see what it contains. For example, if you double-click a work-group computer, you see its shared items, as shown in Figure 8.14. Notice that Vista computers automatically share three folders:

- Public—This folder is open to everyone on the network and provides users with full read/write access.

- Users—This folder is open only to people with an account on the computer.

- Printers—This folder contains the computer's installed printers.

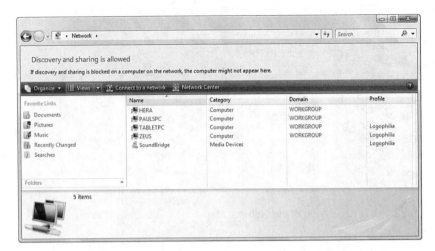

FIGURE 8.13   The Network Explorer shows you the main resources on the network to which you're connected.

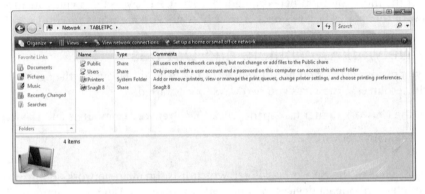

FIGURE 8.14   Double-click a workgroup computer's shared folder to see its contents.

Set Up File and Printer Sharing

Whether it's a folder, disk drive, or printer, networking is all about sharing. To set up sharing in Windows Vista, click the Network Center's View Sharing Settings icon. (Alternatively, open the Control Panel and select Share Files and Folders.) Figure 8.15 shows the Network File and Printer Sharing window that appears.

For general network access, you have two choices:

- **People with a User Account and Password for This Computer**—Select this option to share resources only with people who know the username and password of an account on your computer.

- **Anyone Who Can Connect to My Network**—Select this option to allow any network user to access your shared resources.

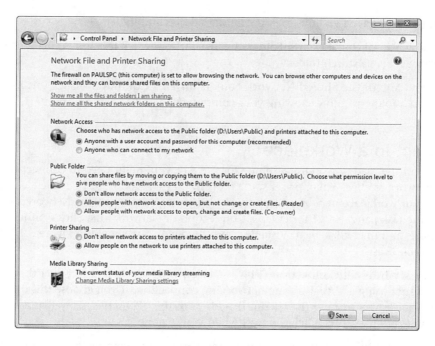

FIGURE 8.15   Use the Network File and Printer Sharing window to set up your computer's options for sharing files, folders, and printers.

To share the Public folder, you have three choices:

- **Don't Allow Network Access to the Public Folder**—Activate this option to prevent sharing the Public folder.

- **Allow People with Network Access to Open, But Not Change or Create Files**— Activate this option to share the Public folder but only allow network users to read files in that folder (Reader permission).

- **Allow People with Network Access to Open, Change and Create Files**—Activate this option to share the Public folder and allow network users to read, edit, and create new files in that folder (Owner permission).

To share the Printers folder, you have two choices:

- **Don't Allow Network Access to Printers Attached to This Computer**—Activate this option to prevent sharing the Printers folder.

- **Allow People On the Network to Use Printers Attached to This Computer**— Activate this option to share your Printers folder.

The Media Library Sharing group is connected to the Library Sharing feature in Windows Media Player. See "Library Sharing" in Chapter 9.

Finally, you also have two links for viewing shared files and folders:

- **Show Me All the Files and Folders I Am Sharing**—Click this link to open the `Shared By Me` search folder.

- **Show Me All the Shared Network Folders on This Computer**—Click this link to open a folder window showing your computer's shared folders and printers.

Connect to a Workplace

If you're on the road or working at home for the day, you might need to connect to your office network to check email or get some files. To do that, you need to create a connection to your workplace network. To do this in Windows Vista, open the Network Center and, in the task pane, click the Set Up a Connection or Network link, click Connect to a Workplace, and then click Next. Vista displays the dialog box shown in Figure 8.16. You have two choices:

- **Use My Internet Connection (VPN)**—Click this option to connect over the Internet using a virtual private networking connection. If you choose this option, Vista asks you to enter the URL or IP address of the VPN server, as well as a username and password. Click Connect when you're done.

- **Dial Directly**—Click this option to connect using your computer's modem and a phone line. In this case, you specify the phone number and your username and password, and then click Connect.

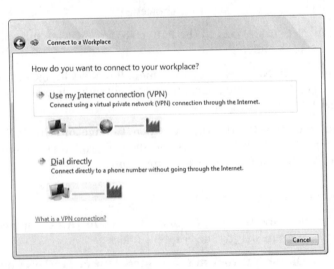

FIGURE 8.16   You can create either a VPN or dial-up workplace connection.

Set Up a Network

If you want to create your own peer-to-peer network at home or in your small office, Windows Vista has a wizard that takes you through the necessary steps. You get started by doing either of the following:

- In the Network Center task pane, click Set Up a Connection or Network, click Set Up a Network, and click Next.

- If you're browsing a network computer's resources, click Set Up a Home or Small Office Network.

In the initial Set Up a Network wizard dialog box that appears, click Next. The wizard then detects your networking hardware, including whether your network configuration includes a router, as shown in Figure 8.17.

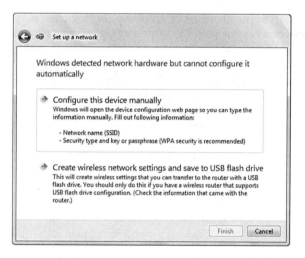

FIGURE 8.17   Vista can detect whether your network is configured with a router.

Click Configure This Device Manually to open the router's home page (usually found at IP address 192.168.1.1 or 192.168.0.1). If your router supports automatic configuration via a USB Flash drive, click Configure Wireless Settings for My Router and Save to USB Flash Drive instead. You then enter a name for the new network (this doubles as your network's SSID and profile name), enter a WPA security key, and turn file and printer sharing on or off.

Then Vista gives you the choice of saving the network settings to a USB Flash drive, as shown in Figure 8.18. After the settings have been saved, you simply plug the Flash drive into another Vista or XP computer that you want on your network. In the AutoPlay dialog box that appears, you choose the Wireless Network Setup Wizard option, as shown in Figure 8.19. This runs the wizard and, by using the settings stored on the Flash drive, sets up the computer on the network in seconds.

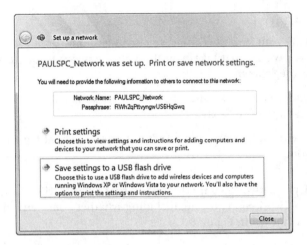

FIGURE 8.18   Vista gives you the option of saving the new network settings to a USB Flash drive so you can apply them on other computers that you want on the same network.

FIGURE 8.19   When you insert the Flash drive in another computer, the AutoPlay dialog box prompts you to start the Wireless Network Setup Wizard.

Add a Computer or Device

Previous versions of Windows showed network resources in either the Network Neighborhood or My Network Places, but those resources were mostly limited to domains, workgroups, and computers. Windows Vista is much more aware of other types of devices connected to the network, including media players, wireless access points, routers, and print servers. These devices usually appear in the Network Map, but some devices might not. To add those devices, open the Network Center and click the Add a Device to the Network link in the task pane. Vista immediately begins searching for network devices. If it finds any, it displays them in a list; you can decide which ones you want to add to your network.

Diagnose Network Problems

Windows XP came with a Repair tool that did a pretty good job of repairing connectivity problems because most networking problems can be resolved by running the Repair tool's basic tasks: disconnecting, renewing the DHCP lease, flushing various network caches, and then reconnecting. However, all too often the Repair would report that it couldn't fix the problem, which usually meant that the trouble existed at a level deeper in the network stack than the Repair tool could go. In an attempt to handle these more challenging connectivity issues, Vista comes with a completely redesigned Network Diagnostics Tool that digs deep into all layers of the network stack to try to identify and resolve problems.

To launch the Network Diagnostic Tool, Vista gives you several methods:

- Right-click the notification area's Network icon and then click Diagnose.

- In the Network Center, click View Status, and then click Diagnose.

- If you lose a connection to a network share, Vista displays a dialog box to let you know, as shown in Figure 8.20. Click the Diagnose button.

- In the Network Connections window (see "Manage Network Connections," later in this chapter), click the broken connection and then click Repair This Connection.

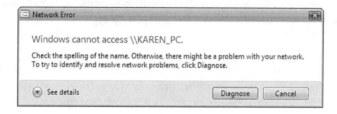

FIGURE 8.20   Vista can search for other devices connected to your network.

Manage Networks

If you connect to multiple networks, Vista enables you to manage the network profiles. For example, if you sometimes connect to a particular network using a wired connection and other times with a wireless connection, you can add both to the network profile.

To get started managing your networks, Vista gives you two choices:

- In the Network Center, click Network List.

- In the Control Panel, select Network and Internet, Network List.

Either way, the Network List window appears, as shown in Figure 8.21.

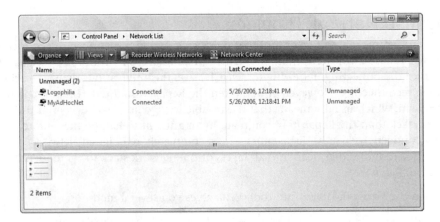

FIGURE 8.21   Use the Networks List window to manage your networks.

When you click a network, the Network List window offers three tasks for managing your networks:

- **Reorder Wireless Networks**—Click this task to change the order in which Vista attempts to connect to your wireless networks when they're within range. Figure 8.22 shows the Reorder Wireless Networks window that appears.

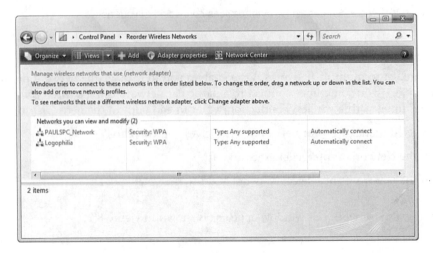

FIGURE 8.22   Use the Reorder Wireless Networks window to change the order that Vista uses to connect to your wireless networks.

- **View Status and Properties**—Click this task to change properties of the network profile.

- **Network Center**—Click this task to open the Network Center.

Manage Network Connections

The final Network Center task is Manage Network Connections, which displays the Network Connections window, shown in Figure 8.23. This window shows you the basic status of each connection (Connected or Not Connected) and gives you the following task options:

- **Connect To**—Click this task to connect to or disconnect from a wireless network. (This task is available only when you click a Wireless Network Connection icon.)

- **Disable This Network Device**—Click this task to enable or disable the current network device.

- **Diagnose This Connection**—Click this task to launch the Network Diagnostics Tool (see "Diagnose Network Problems," earlier in this chapter).

- **Rename This Connection**—Click this task to edit the connection name.

- **View Status of This Connection**—Click this link to see more detailed information about the connection status.

- **Change Settings of This Connection**—Click this link to display the connection's property sheet, where you can configure the network adapter; install, uninstall, or configure network items (such as TCP/IP); and activate Internet Connection Sharing.

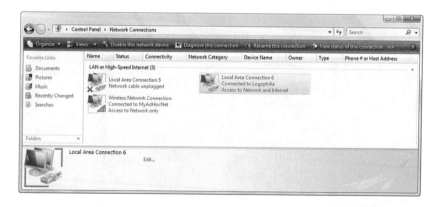

FIGURE 8.23   Use the Network Connections window to view and modify your network connections.

Windows Meeting Space

Vista's replacement for NetMeeting is an entirely new program called Windows Meeting Space (which goes by the name Windows Collaboration in Beta 2). As in NetMeeting, you can use Windows Meeting Space to show a local program or document to any number of remote users, and you can collaborate on a document with remote users. Windows Meeting Space uses several new Vista technologies, including Peer-to-Peer Networking, Distributed File System Replicator (DFSR), and People Near Me. The next few sections show you how Windows Meeting Space works.

People Near Me

To use Windows Meeting Space, you must first sign in to People Near Me. You do this either by starting Windows Meeting Space (see "Starting Windows Meeting Space," later in this chapter) or directly via the Control Panel. For the latter, you have two choices:

- In Category view, click Network and Internet, and then click the Sign In link below the People Near Me icon.

- In Classic view, double-click the People Near Me icon.

In the People Near Me dialog box that appears, display the Sign In tab and activate the Sign In to People Near Me option. Before you click OK, you might want to take a look at the Settings tab, which enables you to change the name and picture that other people see and to control various other People Near Me options, as shown in Figure 8.24.

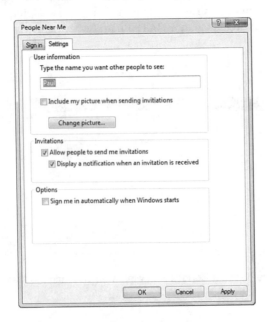

FIGURE 8.24   Use the Settings tab to configure People Near Me.

When you first sign in, Vista displays the People Near Me privacy policy, which states that the People Near Me feature discloses only your name, your computer name, and your computer's IP address. Click OK to continue.

Starting Windows Meeting Space

When you're signed in to People Near Me, you can launch Windows Meeting Space by selecting Start, All Programs, Windows Meeting Space. The first time you do this, the Windows Meeting Space Setup dialog box appears. For Windows Meeting Space to work, the data must be allowed to pass through the Windows Firewall—to do that, there must be Windows Firewall exceptions for the Meeting Space Infrastructure and the DFSR. If you click Enable File Synchronization and Windows Firewall Exception, Vista does this for you automatically.

The Windows Meeting Space window appears, as shown in Figure 8.25. From here, you either start a new collaboration session or join an existing session, as described in the next couple of sections.

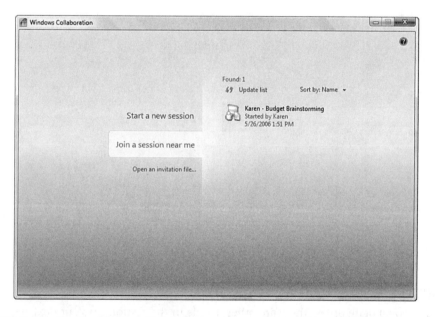

FIGURE 8.25 Use the Windows Collaboration window to start and join collaboration sessions.

Joining a Meeting Space Session

If you know that another person has a collaboration session running, but you didn't receive an invitation, here are the steps to follow to join that session:

1. In the initial Windows Meeting Space window, click Join a Session Near Me. Windows Meeting Space displays a list of running sessions.

2. Click the session you want to join. Windows Meeting Space prompts you to enter the session password.

3. Type the password and press Enter. Windows Meeting Space verifies your password and then joins the session.

Starting a Meeting Space Session

If you want to start your own collaboration session, click Start a New Session. Windows Meeting Space prompts you to enter a session name and password, and then starts the new session, as shown in Figure 8.26.

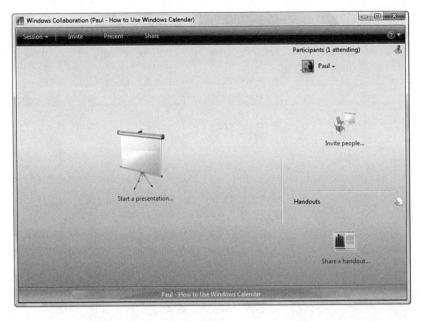

FIGURE 8.26   A new collaboration session, ready to begin.

Inviting People to the Session

You can't collaborate unless there are other people in the session, so your next step is to send invitations to those people you want to join the session. Click Invite in the menu bar or click the Invite People icon to display the Invite People dialog box shown in Figure 8.27. Select all the people you want to invite and then click Send Invitations.

A user who receives your invitation first sees the notification shown in Figure 8.28. After a few seconds, this fly-out disappears and you see the Invite dialog box shown in Figure 8.29. In both cases, you click Accept to join the session (this also loads Windows Meeting Space on the user's machine), Decline to refuse the invitation, or Dismiss to do nothing.

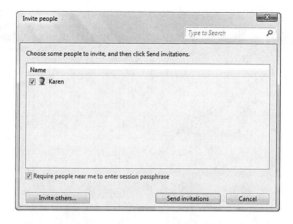

FIGURE 8.27   Use the Invite People dialog box to send invitations for people to join your session.

FIGURE 8.28   You see this notification when a session invitation first arrives.

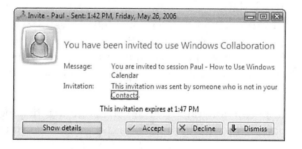

FIGURE 8.29   This dialog box appears a few seconds after the invitation arrives.

As people accept the invitations, their People Near Me name appears in the Windows Meeting Space Participants list.

Share a Handout

Before getting to the presentation, you might have some notes, instructions, background material, or other handout that you want to share with each participant. You do this by clicking Share in the menu bar or by clicking the Share a Handout icon. Select your file and then click Open. The file appears immediately in the Handouts area, which shows the filename and the name of the person who shared it, as shown in Figure 8.30.

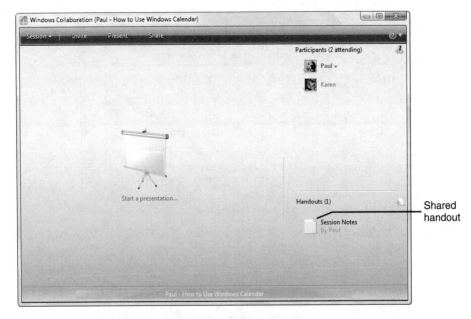

FIGURE 8.30   When a participant shares a handout with the session, the filename and sharer appear in the Handouts section.

Start a Presentation

When all your participants have joined the session and you've shared your handouts, it's time to start the presentation. In Windows Meeting Space, a presentation involves one of the participants performing some sort of action on his or her computer; the other participants then see the results of those actions within their session window. You can perform three basic actions:

- **Demonstrate a specific program**—This involves running the program on your computer so that other people in the session can watch what you do.

- **Collaborate on a document**—This involves running a program and opening the document. The person who starts the presentation initially has control over the document, but you can pass control to any participant.

- **Demonstrate any action**—This involves sharing your desktop, which means that the other participants see anything you do on your computer.

If you're going to demonstrate a specific program or collaborate on a document, first start the program or open the document. Then you initiate a presentation by clicking Present in the menu bar or by clicking the Start a Presentation link. In the Start a Presentation dialog box (see Figure 8.31), you then select the program you want to present, or select Desktop, and then click Present.

TIP

To present your handout, right-click the handout and click Present to Session.

Start a presentation

Choose an option below, then click "Present" to share your desktop, a document on your computer or a running application.

Inbox - Windows Mail
MSN.com - Windows Internet Explorer
Windows Calendar - Paul's Calendar

Browse for a file to open and share...
Desktop

[Present]   [Cancel]

FIGURE 8.31   Use the Start a Presentation dialog box to select the item you want others to view in your presentation.

Controlling the Presentation

After you begin a presentation, the Meeting Space window displays a "You are presenting" message and offers two links:

- **Show Me How the Presentation Looks on Other Computers**—Click this link to see your presentation from the point of view of a remote computer.

- **Stop Presenting**—Click this link to shut down the presentation.

Vista also displays a "You are presenting message" as well as the session title in a title bar across the top of the screen, as shown in Figure 8.32. You can use the controls in this bar as follows:

- Click Pause to temporarily stop the presentation.

- Click Control, Give Control To, and then a participant's name to give that person control of the presentation.

- Click Control, Take Control to resume control of the presentation.

- Click Options, Shows Windows Meeting Space Window to switch to the Windows Meeting Space window.

- Click the Close button to stop the presentation.

Pause

 —Exit

FIGURE 8.32   This bar appears at the top of the screen after you start a presentation.

Figure 8.33 shows what the presentation looks like on a remote computer.

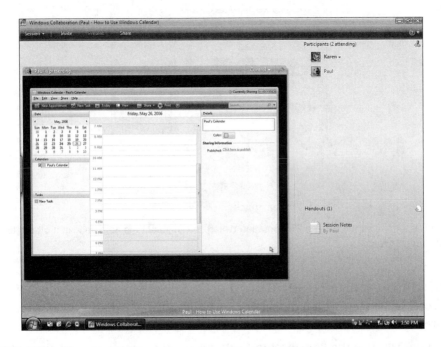

FIGURE 8.33   The presentation as seen on a remote computer.

The Sync Center

One of the main advantages of setting up a small network in your home or office is the ease with which you can share files and folders with other users. You simply share a folder with the network, and others can use the Network Explorer to open the shared folder and work with the files.

However, this benefit is lost when you disconnect from the network. For example, suppose that you have a notebook computer that you use to connect to the network while you're at the office. When you take the notebook on the road, you must disconnect from the network. Fortunately, you can still get network access of a sort when you are disconnected from the network (or *offline*). Windows Vista offers an Offline Files feature that enables you to preserve copies of network files on your computer. You can then view and work with these files as though you were connected to the network.

Vista's Offline Files feature is similar to the feature with the same name in XP Pro, but the Vista version is activated by default and is much easier to use. In fact, in Vista, all you have to do is right-click the network share and then click Always Available Offline. You no longer have to deal with the Offline Files Wizard, so creating offline files in Vista is a two-click operation.

To keep the offline files up-to-date, Vista offers a new tool called the Sync Center, which you open from the Control Panel by launching the Sync Center icon. Figure 8.34 shows the Sync Center window, which usually shows one or both of the following:

- **Folders**—These are folders that you've set up for synchronization. When you make a network share available offline, it appears in the `Offline Files` folder.

- **Devices**—These are removable devices—such as USB flash drives—attached to your computer that you can set up sync partnerships with.

To synchronize, you have two choices:

- To synchronize everything, click the Sync All button.

- To synchronize a specific folder or device, click the item and then click the Sync button.

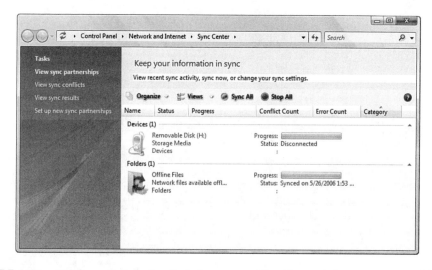

FIGURE 8.34   Use the new Sync Center to keep your offline files and other sync partnerships synchronized.

From Here

Here are some other sections in the book where you'll find information related to the topics in this chapter:

- For more information on Network Access Protection, see the section "Network Access Protection," in Chapter 6.

- Vista's new Network Presentation feature enables you to make a notebook presentation of a networked projector. I discuss this feature briefly in the section "Presentation Settings," in Chapter 7.

Digital Media in Windows Vista

The English language is a veritable factory of new words and phrases. Inventive wordsmiths in all fields are constantly forging new additions to the lexicon by blending words, attaching morphemic tidbits to existing words, and creating neologisms out of thin air. Some of these new words strike a chord in popular culture and go through what I call the "cachet to cliché" syndrome. In other words, the word is suddenly on the lips of cocktail party participants and water-cooler conversationalists everywhere, and on the fingertips of countless columnists and editorialists. As soon as the word takes root, however, the backlash begins. Rants of the if-I-hear-the-word-*x*-one-more-time-I'll-scream variety start to appear, Lake Superior State University includes the word in its annual list of phrases that should be stricken from the language, and so on.

The word *multimedia* went through this riches-to-rags scenario a few of years ago. Buoyed by the promise of media-rich interactive applications and games, techies and nontechies alike quickly made *multimedia* their favorite buzzword. It didn't take long, however, for the bloom to come off the multimedia rose.

Part of the problem was that when multimedia first became a big deal in the early '90s, the average computer just wasn't powerful enough to handle the extra demands made on the system. Not only that, but Windows support for multimedia was sporadic and half-hearted. That has all changed now, however. The typical PC sold today has more than enough horsepower to handle typical multimedia-related tasks, and Windows Vista has a number of slick new features that let developers and end users alike incorporate multimedia seamlessly into their work. Now it doesn't much matter that the word *multimedia* has more or less been replaced by the phrase *digital media*—what really matters is that people can get down to the more practical matter of creating exciting media-enhanced documents.

Easier AutoPlay Defaults

The AutoPlay feature dictates the program that runs automatically when you insert removable media into a slot in the computer. We've had AutoPlay for CDs since Windows 95, and Windows XP added AutoPlay support for most types of removable media, including DVDs, Flash drives, and memory cards.

AutoPlay has become more sophisticated over the years, to the point that XP offered several choices when you inserted removable media, and those choices depended on the contents of the media. For music files, for example, AutoPlay could play or rip the files in Windows Media Player or just open a folder window to view the files. For pictures, AutoPlay could launch the Scanner and Camera Wizard, start a slide show, launch the Photo Printing Wizard, or view the images. Also, many third-party programs could tie into the AutoPlay feature and add their own actions to the AutoPlay menu (for example, to play music files in a different program or to edit pictures in an image-editing program).

However, customizing AutoPlay has never been easy. You could always choose a default action when the AutoPlay window appeared, but what if you wanted to change the default?

In XP, you configured AutoPlay by opening the property sheet for a drive and then displaying the AutoPlay tab. You then used a drop-down list to choose the content type, clicked the default action, and then clicked Apply. From there you had to repeat this procedure for all the different content types: music files, pictures, video files, mixed content, music CD, DVD movie, and blank CD. Finally, you had to run through all of these steps for all the other removable drives on your system. No doubt sensing that users had better things to do, Microsoft has greatly streamlined the customization of AutoPlay defaults in Windows Vista.

Before getting to the customization feature, I should point out that Windows Vista also implements an improved AutoPlay window. Figure 9.1 shows an example. As you can see, Vista's AutoPlay window divides the options into two sections: The top section contains actions specific to the dominant content type on the media, and the bottom section—General Options—contains non-content-related actions.

To customize the AutoPlay defaults, you have two choices:

- If the AutoPlay window is onscreen, click the Set AutoPlay Defaults in Control Panel link.

- In the Control Panel, select Hardware and Sound, AutoPlay (or just launch the AutoPlay icon if you're using Classic view).

FIGURE 9.1   Vista revamped the AutoPlay window and divided the suggested actions into content-related and non-content-related sections.

Either way, you end up at the AutoPlay window shown in Figure 9.2. This page lists 16 different content types, from Audio CD to Video Files, to Super Video CD. Each content type has its own drop-down list, and you use that list to select the default action for each type.

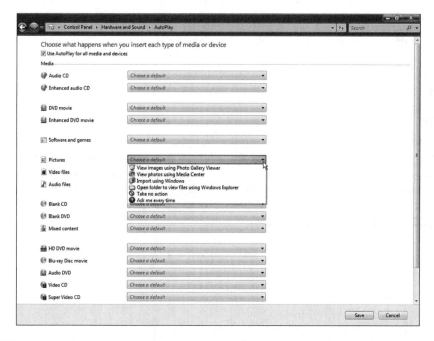

FIGURE 9.2   Use the new AutoPlay page to set the default actions for 14 different content types.

Windows Photo Gallery

Over the past few years, digital cameras have become the photography tool of choice for everyone from novices to professionals. And it's no wonder: Digitals give photographers tremendous freedom to shoot at will without having to worry about paying processing costs or running out of film. If there's a downside to all this photographic freedom, it's that most of us end up with huge numbers of photos cluttering our hard drives. The result has been a thriving market for third-party programs to import, view, and manage all those digital images.

Digital-image management seems like the kind of thing that ought to be part of the operating system. However, although Windows has had programs such as the Windows Picture and Fax Viewer, it has never had a program designed to perform the full range of image-management tasks, from importing and viewing to organizing and burning.

Windows Vista changes all that by introducing a new program called Windows Photo Gallery (WPG). This program can import images and videos from a camera, a scanner, removable media, the network, or the Web. You can then view the images, add metadata such as captions and tags, rate the images, search for images, and even apply common fixes to improve the look of photos. You can also burn selected images to a DVD.

You launch the program by selecting Start, All Programs, Windows Photo Gallery. WPG immediately begins gathering the images on your hard disk. You can also import images by hand using the following File menu commands:

- **Add Folder to Gallery**—This command displays the Add Folder to Gallery dialog box, which enables you to import images from a specific folder.

- **Import from Scanner or Camera**—This command launches the Scanner and Camera Wizard, which takes you step by step through the process of importing images from a digital camera, a document scanner, or a removable medium.

Grouping Images

By default, WPG groups the images by folder, but you can change that using the View, Group By command, which enables you to group on a number of metadata properties, including Date Taken, File Size, Image Size, and Camera. You can then select View, Table of Contents to see links that take you to each group. For example, Figure 9.3 shows images grouped by File Size with the Table of Contents showing links to each group (Largest, Larger, Medium, and so on).

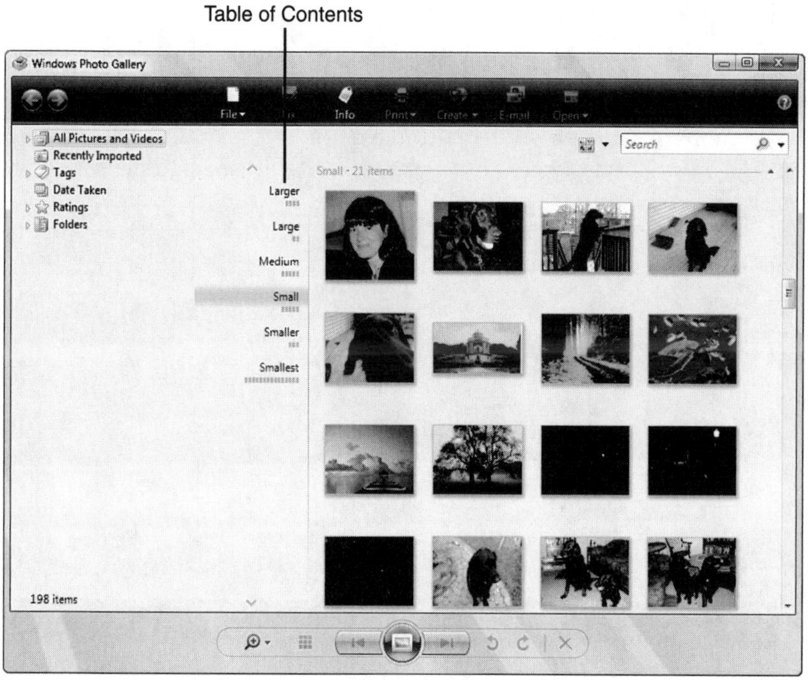

Table of Contents

FIGURE 9.3   Vista's new Windows Photo Gallery program enables you to import, view, organize, and burn images and videos.

Image Metadata and Tagging

You can also create your own metadata for each image. WPG enables you to change four properties: Caption, Date Taken, Rating, and Tag. The Tag property enables you to add one or more descriptive keywords—*tags*—to the image, similar to what you do at photo-sharing websites such as Flickr (www.flickr.com). In WPG, you click the image you want to work with, display the Info pane (click Info or Tags, Create a New Tag), click Add Tags, type the tag, and press Enter. Figure 9.4 shows an image with a couple of tags added. Notice that the tag you create also appears in the Tags list, which enables you to filter the images based on the tag you select. (You can also filter images based on the Date Taken and Ratings properties, as well on Recently Imported and Folders.)

Instant Search

As with so many other Vista windows, WPG comes with an integrated Instant Search box that supports as-you-type searches. After you type text in the Instant Search box, WPG searches filenames and all metadata (including your tags) for matching images and then shows the results in the WPG window. Figure 9.5 shows an example.

Tags appear here for filtering

Tags

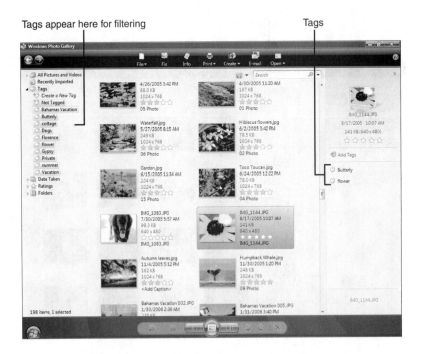

FIGURE 9.4 You can apply descriptive tags to each of your images.

Instant Search box

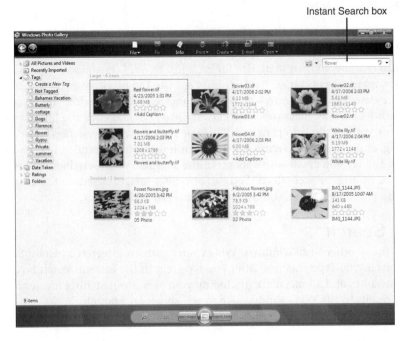

FIGURE 9.5 Windows Photo Gallery supports as-you-type searches on filenames and metadata properties.

Image Editing

WPG also comes with a limited set of tools for altering images. Click the image you want to work with and then click Fix to display the image in the window shown in Figure 9.6. Here you get sliders to adjust the Brightness, Contrast, Color Temperature, and Tint. (You can also click Auto Adjust to have WPG make the adjustments for you.) In all WPG windows, you can also rotate the image, as pointed out in Figure 9.6.

Play Slideshow | Rotate Clockwise
Rotate Counterclockwise

FIGURE 9.6   Click Fix to adjust image qualities such as brightness, contrast, and tint.

More Tools

WPG also supports the following features:

- To preview any image, double-click it.

- To view a slide show, click the Play Slideshow button (see Figure 9.6). Note that the Vista slide show engine comes with 15 different playback modes. During the slide show, move the mouse to display the controls, and then click Themes to choose the playback mode you prefer.

- To set an image as the desktop background, right-click the image, and then click Set as Background.

- To burn images to a DVD disc, select Create, DVD.

What's New in Windows Media Player 11

Windows Media Player (WMP) is your computer's one-stop media shop, with support for playing digital music, audio CDs, digital videos, DVD movies, Internet radio, and recorded TV shows; ripping music from CDs; burning files to disc; synchronizing with external audio devices; and much more. Vista ships with a new version of this popular program—Windows Media Player 11—that offers a few nice improvements over WMP 10.

The first thing you notice when you launch WMP 11 is that the overall interface is a bit simpler than previous versions (see Figure 9.7). There are still a few too many small, undecipherable icons scattered around the window, but these are small blemishes on an otherwise clean look.

FIGURE 9.7   Windows Media Player 11 offers a simpler, cleaner interface than its predecessors.

Navigating the Library

One of the things that makes the WMP 11 interface so much simpler than older versions is that you see only one category at a time in the Library. By default, WMP displays the Music category at startup. However, you can change to a different category (Music, Pictures, Video, Recorded TV, or Other Media) using either of the following techniques:

- Click the Select a Category list (pointed out in Figure 9.8) and then click the category you want.

- Drop down the Library tab list (see Figure 9.8) and then click the category you want.

The path information beside the Select a Category list tells you the name of the current category, folder, and view, as pointed out in Figure 9.8.

FIGURE 9.8   You navigate to a different category using either the Select a Category list or the Library list.

Album Art and the WMP Interface

Another thing you'll notice about the WMP 11 interface is that it features graphics much more predominantly than in older versions of the program. If you've downloaded or scanned album art, it appears throughout the WMP 11 interface. For example, if you select the Artist view, the artist stacks use album art images, as shown in Figure 9.9. Even if you switch to a less specific view, such as Genre, WMP uses album art as part of the stack icons.

FIGURE 9.9   Album art appears through the Windows Media Player interface, such as the Artist view shown here.

Grouping and Stacking Media

By default, WMP opens in the Music category's Songs view, which groups songs according to the values in the `Album Artist` property and then by the values in the `Album` property. WMP also offers several other Music views based on media metadata:

- **Artist**—Stacks the albums using the values in the `Album Artist` property (see Figure 9.9)

- **Album**—Groups the albums alphabetically using the values in the `Album` property (see Figure 9.10)

- **Genre**—Stacks the albums using the values in the `Genre` property

- **Year**—Groups the albums by decade using the values in the `Date Released` property

- **Rating**—Stacks the albums using the values in the `Rating` property

Of course, you get a different set of views for each category. For example, you can view items in the Video category by actors, genre, and rating, and you can view items in the Recorded TV category by series, genre, actors, and rating. In each category, you can see even more views by clicking the Library folder (or by pulling down the Library list in the path data), as shown in Figure 9.11.

FIGURE 9.10   The Library's `Album` folder stacks your albums according to the values in the `Album` property.

FIGURE 9.11   Click the current category's `My Library` folder to see a complete list of the available views.

Media Metadata and Tagging

Metadata in Windows Media Player is best dealt with by downloading the relevant information from the Internet. However, most WMP metadata is editable, and you can make whatever changes you need by right-clicking the metadata and then clicking Edit.

A new innovation in WMP 11 is the Advanced Tag Editor, which gives you a front end for much of the metadata available for a particular media file. Right-click the file you want to tag and then click Advanced Tag Editor to display the dialog box shown in Figure 9.12. You can add metadata related to the track and to the artist, and you can also add websites, lyrics (even lyrics synchronized to the music), pictures, and comments.

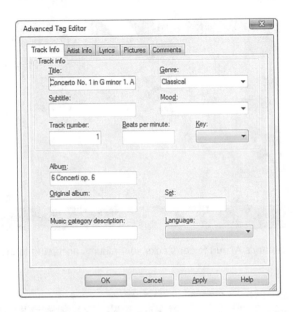

FIGURE 9.12   Use the Advanced Tag Editor to edit the metadata for a media file.

Instant Search

By this point in the book, you won't be surprised to learn that WMP 11 comes with an integrated Instant Search box that supports as-you-type searches. After you type your text in the Instant Search box, WMP searches filenames and metadata for matching media files, and then shows the results in the WMP window. Figure 9.13 shows an example.

Syncing with Media Devices

Syncing items from the Library to a media device is a bit easier in WMP 11. When you insert a WMP-compatible media device, WMP recognizes it and automatically displays the device, its total capacity, and its available space in the Sync tab's List pane, as shown in Figure 9.14.

To create a list of items to add to the device, display the album, song, or whatever in the Contents pane; click and drag the item; and then drop it inside the Sync List. WMP automatically updates the available storage space in the device as you drop items in the Sync List. When you're ready to add the item, click Start Sync. WMP switches to the device's Sync Status folder to display the progress of the sync, as shown in Figure 9.15.

Instant Search box

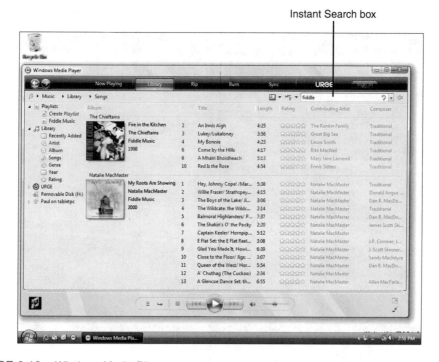

FIGURE 9.13   Windows Media Player supports as-you-type searches on filenames and metadata properties.

TIP

You can "preshuffle" the media files before starting the sync. Pull down the Sync List button and click Shuffle List Now.

WMP 11 supports two-way syncing, which means that not only can you sync files from your PC to a media device, but you also can sync files from a media device to your PC. This is handy if you've purchased music directly to the device or uploaded media to the device using a different application.

To sync from a media device to your PC, you open a view on the media device, find the files you want to sync, and then click and drag them to the Sync List. Alternatively, just click Start Sync to synchronize everything on the device with WMP.

Drag items to sync here

Device info

Device folder

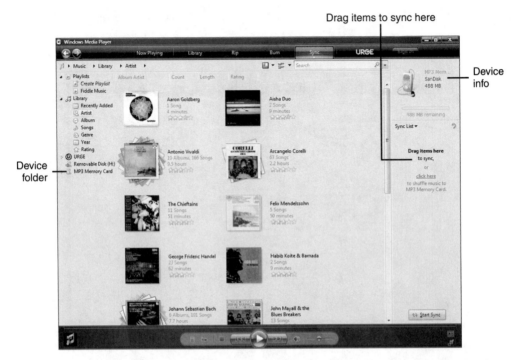

FIGURE 9.14   When you insert a media device, information about the device appears in the Sync tab's List pane.

FIGURE 9.15   The Sync Status folder shows you the progress of the sync.

Easier Ripping

Ripping files from an audio CD is more convenient in WMP 11 because the program gives you easier access to rip settings. For example, if you pull down the Rip tab's list, you can select Format to display a list of file formats, including various Windows Media Audio formats (Regular, Pro, Variable Bit Rate, and Lossless), MP3, and—new in WMP 11—WAV, as shown in Figure 9.16. You can also pull down the Rip menu and select Bit Rate to choose the rate at which you want to rip the media, as shown in Figure 9.17.

FIGURE 9.16   Use the Rip tab's Format menu to select the file format for the ripped media.

FIGURE 9.17   Use the Rip tab's Bit Rate menu to select the quality of the ripped media.

NOTE

The options you see in the Bit Rate submenu depend on the option you select in the Format submenu. If you select a lossless format, then by definition, you cannot select a bit rate (because the media will be ripped at a fixed rate). For WMA Lossless, the fixed bit rate is between 470 and 940Kbps; for WAV, the fixed bit rate is 1411.2Kbps.

Burning Options

Burning music or other media to a disc is more flexible in WMP 11. For one thing, WMP supports burning media to a DVD disc (pull down the Burn tab's menu and select the Data CD or DVD command). For another, WMP 11 comes with a new Burn tab in its options dialog box, as shown in Figure 9.18. You can use the Burn tab to select the burn speed, apply volume leveling to audio CDs, select the file list format for a data disc, and set the file quality.

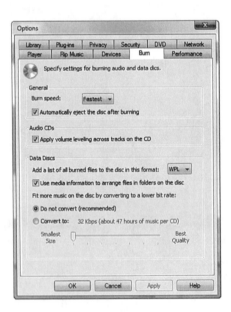

FIGURE 9.18   Use the new Burn tab to set options for burning discs in Windows Media Player.

Library Sharing

It can take quite a while to set up and customize your WMP Library just the way you like it. When you do, however, WMP is a real pleasure to use—so much so that you'll probably be tempted to duplicate your efforts on other computers in your home. Unfortunately, previous versions of WMP gave you no easy way to do that. Basically, you had to copy the media files from your original PC to the second PC, and then build your Library from scratch on the second machine.

WMP 11 changes all that by introducing a welcome new feature called Library Sharing. This feature enables you to share your WMP Library with other network users, just like you'd share a folder or a printer.

To get started with Media Sharing, WMP gives you two choices:

- Pull down any tab menu and select More Options; display the Library tab; and then click Configure Sharing.

- Right-click the Library folder in any category, and then click Library Sharing.

Either way, you see the Library Sharing dialog box onscreen, as shown in Figure 9.19. Activate the Share My Library check box. If you want to control what you share for all devices, click Settings, and then check the media types you want to share. If you want to control the settings for a specific device, select its icon and click Customize. Click the Networking button to open the Network Center if you want to make changes to your network.

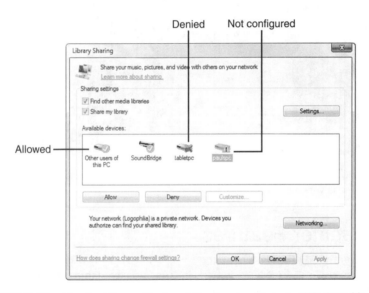

FIGURE 9.19   Use the Library Sharing dialog box to share your Windows Media Player Library with other users on your network.

Note, too, that the Library Sharing dialog box also presents you with a list of available devices with which you can share your library. Click a device, and then click either Allow or Deny. When you click one of these buttons, an applicable icon will appear on top of each device. (For example, a checkmark appears for an allowed device.)

Playing DVDs

As with recent versions of the program, WMP 11 supports the playback of DVD movies, as long as you have compatible decoder hardware or software installed on your system.

However, when you play a DVD in WMP 11, a DVD button is added to the playback controls. Clicking that button displays the DVD menu (shown in Figure 9.20), which offers a much wider array of DVD-related commands than in previous versions. Welcome additions to the DVD arsenal are the capabilities to select audio and language tracks (if available), display subtitles (if any), and capture frames.

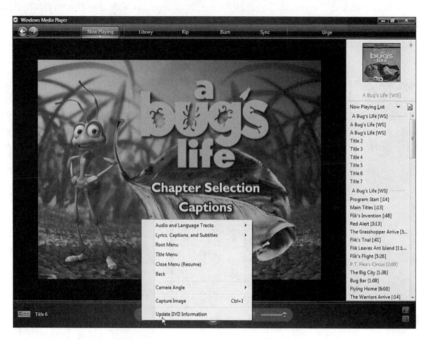

FIGURE 9.20   The new DVD menu in Windows Media Player 11 offers a greater choice of playback options than in previous versions.

New Media Center Features

Prior to Windows Vista, the Media Center program was available only as part of the Windows XP Media Center Edition (MCE), which, in turn, was available only as a preinstalled OS on OEM computers. (XP MCE was also available to MSDN subscribers.) Why no retail version? Probably because the system requirements for XP MCE were quite high (particularly the GPU, which needed to come with hardware acceleration and support for DirectX 9). However, this separate Media Center Edition ends with Vista, which includes the Media Center application in its Home Premium and Ultimate editions.

Interface Enhancements

The version of Media Center that ships with Windows Vista is not radically different from its predecessors. (Early prototypes of the program sported a drastically revised—and reviled—interface, but the protests from dedicated Media Center types forced Microsoft to back down and stick with more incremental changes.) Figure 9.21 shows the initial Media Center screen that appears after you have run through the program's setup chores.

FIGURE 9.21   Windows Vista version of Media Center.

The XP Media Center was widely praised for its simple, easy-on-the-eyes interface, and the Vista version implements several new features to try to improve upon a good thing:

- The top-level tasks (TV, Music, and so on) appear more like a list than menu choices, as they do in XP Media Center.

- When you select a top-level task, Vista Media Center bolds the task text and displays the available second-level tasks below (such as Recorded TV and Set Up TV for the TV option; see Figure 9.21).

- When you select a second-level task, Vista Media Center displays a graphic along with the task text to illustrate the task's function. For example, when you select Pictures + Videos and then the Picture Library task, you see a collection of images, as shown in Figure 9.22.

- As the displayed tasks move away from the center of the screen (whether up or down, left or right), they become progressively lighter. This focuses the user's attention on the task at hand in the center of the screen.

- In keeping with the deletion of the word *My* from most of the Vista interface, XP Media Center's My Videos, My Pictures, My TV, and My Music tasks have been renamed as Pictures + Videos, TV, and Music.

- There is no longer a Shut Down button in the upper-left corner, and the clock has been moved to the top-right corner of the screen.

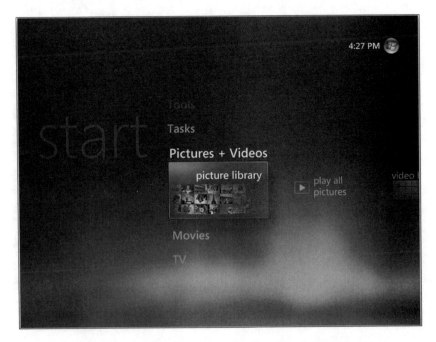

FIGURE 9.22   The Vista Media Center illustrates second-level tasks with graphics.

New Menu Structure

These interface changes make Media Center tasks even easier to navigate. That's a good thing because Vista Media Center has quite a few top-level tasks:

- **Pictures + Videos**—Use this task to access your picture and video libraries. Second-level tasks here are Picture Library, Play All Pictures, and Video Library. (I'm not sure why Microsoft chose to combine these rather different media into a single task, but it does take some getting used to.)

- **Movies**—Use this task (new in Vista Media Center) to work with DVD movies. Second-level tasks are Movie Library (a list of the DVD movies you've watched) and Play DVD.

- **TV**—Use this task to work with your TV tuner. Second-level tasks are Recorded TV (a list of TV shows you've recorded to your hard disk) and Set Up TV (configuring TV options).

- **Music**—Use this task to work with music and radio. Second-level tasks are Music Library (a list of the music files on your system), Play All Music, Radio (listen to radio either through a tuner or via the Internet), and Search (search your system for music).

- **Spotlight**—Use this task to access media online and run other Media Center programs installed on your computer. Second-level tasks are Online Spotlight and More Programs.

- **Tools**—Use this task to access the Media Center settings.

- **Tasks**—Use this task to run other Media Center features. Second-level tasks are Burn CD/DVD, Sync (synchronize content with an external device), Shut Down (close Media Center), and Add Extender (add networked devices such as an Xbox 360 to view your content on those devices).

More Media Center Improvements

Vista's Media Center improvements aren't merely skin deep. The new version also boasts a few new features, including the following:

- Notifications for incoming phone calls. You can set up Media Center to display these notifications for all incoming calls or just for calls with Caller ID.

- Wireless network support. You can now use Media Center to join your computer to an existing wireless network.

- Parental controls to restrict the content that is viewed through Media Center. You can configure controls using TV ratings (see Figure 9.23) and movie ratings.

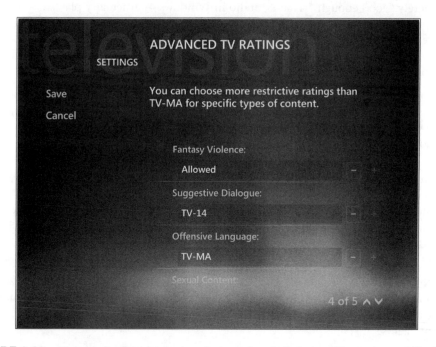

FIGURE 9.23   Vista Media Center introduced parental controls that enable you to use TV ratings and other settings to restrict the viewing of content.

- Program optimization. Vista Media Center comes with an optimization feature that ensures maximum performance from your system. Optimization occurs automatically every morning at 4 a.m., but you can set your own schedule.

Digital Audio in Windows Vista

The reputation Windows has as an audio playback and editing platform has been, not to put too fine a point on it, abysmal. There have been some improvements over the years. For example, the early audio infrastructure (often called the *audio stack*) seen in Windows 3.1 (16-bit) and Windows 95 (32-bit) supported only one audio stream at a time, but Windows 98 enabled multiple playback streams using the Windows Driver Model architecture. However, Windows audio has always suffered from three major problems:

- A poor interface for controlling audio and for troubleshooting audio problems. Tools such as Volume Control, the Sound Recorder, and the Control Panel Sounds and Audio Devices icon had difficult interfaces and limited functionality, and clearly weren't geared for the day-to-day audio tasks that users face.

- Poor quality playback and recording. The Windows audio stack has always been merely "good enough." That is, audio in Windows—particularly playback—was constructed to give the average user a reasonable level of quality. However, the default Windows audio had nowhere near the fidelity audiophiles and professional audio users require, so these users spent much of their time working around inherent audio limitations (or giving up on Windows altogether and moving to the Mac).

- Poor reliability, to the point that audio glitches are one of main causes of system instability. The problem here has been that much of the audio stack code runs in the sensitive Windows kernel mode, where a buggy driver or process can bring down the entire system.

To address these problems, the Vista audio team completely rewrote the audio stack from the ground up. That's good news for both regular users and audiophiles because it means the Vista audio experience should be the best yet. Completely revamping the audio infrastructure was a big risk, but the aim was to solve the three previous problems. We'll have to wait and see if Microsoft accomplished this ambitious goal (not all the new audio features were available as I wrote this), but on paper, things look promising:

- New tools for controlling the volume, recording sounds, and setting sound and audio device properties (discussed in the next three sections) offer a much improved user interface geared toward common user tasks and troubleshooting audio problems.

- The new audio stack offers much higher sound quality.

- Most audio code has been moved from kernel mode to user mode, which should greatly reduce audio-induced system instabilities.

Per-Application Volume Control

The Volume Control tool in previous versions of Windows is a good example of poor audio system design. When you opened Volume Control, you were presented with a series of volume sliders labeled Master, Wave, Line In, CD Player, Synthesizer, Aux, and more. For the average user, most of these labels were, at best, meaningless and, at worst, intimidating. What on earth does the Aux slider control? What's the deal with Line In? Most people ignored all the sliders except Master and just used that slider to control playback volume. However, that Master slider had problems of its own.

For example, suppose you're waiting for an important email message, so you set up Windows Mail to play a sound when an email message comes in. Suppose further that you're also using Windows Media Player to play music in the background. If you get a phone call, you want to turn down or mute the music. In previous versions of Windows, muting the music playback also meant muting other system sounds, including your email program's audio alerts. So while you're on the phone, there's a good chance that you'll miss that important message you've been waiting for.

The Windows Vista solution to this kind of program is called *per-application volume control*. This means that Vista gives you a volume control slider for every running program and process that is a dedicated sound application (such as Windows Media Player or Media Center) or is currently producing audio output. In our example, you'd have separate volume controls for Windows Media Player and Windows Mail. So when that phone call comes in, you can turn down or mute Windows Media Player while leaving the Windows Mail volume as is, so there's much less chance that you'll miss that incoming message.

Figure 9.24 shows the new Volume window that appears when you double-click the Volume icon in the notification area. The slider on the left controls the speaker volume, so you can use it as a system-wide volume control. The rest of the window contains the *application mixer*—this includes sliders and mute buttons for individual programs, and the program's icon. As shown in Figure 9.24, you can get the program's name by hovering the mouse over the icon.

> **NOTE**
>
> When a program stops its audio output, the Volume Control tool removes the program's slider from the application mixer. However, Volume Control waits for a short time before removing the program. Early versions of the application mixer kept icons onscreen for about a minute, which gave you enough time to set the level for programs that produce only occasional sounds (such as Windows Mail). However, more recent versions remove these icons after just a few seconds, which isn't very useful.

9

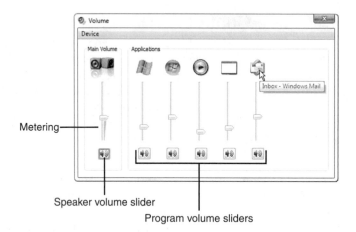

Metering

Speaker volume slider

Program volume sliders

FIGURE 9.24   Windows Vista uses per-application volume control to enable you to set the volume level for each program that outputs audio.

In the old Volume Control tool, when you adjusted the Master slider, the other volume sliders remained the same. In the Vista Volume Control tool, when you move the speaker volume slider, the program sliders move along with it. That's a nice touch, but what's even nicer is that the speaker volume slider preserves the relative volume levels of each program. So if you adjust the speaker volume to about half its current level, the sliders in the application mixer also adjust to about half of their current level.

Volume Control also remembers application settings between sessions. So if you mute Solitaire, for example, it will remain muted the next time you start the program.

The new volume control also supports metering, in which the current audio output is displayed graphically on each slider (see Figure 9.24). This metering appears as a green wedge that grows taller and wider the louder the sound signal is. This is very useful for troubleshooting audio problems because it tells you whether a particular program is actually producing audio output. If you have no sound from a program, but you see the metering in program's volume slider, the problem lies outside of the program (for example, your speakers are turned down or unplugged) .

> **NOTE**
>
> Many notebook computers come with volume controls that enable you to physically turn the computer's speaker volume up or down. Microsoft has talked about tying this physical volume control into the Volume Control program so that if you turn down the sound physically, the speaker volume slider would adjust accordingly. This extremely useful feature was not implemented as I write this, but hopefully it will appear in a later build of Windows Vista.

Sound Recorder

The Sound Recorder accessory first appeared in Windows 95 and has remained a part of Windows ever since. Unfortunately, the Sound Recorder in Windows XP is essentially the same program as the original version, which means the program's annoying limitations haven't changed, either:

- You can save your recording only using the WAV file format.

- You can record only up to 1 minute of sound.

Windows Vista comes with a completely new version of Sound Recorder that does away with these limitations. For example, you can save your recording using the Windows Media Audio (WMA) format, and there is no limit (other than available hard disk space) to the length of the recording.

Having no recording limit might sound dangerous, but the new Sound Recorder captures WMA audio at a bit rate of 96Kbps, or about 700KB for a 1-minute recording. Compare this to a 1-minute CD-quality recording using the old Sound Recorder, which could easily result in a 10MB file!

Figure 9.25 shows the new Sound Recorder window (select Start, All Programs, Accessories, Sound Recorder). Click Start Recording to begin your recording; click Stop Recording when you're done. Sound Recorder displays the Save As dialog box so that you can choose the file location, name, and format.

FIGURE 9.25   The Windows Vista version of Sound Recorder.

Audio Devices and Sound Themes

The Windows Vista replacement for the Control Panel Sound and Audio Devices icon is Audio Devices and Sound Themes (in the Control Panel, select Hardware and Sound, Audio Devices and Sound Themes), shown in Figure 9.26.

The Audio Devices tab shows the playback and recording devices on your system. The first thing to notice is that you now have a visual reminder of the default devices for playback and recording in the form of a green checkmark icon, as pointed out in Figure 9.26. The checkmark means that the device is the default for all uses. However, you can also designate a device as the default for specific uses. As shown in Figure 9.26, if you right-click a device and then click Set as Default For, you get a list that includes All Uses, General Usage, Music and Movies, and Speech and Communications. (Here, "General Usage" means any use that doesn't involve movies, music, speech, and communications.)

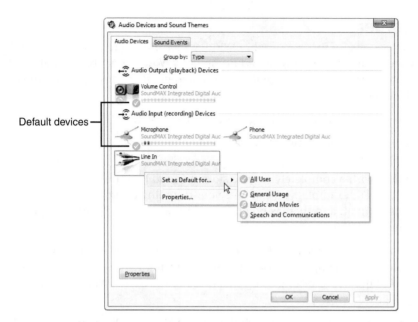

FIGURE 9.26   Open the Audio Devices and Sound Themes icon in the Control Panel to control your system's audio properties.

Windows Vista also implements a more extensive collection of properties for each device. Double-clicking a device displays a property sheet similar to the one shown in Figure 9.27. The properties you see depend on the device. Here's a summary of the tabs you see when you open the default playback device (although note that not all audio playback devices support all of these tabs):

- **General**—Change the name and icon for the device.

- **Configuration**—Specify your speaker setup (Stereo, Quadraphonic, 5.1, and so on), and then test and balance your speakers.

- **Tone**—Set the bass and treble balances.

- **Other**—Configure the device for digital output only.

- **Mixer**—Set the volume levels.

- **Format**—Set the default playback format and latency.

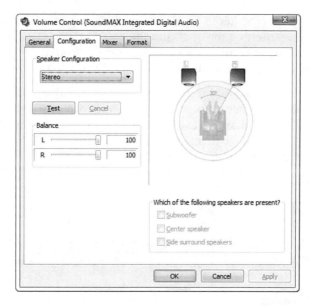

FIGURE 9.27   The audio device Configuration tab enables you to customize how your PC's audio devices work.

DVD Authoring

Previous versions of Windows could rip data from CDs and burn data to recordable CDs, but they had no support for ripping and burning DVDs. (The exception was XP Media Center Edition, which offered support for DVD burning through the Media Center program.) Windows Vista changes that by building DVD-burning capabilities into the following applications:

- Windows Photo Gallery
- Windows Media Player
- Media Center
- Windows Movie Maker

But what about *authoring* actual DVD discs, complete with menus, chapters, and elements of a typical DVD disc interface? Until Vista, you needed to use a third-party program to author a DVD. Now, however, the Home, Premium, and Ultimate editions of Vista come with a new program called Windows DVD Maker, which you can use to author DVDs. The beta version I used had some rough edges but was clearly functional. As you'll see in the section, it's also very easy to use. (Windows DVD Maker is only available in the Home Premium and Ultimate editions of Windows Vista.)

Before you launch the program, insert a recordable DVD disc in your DVD burner (DVD Maker won't work without a disc in the drive). Then select Start, All Programs,

Accessories, Windows DVD Maker to get the program started. (Alternatively, if you see the AutoPlay window after inserting the disc, click Burn a DVD Video Disc using Windows DVD Maker.) DVD Maker operates as a kind of wizard: You work through a couple of windows to add content, create menus, and then burn your DVD.

The opening window is named Add Pictures and Video to the DVD. Click the Add Items button to display the Open dialog box, where you select a video or image file for inclusion on the DVD. When you have several items added, you can use the Move Up and Move Down buttons to rearrange them, and the Remove Items buttons to remove them, as shown in Figure 9.28. You can also double-click any video file to play it in Media Player. When you've added your content, enter a Disk Title and then click Next.

FIGURE 9.28   Use the opening DVD Maker window to add and arrange the videos and pictures that you want on your DVD.

The next window enables you to choose and customize the opening DVD menu. You begin by choosing from one of several predefined menu styles, as shown in Figure 9.29. From there you can perform the following tasks:

- **Menu Text**—Click this button to configure the text that appears on the menu, including the Disc Title, Play Button, and Scenes Button. You can also change the font.

- **Customize**—Click this button to add your own spin to the built-in style you chose. In the window that appears (see Figure 9.30), you can change the menu font, add foreground and background images, specify an audio file to play while the menu is onscreen, choose either Motion Menus or Still Menus, and select a style for the Scenes Buttons. Click Save to update the style, or click Save as New Style to create a custom style.

- **Slideshow**—Click this button if your DVD is a slide show of digital photos. In the window that appears, you can add one or more music files to play in the background, specify the number of seconds to display each photo, select a transition between photos (Cross Fade, Dissolve, Wipe, and so on), and choose whether you want the slide show to pan and zoom the photos.

- **Preview**—Click this button to see an onscreen preview of your menu. You can also use the preview window to play the DVD contents.

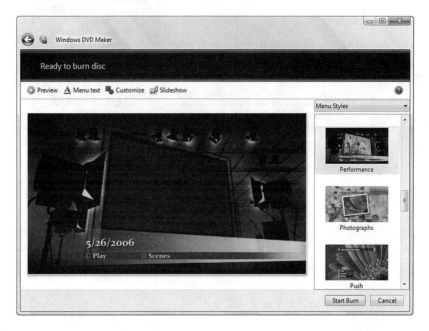

FIGURE 9.29   Use the next DVD Maker window to choose and customize the DVD menu.

When the DVD menu is set up the way you want, click Burn to start the process of your burning the menu and contents to the disk (refer to Figure 9.29). DVD Maker displays a progress window while it encodes the disc, as shown in Figure 9.31.

FIGURE 9.30   You can customize the DVD menu with foreground and background images, music, and more.

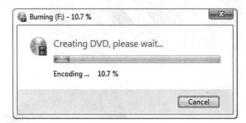

FIGURE 9.31   Click Burn to create your DVD disc.

From Here

Here are some other sections in the book where you'll find information related to the topics in this chapter:

- Videos running in Windows Media Player appear as live thumbnails when you use the Vista cool switches. In Chapter 3, see the section "Better Cool Switches: Flip and Flip 3D."

- WMP videos also appear as live thumbnails in the taskbar. In Chapter 3, see the section "Taskbar Thumbnails."

- For more about metadata and its relation to grouping and stacking files, see the section "Grouping, Stacking, and Filtering with Metadata," in Chapter 4.

10

Windows Vista and Gaming

In his 2005 book *What the Dormouse Said*, journalist John Markoff describes how the 1960s counterculture gave rise to and shaped the personal computer industry. At one point, he tells the story of how engineers at the Stanford Artificial Intelligence Laboratory (SAIL) decided to create their own version of Spacewar, the world's first computer game (invented by MIT hacker Stephen Russell in 1962). SAIL used a time-sharing system in which a number of terminals competed for the resources of a single minicomputer, and this often caused the Spacewar screen to freeze while it waited for processor cycles. To fix this problem, the Stanford engineers invented a new operating system mode that doled out processor resources in sixtieth-of-a-second slices, which improved the performance not only of Spacewar, but also of many other applications. Markoff concludes the story:

> It was called "Spacewar mode" and was one of the earliest examples of how gaming advanced the state of computing.

That incident occurred 40 years ago, and gaming has been leaping ahead of the PC industry and dragging it along it in its wake ever since. Whether it's video hardware, networking advances, or graphics programming, game developers and hardcore gamers continually push PCs to their limits in the quest for higher-quality gaming experiences.

Windows Vista will be known as the first Windows OS that targets gamers directly. Why the sudden focus on gaming? Probably because Microsoft's own research uncovered an interesting and surprising fact: Gaming is the second most popular PC activity, well behind web surfing, but more popular even than email. Amazingly, about 1 in 5 users play games on their Windows PCs, which is a huge user base that Microsoft figures it can no longer ignore. As you'll see in this chapter, Vista includes many new features that are aimed directly at the gaming market, including game developers, the gamers themselves (both hardcore and casual), and even their concerned parents.

The Game Explorer

Your first clue that Microsoft is serious about gaming in Vista is the newly elevated status of the Games folder. In Windows XP, Games was a mere submenu off the All Programs menu, but in Vista it takes a place of pride on the main Start menu along with Documents, Pictures, and Music.

The first time you select Games, you see the Set Up Games Updates and Options dialog box, which displays two check boxes:

- **Download Information About Installed Games**—Leave this check box activated to allow Vista to download information such as game updates.

- **List Most Recently Played Games**—Leave this check box activated to allow Vista to track your game play.

Figure 10.1 shows the default window for the Games folder, which Microsoft is calling the Game Explorer.

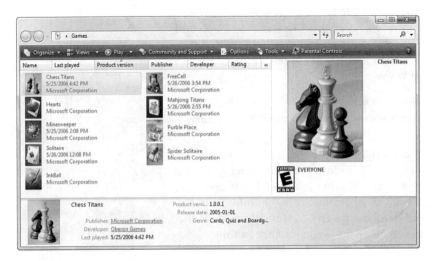

FIGURE 10.1   Windows Vista comes with a new Game Explorer window devoted exclusively to games.

The Game Explorer is a special shell folder that offers several new features for gamers and game developers:

- A repository for all installed games. See "Getting Games into the Game Explorer," later in this chapter.

- Game-related tasks such as launching a game, linking to the developer's website, and setting up parental controls. See "Game-Related Tasks," later in this chapter.

- Support for games metadata such as the game's publisher and version number, and the last time you played the game. See "Support for Games Metadata," later in this chapter.

- Autoupdate of games. With the new Game Update feature, Vista automatically lets you know if a patch or a newer version is available for an installed game.

The Game Explorer is initially populated with the nine games that come in the Vista box. These games include updates to venerable Windows favorites (FreeCell, Hearts, Minesweeper, Solitaire, Spider Solitaire, and InkBall), and a few new additions (Chess Titans, Mahjong Titans, and Purble Place). All the games come with decent user interfaces that take full advantage of Vista's graphics capabilities.

Getting Games into the Game Explorer

Ideally, Microsoft would like to see all installed games show up in the Game Explorer. In practice, however, that's not easy to do because Vista has no reliable way of telling whether you're installing a game.

As a first step toward solving this problem, Microsoft created the *game-definition file* (GDF). This is an XML file that describes various aspects of the game and enables Vista to recognize when a game is being installed so that it can add the game to the Game Explorer. Microsoft is implementing GDFs in three ways:

- It's asking game developers to create a GDF for each new game they create and to embed the GDF in the game's executable file or an associated dynamic link library.

- Microsoft has created GDFs for more than a thousand legacy games and included those GDFs in Windows Vista in the following file:

  `%SystemRoot%\System32\GameUXLegacyGDFs.dll`

- Microsoft and/or game developers will continue to create GDFs after Vista ships, and these GDFs will be added to Vista as updates.

Here's an example of a GDF for a legacy game (Boggle, in this case):

```xml
<?xml version="1.0" encoding="utf-16"?>
<GameDefinitionFile xmlns="urn:schemas-microsoft-com:GameDescription.v1"
xmlns:baseTypes="urn:schemas-microsoft-com:GamesExplorerBaseTypes.v1">
  <GameDefinition gameID="{dc90fdca-aa28-4d13-8401-ad149e4bccae}"
  WMID="{9e6c8124-5159-4aed-a175-a2dd292dfe86}">
    <Name>Boggle"!</Name>
    <Ratings>
```

10

```
    <Rating ratingID="{7a53b0be-b92d-4e8a-a11f-8e6f9f3c575b}"
    ratingSystemID="{768bd93d-63be-46a9-8994-0b53c4b5248f}" />
  </Ratings>
  <Version>
    <VersionNumber versionNumber="1.0.0.0" />
  </Version>
 </GameDefinition>
</GameDefinitionFile>
```

The complete schema for GDFs is much more complex and includes items for the game's release date, box art, genre, and more.

When you install a program, Vista looks either for a pointer to a GDF or for an entry in GameUXLegacyGDFs.dll. If it finds either one, it uses the data in the GDF to add the game to the Game Explorer. For example, Figure 10.2 shows the Game Explorer after installing the game Halo: Combat Evolved.

Game added to Game Explorer

FIGURE 10.2   If a game has a GDF, Vista adds it to the Game Explorer during installation.

Game-Related Tasks

The task toolbar in Windows Vista shell folders such as Pictures, Music, and Videos contain links to tasks related to the folder content. For example, the Pictures folder has tasks such as Slide Show and Order Prints, while the Music folder has tasks such as Play and Play All. The Game Explorer is also a shell folder, so it, too, comes with several content-specific tasks:

- **Play**—Launches the currently selected game.

- **Community and Support**—Displays a menu with two options: Home Page and Support. The Home Page item takes you to the main website of the currently selected game's developer, and the Support item takes you to the developer's main technical support page.

- **Options**—Displays the Set Up Games Updates and Options dialog box.

- **Tools**—Gives you quick access to game-related hardware features in the Control Panel: Hardware, Display Devices, Input Devices, Audio Devices, Firewall, and Installed Programs.

- **Parental Controls**—Starts the Parental Controls feature. See "Parental Controls for Games," later in this chapter.

Support for Games Metadata

As you learned in Chapter 4, "File System Improvements" (see the section "Metadata and the Windows Explorer Property System"), Windows Vista brings metadata into the operating system in a meaningful way that enables you to sort, group, stack, and search based on property values. This new metadata focus shows up in the Game Explorer, as well, which keeps track of 11 properties for each game:

- **Name**—The name of the game

- **Publisher**—The publisher of the game

- **Developer**—The developer of the game

- **Last Played**—The date and time that you last opened the game's executable file

- **Product Version**—The current version number of the game

- **Release Date**—The date the current version of the game was released

- **Genre**—The game genre (such as Shooter or Strategy)

- **Rating**—The game's Entertainment Software Rating Board rating (see "ESRB Game Ratings," later in this chapter)

- **Game Restrictions**—The restrictions that have been placed on running the game (see "Parental Controls for Games," later in this chapter)

- **Content Descriptors**—A word or phrase that describes the game content, as applied by the ESRB

- **Install Location**—The folder in which you installed the game

To view all the metadata, switch to Details view (which doesn't show some metadata, including Release Date and Genre), as shown in Figure 10.3. Unfortunately, there is no editable metadata in the Game Explorer (except, indirectly, the Game Restrictions property, which you "edit" via the Parental Controls feature). It would be nice to have the capability to add comments or keywords, particularly on systems that have dozens of games.

10

FIGURE 10.3   The Game Explorer displays game metadata such as the date and time the game was last played, the game's version, and the game's ESRB rating.

ESRB Game Ratings

Games today range from harmless edutainment and board games to first-person shooter games that feature scenes of intense violence and even sexual content. How are parents supposed to be able to tell the difference? It's a big problem because most homes nowadays have a computer, and many have separate computers for the kids. To solve the problem, in 1994 the Entertainment Software Association established the Entertainment Software Rating Board (ESRB), an independent regulatory body that applies and enforces ratings, advertising guidelines, and online privacy policies for computer and video games.

> **NOTE**
>
> Vista actually supports game ratings from several different organizations, including the Computer Entertainment Rating Organization (CERO) and Pan European Gaming Information (PEGI). ESRB is the default rating system in North America, so it's the one I discuss here. To learn how to change the rating system, see "Parental Controls for Games," later in this chapter.

The ESRB applies to each game one of the following ratings:

- **Early Childhood (EC)**—The game has no inappropriate content and is, therefore, suitable for ages 3 and older.

- **Everyone (E)**—The game has mildly inappropriate content (such as cartoon violence) but is still suitable for ages 6 and older.

- **Everyone 10+ (E10+)**—The game has some inappropriate content (such as cartoon violence and minimally suggestive themes) but is still suitable for ages 10 and older.

- **Teen (T)**—The game has some violence, suggestive content, blood, or strong language that should be viewed only by persons age 13 years and older.

- **Mature (M)**—The game has intense violence, sexual themes, or other content that should be viewed only by persons age 17 and older.

- **Adults Only (AO)**—The game has prolonged scenes of intense violence, sexual themes, nudity, or other content that should be viewed only by persons age 18 years and older.

For some games, the ESRB also applies *content descriptors*, which are words or phrases that describe the game's content in general terms and explain the game's rating. Here's a partial list of the ESRB content descriptors:

- **Blood and Gore**—Depictions of blood or the mutilation of body parts

- **Cartoon Violence**—Violent actions involving cartoonlike situations and characters

- **Crude Humor**—Depictions or dialogue involving vulgar antics, including "bathroom" humor

- **Fantasy Violence**—Violent actions of a fantasy nature, involving human or nonhuman characters in situations easily distinguishable from real life

- **Intense Violence**—Graphic and realistic-looking depictions of physical conflict

- **Language**—Mild to moderate use of profanity

- **Mature Humor**—Depictions or dialogue involving "adult" humor, including sexual references

- **Mild Violence**—Mild scenes depicting characters in unsafe or violent situations

- **Nudity**—Graphic or prolonged depictions of nudity

- **Sexual Themes**—Mild to moderate sexual references or depictions

- **Strong Language**—Explicit and/or frequent use of profanity

- **Strong Sexual Content**—Graphic references to or depictions of sexual behavior, possibly including nudity

- **Suggestive Themes**—Mild provocative references or materials

- **Use of Drugs**—The consumption or use of illegal drugs

- **Use of Alcohol**—The consumption of alcoholic beverages

- **Use of Tobacco**—The consumption of tobacco products

- **Violence**—Scenes involving aggressive conflict

Vista's Game Explorer supports both the ESRB ratings and content descriptors in the metadata for each game. As shown in Figure 10.1, you need to display the Reading pane (select Organize, Layout, Reading Pane) to see the ESRB logo—which includes the rating short form (EC, E, E10+, T, M, or AO)— as well as the rating. You can also use the ESRB data to restrict game usage, as you'll see in the next section.

> **NOTE**
>
> The Preview pane's ESRB logo is also a link that, when clicked, takes you to the ESRB website (www.esrb.com). You can use this site to learn more about the ESRB and to find the ratings and content descriptors for thousands of PC and video games.

Parental Controls for Games

If you have kids, chances are, they have a computer—either their own or one shared with the rest of the family—and, chances are, they play games on that computer. That's not a problem when they are being supervised, but few of us have the time or energy to sit beside our kids for each and every computer session—and the older the kid, the more likely that a hovering adult will be seen as an interloper. In other words, for all but the youngest users, your children will have some unsupervised gaming time at the computer.

To avoid worrying about whether your 8-year-old is playing Grand Theft Auto or something equally unsuitable, you can take advantage of Vista's parental controls that I discussed back in Chapter 6, "Security Enhancements in Windows Vista" (see the section "Using Parental Controls to Restrict Computer Usage"). Specifically, the Parental Control feature has a Game Controls section that enables you to control gaming using ratings and content descriptors.

Before you get started, you need to set up a user account for each child (or a single account for all your children, if that works better for you). When you click the Parental Controls link in the Games Explorer, Vista displays the Parental Control window, shown in Figure 10.4.

Before setting up the controls, you should select the rating system you want to use. Click the Select a Games Ratings System link to display the Game Rating Systems window shown in Figure 10.5. Select the rating system you prefer and then click OK to return to the Parent Controls window.

Click the user you want to work with to display the User Controls window. Activate the On, Enforce Current Settings option, and then click Games to display the Game Controls window, shown in Figure 10.6.

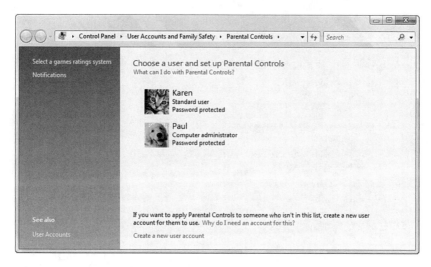

FIGURE 10.4   Use the Parental Controls window to restrict game playing for a user.

FIGURE 10.5   Use the Game Rating Systems window to choose the rating system you want to use with parental controls.

The next three sections run through the three methods you can use to control game play.

10

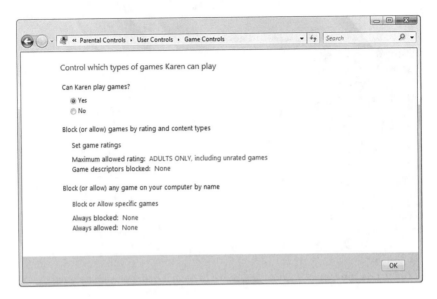

FIGURE 10.6   Use the Game Controls window to set the gaming restrictions for the selected user.

Turn Off Game Play

If your kids are too young to play any games, or if you'd prefer that they spend time on the computer working on more constructive pursuits, you can turn off game playing altogether. In the Can *UserName* Play Games? section, select No to prevent the user named *UserName* from launching any games from the Games Explorer. If you select Yes instead, you can use the techniques in the next two sections to control the games the user can play.

Controlling Games via Ratings and Descriptors

Instead of shutting off all game play, you're more likely to want to prevent each user from playing certain types of games. The easiest way to do that is to use game ratings and content descriptors. In the Game Controls window, click Set Game Ratings to display the Game Restrictions window, shown in Figure 10.7.

Click the rating option that represents the highest rating the user is allowed to play. For example, if you're using the ESRB rating system and you select the Teen option, the user will be able to play games rated as Early Childhood, Everyone, Everyone 10+, and Teen. He or she will not be able to play games rated as Mature or Adults Only.

You can also prevent the user from playing unrated games by selecting the Block Games with No Rating option.

You can also block games based on content descriptors. If you scroll down in the Game Restrictions window, you see the complete set of content descriptors, each with its own check box. For each check box you activate, the user will not be able to run any games that include that content description, even if the game has a rating that you're allowing.

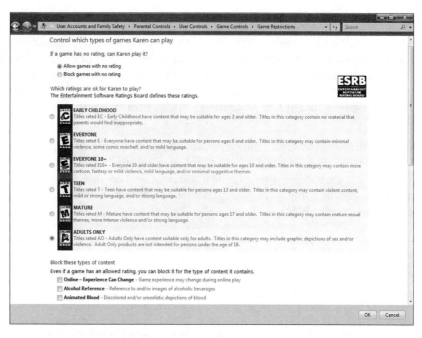

FIGURE 10.7   Use the Game Restrictions window to control game playing using ratings and content descriptors.

FIGURE 10.8   Use the check boxes in the bottom half of the Game Restrictions window to control gaming using content descriptors.

Blocking and Allowing Specific Games

You might want to fine-tune your game controls by overriding the restrictions you've set up based on ratings and content descriptors. For example, you might have activated the Block Games with No Rating option, but you have an unrated game on your system that you want to allow the kids to play. Similarly, there might be a game that Vista will allow based on the ratings and descriptors, but you'd feel more comfortable blocking access to the game.

In the Game Controls window, click Block or Allow Specific Games to display the Game Overrides window, shown in Figure 10.9. The table displays the title and rating of your installed games, and shows the current control status—Can Play or Cannot Play. To allow the user to play a specific game, click Always Allow; to prevent the user from playing a specific game, click Always Block.

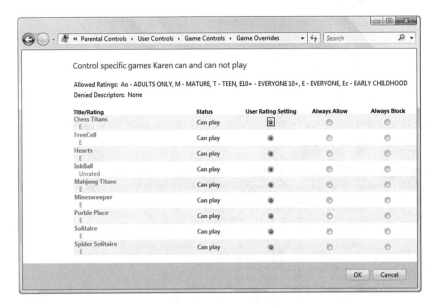

FIGURE 10.9   Use the Game Overrides window to allow or block specific games.

Gaming and WinSAT

Back in Chapter 5, "Vista Performance and Maintenance," I introduced you to Vista's new WinSAT tool (see the "Windows System Assessment Tool [WinSAT]" section). Recall that WinSAT runs during setup and whenever you make major performance-related hardware changes to your system. WinSAT creates metrics for five aspects of your system performance—graphics, Direct3D, memory, processor, and storage—and these metrics are stored as XML data on your system.

The key point here for gaming is that WinSAT also exposes an application programming interface (API) for third-party developers. This API enables a game developer to interrogate the assessments to determine the overall performance of the machine and to examine specific performance metrics, such as Direct3D rendering. This enables the game developer to activate game features that your computer can handle and to deactivate features that would run poorly or not at all on your system.

DirectX 10

Microsoft has said that it's enhancing game performance and the games interface in Windows Vista not only because so many people play games on PCs, but also because it wants to change the perception that the PC is a poor gaming platform. Many people believe that if you're serious about gaming, you need to use a dedicated game platform such as an Xbox or a PlayStation. This has seemed even more true with the release of the Xbox 360 and the forthcoming release (as I write this) of PlayStation 3, which offer spectacular graphics and game features.

Can Vista really compete with these dedicated game consoles? I think it can because Vista has a gaming ace up its sleeve: the Xbox 360 and the PlayStation 3 both use the DirectX 9 hardware to render video and audio. However, Windows Vista supports DirectX 10, the latest and greatest version of the APIs, which has been completely rewritten to take full advantage of the powerful graphics hardware that's now available for PCs.

The specifics of what's in the DirectX 10 package were not known as I wrote this, but Microsoft had let a few tidbits out of the bag:

- DirectX 10 removes many legacy functions and interfaces that were kept for backward compatibility but degraded the overall performance of the APIs. As a result (at least as of this writing), DirectX 10 is exclusive to Windows Vista and won't be supported in Windows XP.

- At the hardware level, games programmed for the DirectX 9 and earlier APIs will not work with DirectX 10. However, DirectX 10 will support these legacy programs via software emulation.

- DirectX 10 requires a graphics card that has a specific set of features for maximum performance, so game developers can assume that those features will be present and don't have to weigh down their code with workarounds and other card-specific code.

- DirectX 10 supports impressive new "shader" functions for both pixels and primitives such as dots, lines, and triangles.

- DirectX 10 supports hardware caching of render states, in which thousands of objects can be held in the cache for easy access. This improves performance not only by making more code quickly accessible, but also by minimizing the number of times the game code has to switch from one render state to another.

These and many other changes should produce a significant improvement in game performance. In particular, PC games developed with DirectX 10 should render scenes with amazing levels of detail, shading, reflections, and other elements that will give these games more of a "real-world" feel (see Figure 10.10).

FIGURE 10.10   DirectX 10 enables game developers to produce scenes with incredible detail and shading.

From Here

Here are some other sections in the book where you'll find information related to the topics in this chapter:

- For the details on metadata in Windows Vista, see the section in Chapter 4 titled "Metadata and the Windows Explorer Property System."

- For more about Vista's parental controls, see the section in Chapter 6 titled "Using Parental Controls to Restrict Computer Usage."

- You might need to mute or turn down the sound on your game. In Chapter 9, see the section "Per-Application Volume Control."

Index

SYMBOLS

A

B

D

G

gadgets

   desktop gadgets, 89

   web gadgets, 88

Game Controls page (Parental Controls), 170

Game Controls window (Games Explorer), 266-268

Game Explorer, 30

Game Overrides window (Games Explorer), 268

Game Rating Systems window (Games Explorer), 264

Game Restrictions window (Games Explorer), 266

gamers, Vista effects on, 37

Games Explorer

   adding games to, 259-260

   blocking specific games, 268

   Community and Support task, 260

   configuring, 258

   ESRB game ratings, 262-263, 266

   GDF, 259-260

   Hardware task, 261

   included games, 259

   metadata support, 261

   Options task, 261

   Parental Controls, 261, 264-268

   Play task, 260

   Preview pane, ESRB logo, 264

   Set Up Games Updates and Options dialog, 258

   turning on/off game play, 266

Games icon (Start menu), 73

gaming

   DirectX 10, 269

   Games Explorer, 258-268

   Spacewar mode, 257

   WinSAT, 268

Gaming Graphics metrics (WinSAT), 121

GDF (game-definition files), 259-260

General area (Network Center), 203

General Settings page (Windows Defender). See Options page (Windows Defender)

General tab

   playback devices, 252

   Preview pane, 137

   System Configuration Utility, 138

Genre view (WMP 11), 236

Gestures tab (Tablet PC Input Panel), 191-192

"ghosting," 51

Global Logs pane (Event Viewer), 136

graphics

   improvements to, 20

   memory, 45

   primitives, 66

   raster graphics, 66

   requirements, 44-45

   vector graphics, 66

Graphics metrics (WinSAT), 121

Group By command (WPG), 230

Group command (Windows Explorer), 103

group policies, customizing User Account Control, 163-164

grouping

   files, 102-103

   images in WPG, 230

   media, WMP 11, 27, 236

   metadata, 15

GUI, System Image Manager, 33

H

handouts (presentations), Share a Handout icon (Windows Meeting Space), 221

Handwriting Personalization tool, 196-197

Handwriting tab (Tablet PC Settings dialog), 189-190

handwritten text (Tablet PCs), 191-192, 196-197

hard disks

   Check Disk tool, 52

   cleanups, 51

   defragmenting, Vista pre-installation checklist, 52

   inefficiency of, 52

How can we make this index more useful? Email us at indexes@sampublishing.com

O – P